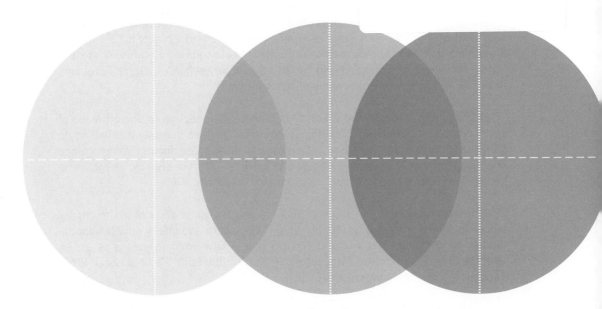

How to be a Social Worker

"There are many introductory textbooks available in social work, but *How to be a Social Worker* is unique because of how it manages to combine deep intelligence with practical relevance. It skilfully draws on a wide range of theories from sociology, pyschology, and social work itself and applies them in a highly accessible but never simplistic way to practice and the challenges of acquiring a professional identity in social work. It deserves to be an instant bestseller." – Harry Ferguson, Professor of Social Work, University of Nottingham, UK

"This is a highly readable and practical first-steps introduction to doing the job of social work. The content is eminently usable and digestible in a way that will equip students with essential ideas and knowledge and an appreciation of the importance of thought and reflection in doing social work." – Martin Sheedy, Programme Leader for Social Work, Liverpool John Moores University, UK

"This text provides students and practitioners with a critical account of the importance of self and professional identity within social work and offers valuable opportunities to challenge assumptions, reflect and review what it means to be an effective professional in the 21st century." – Steve Hothersall, Head of Social Work Education, Edge Hill University, UK

"A useful exploration of the development of the professional self in social work, particularly for students." – Sharlene Nipperess, Lecturer in Social Work, Deakin University, Australia

"This book will be a useful reference for those contemplating a career in social work through to those newly employed. In particular, the case studies used throughout are interesting and illustrate the complexity of social work and the dilemmas faced on a daily basis." – Louise Houston, Practice Educator in Social Work, University of Plymouth, UK:

"This is an extremely well laid out, easy to read book which came in particularly useful when I was writing an assignment on communication skills in social work. It was a valuable tool in helping me to understand the theories I was drawing on during my first placement setting, too." – Matthew Caunce, Year 2 BA Social Work student, Lancaster University, UK

Priscilla Dunk-West

How to be a Social Worker

A Critical Guide for Students

palgrave
macmillan

First published 2013 by
PALGRAVE MACMILLAN

Palgrave Macmillan in the UK is an imprint of Macmillan Publishers Limited, registered in England, company number 785998, of Houndmills, Basingstoke, Hampshire RG21 6XS.

Palgrave Macmillan in the US is a division of St Martin's Press LLC, 175 Fifth Avenue, New York, NY 10010.

Palgrave Macmillan is the global academic imprint of the above companies and has companies and representatives throughout the world.

Palgrave® and Macmillan® are registered trademarks in the United States, the United Kingdom, Europe and other countries

ISBN: 978–0–230–37016–6

This book is printed on paper suitable for recycling and made from fully managed and sustained forest sources. Logging, pulping and manufacturing processes are expected to conform to the environmental regulations of the country of origin.

A catalogue record for this book is available from the British Library.

A catalog record for this book is available from the Library of Congress.

This book is dedicated to Penny:
sister extraordinaire

Contents

List of Figures

Acknowledgements

This book has emerged from almost a decade of teaching social work to students in Australia and England and my subsequent desire to create a text that brought together the varying strands of the curriculum in a new way. This desire turned into a reality with the assistance of Lloyd Langman, Commissioning Editor at Palgrave Macmillan. Lloyd's enthusiasm has endured throughout this project and he has been a joy to work with. Similarly Katie Rauwerda, Assistant Editor at Palgrave Macmillan, has provided skilful and critical insights and support at crucial times throughout the writing process.

I have been incredibly fortunate to have taught so many inspiring students over the years: thank you to each and every one of you for helping me develop my teaching skills and knowledge. Students energise me to remain curious about the world of social work. Working with a diverse bunch of students over a number of years has highlighted the need for learning resources to be flexible and to offer various methods of knowledge delivery. I deliberately used visual methods and reflective prompts alongside traditional writing in the hope that this book opens up new opportunities for reflexivity and creativity and that it will appeal to former and future students of social work.

The central theoretical idea contained in this book comes from George Herbert Mead, an early figure in what we refer to as the symbolic interactionist tradition in sociology today. The idea that the self is 'made' through social interactions has been influential for me in that it has helped me better understand the professional world of social work. I first encountered G. H. Mead through my early studies in sociology. More recently, scholars in sociology have applied his work to intimacy studies, so my PhD research in the area of the everyday sexual self in sociology led me to think about his theory and its application to both my own research as well as to my profession of social work. It is therefore these shoulders upon which I stand in making the claim for the application of Mead to social work.

I have also been fortunate to work with a number of scholars whose wisdom and passion has inspired me and whom I wish to thank. These include: Professor Fiona Verity, Dr Trish Hafford-Letchfield, Dr Gill Cressey and Professor Lesley Cooper. Thanks are equally due to Elaine Bourne and Sue Maywald who shared their wisdom about practice learning and education and helped me to understand the world of placement learning in my initial years in the university setting. I have had institutional support in the writing of this book from the University of South Australia and my brilliant new colleagues, for which I am very grateful.

Andrew Dunbar, I sincerely appreciate you allowing your work to be reproduced and applied to social work learning. Thank you to the excellent Trilby and her folks for the child development photograph. Laura Varley, who helped with administrative tasks associated with this project, provided crucial, and timely, assistance and helped with the final push to get everything together in time. Veronica Gubbins has always, over a great number of years, encouraged the writer in me: thank you. Thanks are also due to Jan and Gary Dunk for their continuing support across continents. Last, but by no means least, Blake and Paxton: thank you for being two wonderful people in my life. Brad: thank you for everything, including for being you.

Priscilla Dunk-West

The author and publishers wish to thank the following for permission to reproduce copyright material:

– Andrew Dunbar for Figures 1.1 and 2.1
– Trilby's parents for 'Trilby painting', 2011 (Figure 2.2)

Every effort has been made to trace rights holders, but if any have been inadvertently overlooked the publishers would be pleased to make the necessary arrangements at the first opportunity.

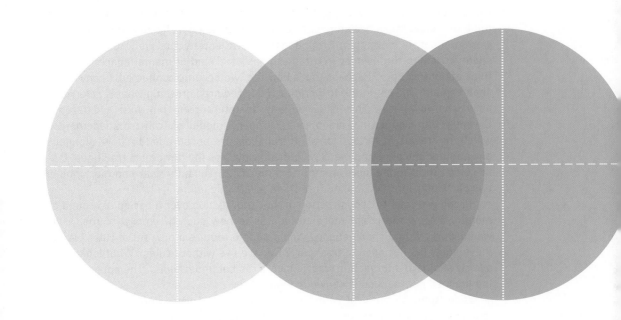

Introduction

During the conceptualisation of this book I held an academic post at Coventry University, England. Given the multiple roles the contemporary academic must fulfil, mundane tasks become opportunities for thinking, reflection and planning. It was a deliberate merging of a mundane task with intellectual work to use my time spent travelling to Coventry in the mornings as a kind of mental space for me to think about this book. Perhaps that's how the two became connected. In any case, I shall explain. The commute to work each day required crossing what is referred to as a 'shared space'. This is essentially an intersection but with a difference. Coventry City Council has adopted a European model of traffic management in which the travels of various forms of transport are encouraged to 'flow' alongside one another. Encouraging the 'flow' of traffic involves the removal of traditional traffic rules (Chris Young, pers. comm. 18 June 2012). Thus, there are no markings on this particular intersection, nor are there any traffic lights.

Having watched the construction of this intersection over a period of around six months, I grew more and more curious as to how such a removal of road rules would work. Would chaos ensue? Would people require a new set of rules? Would these apply to all modes of transport? Can we live without rules? What looked like a fairly standard intersection was, in fact, a radical undertaking. The appearance of the finished intersection is shown in Figure 0.1.

Aside from the physical connection between my journey into Coventry and my thinking about this book, what does traffic have to do with social work? Our everyday

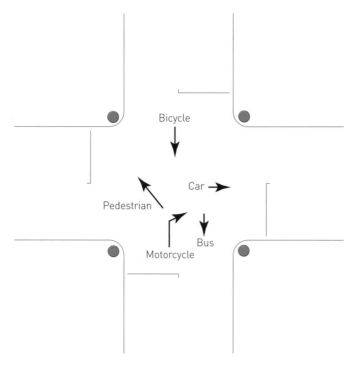

FIGURE 0.1 The intersection: What happens when our rules are removed?

activities, I believe, help us understand not only our external world, but our internal perceptions. Hopefully as you read this, the traffic metaphor will begin to make sense and will assist in providing some insight into the theoretical orientation upon which this book has been developed. But first, some overview as to how the book relates to social work students is needed.

In short, this book aims to teach the reader how to develop and establish their professional social work identity. This means not only learning how to be a social worker but also understanding how identity is made and appreciating how this self is related to its broader society. It is only through this awareness of the self that we can consciously fashion a *social work self*—and this is a process which continues throughout our careers. The ways in which we engage in this process shape the local, national and even international social work identity.

The book brings together the subjects studied during qualifying courses as well as engaging the reader in key debates and tensions in social work. A critical awareness of these, and their manifestations in practice, is vital to a positive social work identity. In this introductory chapter we will begin to examine how the social work identity is 'made'. In order to understand this it is crucial to examine the self.

From the very beginning of study to completing the award, social work students can find it difficult to connect up the subjects they study in university with the experiences they have in placement, and often this continues well into one's social work practice career. The subjects studied—which range from human development to communication skills to research—can feel somewhat separate from one another. This book aims to develop in the reader an understanding that the learning process is concerned with the construction or 'making' of the social work self.

Back to our traffic metaphor. The experimental intersection held my interest because, as a social scientist, I am curious about the ways in which everyday rules shape our behaviour. I watched others' reactions as they drove, cycled, walked into this new shared zone. I also drove and walked through the area.

What I noticed is that despite the absence of rules, people were required to enter the zone at a slower speed than on traditional roads. Generally speaking, the people I observed on my daily trek to work would approach the intersection as though diving into the unknown. When approaching a roundabout, for example, we have an understanding of the rules: giving way to traffic to one's right, waiting until there is a clear path, signalling direction through the use of indicators—these are all examples of the expected rules which help us negotiate our path on traditional roads. A traffic light is a very clearly defined set of rules with colours signalling certain actions. So the shared space was very different from these other types of intersections. The reduced speed on approach to the intersection was prompted by a lack of knowledge about what the rules were, and yet in the shared zone there are still rules. Motorists give way to others, people look to see if there is oncoming traffic, people allow others to proceed before them. There are rules in this system—they are just different from those on traditional roads.

Similarly, the beginning social work student enters university without an understanding of the 'rules' of social work. On the surface, entering into the world of social work entails a letting go of previously held values, ideas, theories and knowledge. Learning about social work can feel like being in a space with unknown rules and boundaries. Being on placement, for example, can be enormously confronting for a person who has developed a successful career elsewhere, either in paid or non-paid work.

Studying social work can feel like starting all over again. Yet as the social work student progresses through their studies, they find some confidence in developing a social work self which incorporates knowledge and values that were previously held. Many social work students have a long-held interest in social justice, for example, and this value resonates through social work ethics, theory and practice. Making connections between the self who comes to social work and the social work self is inherent to the learning that occurs throughout the social work degree.

It is also the task of the social work student to try to navigate their way through their classroom social work education and the practice that occurs through placements. Although it can feel like drifting amongst oncoming traffic, this journey is one that occurs through navigating theoretical frameworks in the real world of practice. Your fellow learners are a source of support in your social work journey, and key ideas and theories enable the traveller to gain momentum in their journey to become a competent social worker.

Similarly, lectures, seminars and other facilitated learning assists in the process whereby the social work self is constituted. This book has been written as a support to all of these 'anchors' to learning in the hope that it will make navigating your path through the seemingly chaotic intersection a little easier and clearer.

There is another way the new traffic management model I have described is comparable to becoming a social worker. Our behaviour as motorists, motorcyclists, pedestrians in using traditional forms of management becomes, as George Herbert Mead might say, 'routinized'. We engage in routine behaviours in our everyday lives: these are formed through repetition over time until the behaviours become so familiar that you become unaware of them. If you have ever arrived at a destination and been unable to recall your journey in specific detail (Did you wait at that set of traffic lights, or were the lights green? Was it easy this morning to turn right on the usually congested road?), you have experienced an example of routinized behaviour. It can seem as though you were, for example, driving *without thinking* (Chris Young, pers. comm. 18 June 2012). The new model of shared traffic management seeks to interrupt this routinization by removing familiar cues and force active engagement with what is occurring within the shared space. It therefore becomes impossible to drive in this space passively, or *without thinking*. This is because the environment is constantly changing and there are multiple forms of modes of transport and directions travelled.

The underlying theoretical idea in this book is Mead's theory which argues that our selves are constructed through our interactions with others. Most of the time we are unaware of our selves or our identities when we engage in these interactions (Mead 1934).

In social work, we have long been concerned with reflexivity or the ability to think back or reflect on our behaviour and change our subsequent behaviour according to our desires. This book contains material to assist in this tradition of reflexive practice, and in particular how it relates to your emerging social work self. It is important in social work to disrupt practice with reflexivity so that our practice is constantly positively engaging in the dynamic terrain in which we find ourselves.

Subjects taught in social work curricula can feel disjointed. Although this book deals with each subject in a chapter format, there is a common approach to all of these seemingly separate topics. In order to develop the social work self, the learner is required to:

- Actively engage in critical reading, thinking, listening and talking about issues related to social work, including the broader social sphere
- Use personal biography and experiences in everyday life in making sense of social work topics. This, in turn, requires students to
- Engage in reflexive exercises based on theoretical material

In facilitating the above, this book is a little different from other social work text-books. The key idea in this book—that the self is constructed through social inter-action—is a forgotten idea in social work (Forte 2004a, 2004b). There is much to be gained through the application of such a theory of self to social work learning. In this vein, this book is an attempt to stimulate the reader's thinking—both about one's self and about one's everyday life—in new ways, and to relate this knowledge to social work. Theoretical material, reflexive exercises and active engagement in the curriculum enable students to surrender their 'routinized behaviour' so that new skills and knowledge may be developed.

The book is designed in such a way that chapters can be read either as stand-alone text, from beginning to end, or in an order which fits the reader's purpose. It is hoped it will be a book which accompanies students from the beginning of their course to the end of their course and into their social work career. I will now outline how the book is set out and then explore how the material in each chapter fits with the task of helping people to *be* social workers.

Chapter 1 examines the concept of selfhood and relates this to social work learn-ing and self-making. Social work is a profession which is committed to the under-standing that the social environment, including the cultural setting, has an enormous impact on individual experiences. In Chapter 1 we therefore spend some time exploring some of the automatic assumptions we make about others due to our socially situated knowledge. The 'self' is a central term used in this book so in Chapter 1 we explore how understanding professional practice through the analysis of self is important to social work as a profession as well as to one's emerging iden-tity as a social worker. The role of reflexivity is examined in relation to the self and social work. In social work, being able to progressively get 'better' in one's practice is an accepted outcome from reflexive engagement. Chapter 1 outlines what this means for one's own developing professional self.

With Chapter 1 laying the conceptual foundations for the book, Chapter 2 commences with an engagement with theoretical material which helps social work-ers make sense of individual circumstances. Thinking about individual problems through a life course or lifespan approach involves compartmentalising life stages. Generally speaking, the life stages are birth, early childhood, middle childhood, adolescence, adulthood, older age and death. This is a linear model of life: as one grows older, one moves on to the next category. Scholarship derived from the disciplines of developmental psychology, sociology and social work has contributed to our current knowledge of the life course. All of these approaches inform the knowledge-base discussed in Chapter 2. In this chapter we consider how knowledge about human development assists both in contextualising individual problems within broader social and age contexts and in helping to frame the different roles social work plays in helping to meet the age-related requirements which emerge in each life stage. In Chapter 2 the reader is encouraged to engage in thinking about one's own self and life stages. The key ideas which underpin Chapter 2 are that in order to be a competent social worker, one must understand the key developmental theories, be able to apply them to particular client scenarios and be able to understand and apply theories of normative development in the context of social and cultural norms.

Chapters 1 and 2 may describe knowledge new to the reader whereas in Chapter 3 we move on to consider one of the fundamental skills used in everyday life. Communication skills involve the exchange of information between one person and another. Since social work is a profession in which relationships are fundamental, knowledge about and abilities in communication are essential. Being able to 'read' situations, verbal and non-verbal cues, for example, is central to social work practice in all settings. In Chapter 3 the differing types of communication are outlined and the reader is encouraged to reflect on particular scenarios and think about how meaning is conveyed, and what the social work role might be. They are also invited to 'read' situations using their knowledge about communication. Invariably, students of communication skills tend to have a heightened awareness about the ways in which they and those around them communicate. This appreciation is encouraged in this book, for it is through everyday life—noticing the day-to-day events, exchanges and communications around us—that new insights emerge. In Chapter 3, communication and skills relating to communication are seen as occupying a central role in social work. Combining the social work purpose alongside communication skills enables students to practise how to be a social worker. As we shall see in Chapter 6, placement enables students to put their communication skills to use. But before these skills can emerge, a theoretical framework for practice needs to be developed.

Chapter 4 outlines some of the central theories used in contemporary social work practice. These include cognitive behavioural therapy, humanistic approaches, systems theory/ecological perspectives, feminist social work theory, critical and structural approaches and sociological social work. Each of these theories is outlined and placed in context compared with the others. For example, the view that individual thoughts affect behaviour influences some theoretical traditions whereas in other traditions, social and cultural values and institutions are seen to play a key role in limiting individual opportunities. Therefore the answer to the question: 'what is the role of the social worker?' will differ depending on which theoretical position is taken. Increasingly, organisations are aligning themselves with particular traditions, which has meant the dominance of a set of theories in particular areas of practice. For the social work student, this can be confusing. This chapter suggests choosing a theoretical tradition or approach which appeals to the reader and exploring why it fits. Social workers' development throughout their practice often means engaging with new theoretical traditions and evaluating one's own current ones. In this way, knowledge about theory can be 'scaffolded' or constructed upon a firm foundation. Chapter 4 begins this process through identifying groupings for theories and suggesting ways in which individuals can accommodate a tradition alongside their emerging professional self.

Just as with social work theories, the ethical basis of social work must be considered alongside the emerging social work self. Chapter 5 therefore explores values and ethics and notes that decisions we make in our everyday lives are derived from our own framework of values and ethics. Ethics relate to the rules we employ in making decisions about how we live. In social work, ethics are foundational for practice, alongside our theoretical perspectives. Chapter 5 outlines some of the key philosophical orientations used in social work. These include utilitarianism, Kantianism, virtue-based ethics, care ethics, bioethics and a human rights approach. The chapter examines governing bodies and their role in institutionalising and policing social work ethics. It looks at some ethical issues which can emerge in practice including ethical dilemmas, organisational ethical issues, impaired workers and dual role relationships. Just as with the material explored in Chapter 4 which related to theories, in Chapter 5 the reader is invited to consider: 'what roles do values and ethics play in one's everyday life?' Developing these alongside social work values and ethics is a key task in the emergence of the social work self.

In Chapter 6 we consider the complex world of placement. Field education, or placement, requires students to enter an organisational setting and begin to practise their social work skills and use their social work knowledge for purposeful action and interaction. Because this type of knowledge acquisition is derived through an experiential means—that is, students are 'doing' social work in a real setting—placement can feel separate from other types of knowledge acquired during social work study. In fact, placement is an opportunity to bring together learning from classroom-based subjects. We also discuss assessment. Assessment is a core social work skill and is evident in virtually all practice settings, and in this chapter we consider ways in which assessment skills can be applied to client scenarios. The role of the supervisor concludes Chapter 6.

As we see in Chapter 7, research is increasingly used in social work practice settings. The ability to think about issues as a researcher is first explored, through the concept of 'research mindedness'. For the social work student, it is essential to develop an understanding of research in the context of the profession. Therefore in this chapter the following are explored since they are foundational to carrying out research: research questions, aims and scope, epistemology, research methodology and methods, interviews, focus groups, questionnaires, observation and ethnography, ethics, sampling, data analysis and literature reviews. Not only is it important for social workers to consider research as a potential dimension to their social work role, but it is crucial that social workers understand how to apply social work research. This skill is encouraged using targeted exercises in Chapter 7.

Chapter 8 concludes *How to be a Social Worker*. In this final chapter there is some consideration of how, post qualification, social workers' identities are continually forged. Although the chapter brings the book to its conclusion it is also designed to assist newly qualified graduates to understand and continue to develop their social work selves. Positioning reflexive moments in the world of practice is argued to provide social workers with the tools to appreciate and grow the social work self. Finding the ethical and theoretical framework to carry social work practice into the future is also important to maintaining passion and interest in this profession. We consider some of the ongoing challenges in social work and how we can respond to the changing world around us. Understanding selfhood is argued to have important benefits to social work identity on a personal level as well as for the collective identity that we hold as a profession. In this final chapter we see that it is important to understand who we are and what we do in social work.

Now that we have briefly explored the content of the chapters, it will be useful to understand the ways in which the material comes together. The two common threads which tie all of the chapters together in this book are (i) the importance of relationships and (ii) the centrality of the everyday.

Firstly, relationships are central to social work. Social relations are also essential to selfhood, as we shall see throughout this text. Additionally, a student's engagement in learning about social work requires understanding the relationships between themselves and formal knowledge, themselves and their own values and those of the profession, as well as understanding how existing skills in communication are transferred into social work practice. Thus, those chapters which explore skills and values are oriented towards student engagement with the ways in which their own relationships have developed and are characterised. Understanding the ways in which one's own values and beliefs shape one's interaction with others, for example, helps to frame the ways in which social work values are central to social work practice, theory and research. A student's relationship with formal knowledge such as theoretical material is made stronger through reflexive engagement in the subject matter. For this reason, theory is outlined in relation to the social world and students are invited to consider the relationship between theories used in social work and the needs of others. Identifying the relationships—that is, the connections and synergies between practice, theory and the emerging social work self—is of central concern to this book.

Secondly, throughout this text the reader is encouraged to reflect upon their lived experience. Day-to-day or everyday life is used to help student engagement with social work. The everyday level of analysis, combined with the emphasis on relationships, promotes critical engagement with issues of central concern to social workers. Since social work is concerned with working with people, the ways in which we engage in the world around us prior to studying social work require reflection and analysis. It is through the engagement with the everyday that we can begin to unravel the embedded assumptions, values and social norms which characterise our social setting.

As we shall see throughout this book, becoming a social worker occurs through the intersection of one's life circumstances and experiences or biography, the broader scholarly ideas held by our profession, our own imagination and engagement in reflexivity. In order to participate in these interactions, we must understand the role of human interaction (Mead 1934). What brings social work students to social work differs greatly, but there is often a 'personal' experience which propels people into the work. This book offers opportunities to better understand the connections between who we are as a 'private' person and who we are as a professional and how these intersect and play out in the work that we do. At the beginning of studying social work it can be difficult to see what the future social work self will look like in everyday practice.

As a beginning social work student you are therefore entering a period of time and space where you will learn and fashion your social work self. The interaction between older ways of thinking and relating and newer ways which develop as you gain additional knowledge will be reflected upon. Your social work self is very much a part of who you already are. I leave you with the words of C. Wright Mills, who sums up this connection between our work and our selves. Here he urges students to view their intellectual endeavours as very much a part of their personal lives. In social work we bring our selves to our role and in this sense, the nexus between the personal, biographical, political and social holds the key to incorporating new knowledge about social work. Social work cannot be practised well without a personal commitment to fighting inequality and injustice.

It is best to begin, I think, by reminding you, the beginning student, that the most admirable thinkers within the scholarly community you have chosen to join do not split their work from their lives... What this means is that you must learn to use your life experience in your intellectual work: continually to examine and interpret it. In this sense craftsmanship is the centre of yourself and you are personally involved in every intellectual product upon which you may work. (Mills 1959, p. 196)

1

The Social Work Self

This chapter:

- Introduces social work

- Explains what is meant by the term 'self'

- Promotes reflection about the self and assumptions

- Introduces the concept of reflexivity

- Outlines the theoretical orientation featured in this book

Imagine you are asked the question: 'who are you?' You might answer this by describing the way that you see yourself or you might imagine what others would say about you. The kinds of words you might use may well suggest a particular kind of 'personality'. Words such as 'easygoing' or 'shy' or 'kind' or even 'extrovert' or 'introvert' might spring to mind, for example. Yet the concept of a personality is just that: a concept. It is merely a theory to explain the self. Additionally, the ways in which we describe ourselves will change over time, alongside new and varied life experiences.

Think about how you would have been described when you were aged nine compared to your current age. Do you think you will use the same kinds of words to describe yourself when you are in your 80s? In this chapter we will critically challenge the notion of 'personality' through examining the idea that our self is always changing and in flux because it is produced through our interactions with others (Mead 1934). In social work, there is much to be learned about identity, or what we call 'the self', because the ways in which we think about our own identities help to shape how we approach others.

In this chapter we therefore begin to examine what this ongoing process of 'making' the social work self entails and specifically how identity is 'made'. In the same way that we can reflect upon and describe ourselves in everyday life, for example in the articulation of a 'personality' and its associated traits, so too can the professional social work self be described in specific terms. Whilst the ways in which we present ourselves as social workers will differ from person to person, there is also a broader social work identity which draws all social workers into a shared set of values, theory base and purpose. Before examining how individual social work identity is constituted, it is important to understand social work more broadly.

UNDERSTANDING SOCIAL WORK

The term 'social work' provokes varying responses, depending on the context within which the words are uttered. As Payne points out, 'there will never be a final answer that says social work is one thing' (2005, p. 11). This is due to a range of factors. For example, national policies can frame and determine the scope of social work roles and international social work practices vary markedly. Similarly, social work varies at certain temporal points in history. Social work in today's economic and social climate differs from the social work being practised decades ago. Exactly what I mean by social work may not be exactly what others mean. Yet despite all of these influences on social work, we can still make some general statements about what it entails. Social workers share similar professional values and work from a shared theory base. Social workers work to address inequality and injustice across a range of differing settings, roles and foci. Despite some differences in the ways social work is practised, experienced and even articulated, it does have a clear identity.

Social work involves working with people. Social workers see people in their social and cultural contexts and work to promote the well-being of others. This means that social workers share the view that inequality and oppression ought to be challenged and the rights of vulnerable people promoted. Yet what does this mean in practice? What do social workers *do*? The International Federation of Social Workers (IFSW) describes some of the *practices* that social workers engage in:

> Social work addresses the barriers, inequities and injustices that exist in society. It responds to crises and emergencies as well as to everyday personal and social problems. Social work utilises a variety of skills, techniques, and activities consistent with its holistic focus on persons and their environments. Social work interventions range from primarily person-focused psychosocial processes to involvement in social policy, planning and development. These include counselling, clinical social work, group work, social pedagogical work, and family treatment and therapy as well as efforts to help people obtain services and resources in the community. Interventions also include agency administration, community organisation and engaging in social and political action to impact social policy and economic development. The holistic focus of social work is universal, but the priorities of social work practice will vary from country to country and from time to time depending on cultural, historical, and socio-economic conditions. (IFSW: http://ifsw.org/policies/definition-of-social-work/)

Therefore some of the roles of a social worker entail: providing education; providing assistance to those in crisis; advocating for the rights of others; promoting the well-being of communities; providing clinical services such as individual, family and group therapeutic counselling services; working in partnership with others to advance political rights movements; designing services for communities based on needs; working with vulnerable persons to promote their safety and help them thrive; working in social policy and engaging in research.

There are some terms which help categorise the work which social workers undertake and these are primarily associated with particular groups of people. Therefore social workers often talk in a kind of 'shorthand' about their work. For example, a social worker may say they 'work in mental health'. Although the specific focus of their mental health work will depend on the type of organisation they work for (Is it government or non-government? Does the organisation work with people who self-refer or do people need a referral from another professional?), it is useful to understand the ways in which social work is divided according to themes or fields. Some of the key terms used to denote a particular social work focus are listed in Table 1.1.

TABLE 1.1 Some key terms used to denote a particular social work focus	
Field of practice	**Description**
Youth offending	Social work in youth offending involves working with young people who have committed criminal offences. Some organisations work with young people to try to prevent reoffending while others work to address broader issues such as safety, housing, employment and other needs.
Mental health	This area involves working with people with mental illness/mental health concerns. It can include those with diagnosed mental health conditions, those at risk of mental illness and their families and/or carers. Depending on the context, work can be with individuals, groups, families or communities. Services such as Child and Adolescent Mental Health Services (CAMHS) cater for mental health needs in children and teenagers whereas other services cater for adults.

TABLE 1.1 *continued*

Field of practice	Description
Substance misuse	This area involves working with people who have substance misuse issues such as drug and alcohol dependency/addiction. Work can be with a range of client issues/groups including individuals, families, groups and communities.
Older people	Social work with older people can include addressing health and/or accommodation needs, for example assessing and arranging residential aged care facilities. Depending on the organisational context, it can include working to prevent and/or protect against abuse ('safeguarding'), working with families, groups or communities.
Disability	Disability services can be divided according to age groups or for particular disabilities. For example, the needs of people with acquired brain injury will differ markedly from those of people with learning disabilities.
Children and families	Child protection, for example, involves working with children, young people and their caregivers towards protecting children and young people from harm, which includes abuse, violence and neglect. There are various services in this area, which determines the agency focus. Work can therefore span working with children, young people and their families, foster carers and carers, groups and communities. Work can be preventative, for example parenting programmes aimed at reducing child abuse, or can be in response to community need.
Sexual health	Sexual health services include specialist programmes such as those directed towards reducing teenage pregnancy, reducing sexually transmissible infections and issues relating to sexuality or sexual identity. Client groups can include school-based programmes, individual work and group work in community settings.
Domestic violence	Domestic violence involves control and the misuse of power through violence towards an intimate partner. Domestic violence can take the form of actual or threatened violence. This violence can be verbal, emotional, financial, sexual and/or physical. Services relating to domestic violence include shelters for people escaping domestic violence, counselling services, and programmes for perpetrators of domestic violence. Depending on the agency context, social workers can work with individuals, groups or communities.
CALD	This field of practice refers to working with people who are from Culturally And Linguistically Diverse backgrounds (CALD). The term NESB is also used for this client group (people from Non English Speaking Backgrounds). Some social workers describe their work according to this category, which can include work with refugees, particular ethnic communities, diaspora communities and people from particular cultural and religious groups.
Community	Community-based intervention targets a particular issue. For example, working towards prevention of stroke within the community might include encouraging smoking cessation, increasing community awareness about stroke symptoms and risk factors and working with other organisations to undertake early screening for risk factors. Community development encompasses work in national and international contexts and intervention occurs with the community rather than at an individual level.
Advocacy	Social workers in advocacy represent and work in partnership with clients so that they may gain access to services and opportunities. Rights-based intervention seeks to redress oppression. There are a number of client groups in this area, including the general population. Some organisations represent one particularly vulnerable and oppressed group of people. For example, the social model of disability recognises that the environment 'disables' people through its lack of design or accommodation for people with disabilities and this model can be used in individual, group and community work aiming for political and social change.

TABLE 1.1 *continued*	
Field of practice	**Description**
Health	Social workers within health can work towards preventing illness as well as alongside other health professionals on a range of programmes. Social models of health highlight the important contextual role that one's social setting, class, gender and other 'determinants' of health play in how well-being and health are experienced by individuals. Social work is well placed to work within a social model of health. Practitioners in this area may be employed in acute services such as hospitals and specialist clinics as well as in organisations working to prevent ill health.
International development	International development activities can encompass community work, individual work and group work. International development will involve a particular issue, such as reducing HIV transmission or assisting in peace-building. The work occurs in the country in which the development is targeted.
Policy	Policy refers to government-endorsed decisions about a particular issue. Working in policy can entail researching an issue and canvassing viewpoints from key individuals and groups about that issue. Policy working often involves communicating through written material such as reports, and work can be undertaken through both government and non-government organisations.
Research	Research entails a deeper understanding of a particular issue. Social workers who work in research can be employed in government and non-government organisations. They can carry out very large scale surveys as well as small scale studies such as those evaluating social work services.
Self-employed	Some social workers can work through consultancy. For example, those who have acquired particular expertise in an identifiable area of practice may offer services in such an area. Whether a social worker is able to sustain employment through working for themselves depends on the national context: social workers in some countries are more able to go into private practice than in other countries.

WORKING WITH OTHERS

Throughout this book we will explore some of the differing practice contexts and issues which relate to working with other professional groups. In understanding social work we also need to place the profession within its multidisciplinary context. Multidisciplinary, interdisciplinary or allied professionals working together all mean the same thing. These terms refer to the ongoing relationships between other professions and social workers. Multidisciplinary approaches entail working alongside, or in partnership with, various disciplines besides social work. The types of professions engaged in interdisciplinary working vary according to the field of practice. Table 1.2 takes the fields of practice from Table 1.1 and matches them to the key professions with whom social workers in the area may work.

Alongside these professionals, social workers can expect to work with carers and volunteers in a variety of settings. Social workers can also become specialised in their particular field, which differentiates them from other social workers whose work may be more generic. For example, mental health social

TABLE 1.2 The key professions with whom social workers in each field of practice may work

Field of practice	Working with others: Social workers work with...
Youth offending	Lawyers General practitioners (GPs) and specialists Teachers in educational institutions Youth workers Psychologists Interpreters
Mental health	Nurses Psychiatrists Psychologists General practitioners (GPs) Diversional therapists Interpreters
Substance misuse	Specialist medical professionals including nurses and doctors Interpreters Counsellors
Older people	Occupational therapists Speech therapists/speech pathologists Physiotherapists General practitioners (GPs) and specialists Podiatrists/chiropodists Psychologists Dieticians Exercise physiologists Interpreters
Disability	Occupational therapists Physiotherapists Speech therapists/speech pathologists General practitioners (GPs) and specialists Podiatrists/chiropodists Interpreters
Children and families	Teachers and educational institutions Police Community-based workers General practitioners (GPs) and specialists such as paediatricians Health Visitors Speech therapists/speech pathologists Lawyers Interpreters Family therapists Developmental psychologists
Sexual health	Nurses General practitioners (GPs) and specialists such as sexual health physicians, gynaecologists, obstetricians and midwives Community development workers Teenage pregnancy coordinators Health Visitors Interpreters

TABLE 1.2 *continued*	
Field of practice	**Working with others: Social workers work with...**
Domestic violence	General practitioners (GPs) and specialists Interpreters Counsellors Health Visitors
CALD	Interpreters Government and non-government workers Health professionals including general practitioners (GPs) and specialists
Community	Interpreters Government and non-government workers Community development workers
Advocacy	Interpreters Government and non-government workers Councillors/Members of Parliament (MPs)
Health	Occupational therapists Speech therapists/speech pathologists Physiotherapists General practitioners (GPs) and specialists Podiatrists/chiropodists Psychologists Health Visitors Dieticians Exercise physiologists Interpreters Diversional therapists
International development	Interpreters Policy-makers Epidemiologists Medical doctors and nurses Medical specialists such as obstetricians and gynaecologists Teachers Community workers
Policy	Government and non-government workers Advocacy groups Experts such as researchers Medical experts such as epidemiologists Interpreters
Research	Statisticians Social scientists Psychologists Interpreters Funders such as government and non-government employees

workers (also referred to as 'approved social workers/approved mental health practitioners') have particular roles within mental health and may be involved in the clinical assessment of people with mental health conditions. Similarly, social workers can work as counsellors and may gain further qualifications to specialise in therapeutic practice. Specialisms in social work can allow people to continue to develop their expertise in a particular area, which is an important aspect of professional self-development.

Although the idea that social workers work alongside or in partnership with other professionals can sound relatively straightforward, in fact there are many complexities relating to interdisciplinary working. Looking at Table 1.2, note in how many fields of practice social workers work alongside health professionals. What do you think might be the issues when working with other professions? For example, which professions are more respected or hold more power? Do social workers have less status than health professionals?

Recent research into the mental health field found that social workers were indeed worse off than other colleagues in relation to their professional identity and subsequent status (Bailey & Liyanage 2012). The researchers found that despite mental health social workers having gained expertise in the area, they have 'reduced status' (p. 1113) compared to other professional groups. This research resonates with earlier work which explored the relationship between medical doctors and social workers, and found that the respective world-views of each of these professions differed markedly (Huntington 1981). Yet differences can be productive, allowing each profession to bring new ideas which, when combined, benefit others (Lymbery 2006, p. 1122). Conflict as a result of interprofessional working can lead to creative responses to problems which might otherwise have been overlooked (Quinney & Hafford-Letchfield 2012). However, further complicating matters is the organisational context within which professions work together.

Broadly speaking, there are two aspects to interdisciplinary working. The first relates to the interpersonal relationships between professional staff. For example, some interdisciplinary team members are situated together in the work environment. The ways they communicate with one another will depend on a range of factors, but the portrayal of the profession of social work in that exchange depends on the profession's own identity as well as how that social worker understands and practises social work. Secondly, the funding models devised by governments and policy-makers along with the organisational settings, including the non-government or voluntary sector, impact on whether interdisciplinary work is effective and positive. This aspect to interdisciplinary working is more *structural* whereas the former is *interpersonal*. The structural setting and interpersonal relationships influence the service clients receive.

Bywaters (1986) argues that medical professionals and social workers cannot work together unless the medical profession adapts its world-view to include an appreciation of *social* models of health (Bywaters 1986, p. 663 cited in Lymbery 2006, p. 1122), rather than simply viewing work with others, as it has done historically (Lymbery 2006, p. 1125), through a strictly medical lens. Bywaters' position raises an important question: is it necessary to have shared world-views or epistemologies in order to work effectively together? This is something we will consider throughout the book. Importantly, what is the impact on the client of professions working alongside each other? Let's consider Case Study 1.1.

CASE STUDY 1.1 Samuel Carey

Imagine you are a social worker in a mental health hospital setting. As part of your role, each week you attend a case allocation meeting. This meeting is chaired by the medical Consultant who is the head of the medical team. Other attendees include other medical doctors, occupational therapists, physiotherapists, mental health nurses and social workers. You learn the following information:

Samuel Carey is a white British male in his late 50s. He is in a long-term relationship with Sarah, aged 59, and they have two children who are both aged in their 30s. Samuel and Sarah live in a two bedroom flat in an upmarket area of town. Until recently, Samuel worked in the IT industry but he recently became retrenched. Sarah has Ehlers-Danlos syndrome which means that she has mobility problems. Sarah sees a physiotherapist privately for this condition, which is expected to worsen as she ages. Samuel has come to the attention of the unit after being arrested by the police one day prior to this referral. Samuel was reportedly seen damaging property after assaulting one of his former employees. The police reported that Samuel was 'psychotic' when he was incarcerated and they would like him to be detained and assessed by the unit. Although Samuel has been hostile since his contact with the police, he has no criminal history and has been described by former employees as 'a lovely guy who wouldn't hurt anyone'.

Consider what information might be important to take into account in deciding how to act. For example, consider:

- What might the physiotherapists be interested in learning more about?
- What might the mental health doctors and nurses be interested in learning more about?
- What might the social workers be interested in learning more about?

In this case study, it is somewhat easy to assume that the physiotherapists would be interested to hear more about the impact the Ehlers-Danlos syndrome is having on Sarah and how this will be managed in the future. Similarly, the occupational therapists may be interested in better understanding the limitations of mobility and related mental health issues and how these might be overcome in day-to-day life. Similarly, the mental health doctors and nurses may be interested in investigating further in order to undertake an assessment with a view to diagnosing Samuel so they can meet his needs through medication or therapies. The social worker might be approaching the situation wanting to understand how and why Samuel's behaviour has changed so markedly and what the impacts are for Sarah.

Yet all of the above are assumptions. The assumptions include that medical staff (including doctors, nurses and physiotherapists) are only interested in medical issues whereas the other professions are more interested in the social contexts (occupational therapists, mental health social workers). A more realistic and optimistic perspective is that each profession can apply their specialist knowledge in their work in order to help their client. In working with other professions, any one professional can recognise other areas where a client can benefit from others' expertise. Given the case study described a case allocation meeting, it is important to recognise that usually in these meetings a plan of action is decided. Consider, for example, that the medical doctor wanted to see Samuel immediately to make an assessment whereas the social worker wanted to see Samuel and Sarah together first. Both professions want to undertake their own assessment, but they will need to decide upon an agreed course of action. Similarly, the other professions will need to agree on what to do next. There are many potential ways to respond to this scenario. Assessing using some of the longer-term questions might consider: is there a risk of Samuel harming others? How will Sarah's mobility needs be met in the future? What are Samuel's needs and how will these be met?

Research has identified the tensions and complexities in interprofessional working (Bailey & Liyanage 2012; Bywaters 1986; Carpenter *et al.* 2003; Lymbery 2006). Multidisciplinary working may be more prevalent in the future, or it may become less common, but it is clear that the social work profession will need to continue to work with other professionals in the immediate future. One aspect which affects the status of a profession and its portrayal to other professional groups is the identity of social work itself. We now consider what is meant by identity, or *self*, and how this is relevant to becoming a social worker.

WHAT IS THE SELF?

Take a look at Figure 1.1 on page 22. What do you see? Take a few moments to really reflect upon this image and begin to think about the identity of the subject. Who do you think is featured in this image? Does the ear belong to a man or a woman? What makes you think about them as gendered? From this image are you able to draw any conclusions about the person's age? Do you think they are aged in their teens, for example, or are they in older age? What clues are there to help you decide their age group? Do you see the person as wealthy, or working class? What kind of house do they live in and are they employed? Can you tell what their cultural background is? Are they part of a large family, do they have siblings and how might you characterise their peer group?

Even though what is featured in the photograph is only a fragmented image of a person, when you first began to study the image you already began to connect the ear with an individual. Through looking at the image you started to piece together experiences unique to you—your life, the people around you such as your friends and family—and think about how you might categorise the person featured in the photograph in relation to these. For example, from studying this image you may imagine that the subject is male, that because of his piercing he is a young person and perhaps he is image conscious. You can then begin to create a mental image of the person by linking together your own experiences in everyday life with the imagined identity of the subject in the photograph. Perhaps you know a young man whom you are basing your image upon. Or maybe you are drawing your knowledge and inspiration from images you see in the media. Your experience of social interaction—or sociality—helps you to make some initial assumptions about the identity of the person featured in this image. Human interactions take place in everyday life and include conversations and communication with others in a range of daily activities.

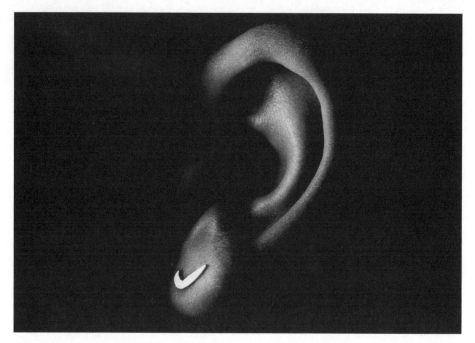

FIGURE 1.1 What and who do you see?

© Andrew Dunbar

Without these interactions, society would cease to function. Not only are these inter-actions central to a functioning society—sociality is also central to creating the self (Mead 1934). Let us take a closer look at sociality and what it means for selfhood.

SOCIAL INTERACTION OR SOCIALITY

George Herbert Mead's scholarship has provided a significant, and continuing, contribution to sociology (Alexander 1989; Joas 1997). His work is usually associ-ated with a particular tradition in sociology called symbolic interactionism. Symbolic interactionism 'directs our attention to the detail of interpersonal interac-tion, and how that detail is used to make sense of what others say and do. Sociologists influenced by symbolic interactionism often focus on face-to-face interaction in the contexts of everyday life. They stress the role of such interaction in creating society and its institutions' (Giddens 2005, p. 18). As we shall see, Mead (1934) argues that the self is created through social interactions.

There are strong historical links with Mead's theory-building about interpersonal relationships and social work, with Mead having been involved in many of the hous-ing and rights struggles of early social work figures such as Jane Addams (Forte 2004a, p. 393). For this reason, Mead is also associated with a type of early sociol-ogy in which social problems were not only theorised or thought about by scholars but were acted upon through social action and activism.

Mead's conception of self is useful for understanding the professional social work self. Broadly speaking, interactionism emphasises the power produced through relationships between people. Since social work is also focused on relationships and their meanings for individuals, groups and communities, it makes sense that person-to-person interaction and understanding the person themselves is an area of intellectual inquiry. Mead's theory of self resonates with early social work literature ranging from Mary Richmond's notion of self to Siporin's (1972) appreciation of the self in its social context (Forte 2004a, p. 394). As we will see throughout this book, Mead's theories are relevant to social work. Yet it is important to understand what we mean by social interaction. This involves understanding the link between social interaction and selfhood.

In *Mind, Self and Society* Mead (1934) argues that the self is 'made' through *sociality* which consists of social interactions and relationships with others. Thus we only create our identities or selves through these relationships. As we shall see, this idea is in direct contrast with psychoanalytic notions of the self, which primarily see identity as being complex and compartmentalised. For example, Mead rejects the notion that people have a mind—the only mind, he says, is that which is produced through external relationships with others. Mead says that the mind is not internal to individuals but is a concept which is reinforced through our interactions with others. This idea—that the mind is outside our selves rather than inside—goes against what is popularly accepted to be 'true'.

At the beginning of this chapter you were invited to think about how you would respond to the question: 'who are you?' Your response would have most likely drawn from the idea that people's identities can be defined through the notion of personality. Yet a personality is simply an idea in which the self is represented as an internal, quantifiable and descriptive entity. Mead's notion of self (1934) rejects the view that people have personalities and he argues that there is no such thing as a 'mind' beyond the idea shared between people. Instead, social interaction is central to 'producing' the self. There are some examples of ways people display a sense of self which is external to their thoughts or minds. Imagine you were to make a collage of images, for example on a pin board or a social media website, to represent yourself—this would be an example of how we like to pictorialise our selves and present this to others for them to see. Mead's idea about self being external to our minds is similar to this idea in that we describe ourselves to others and think about ourselves only in relation to others and the rest of society.

According to Mead (Mead 1934; Da Silva 2011), all social interactions—interactions involving more than one person engaged with another through gestures and language, conversations and behaviours—are constitutive of the self. Whereas in psychoanalytic theory the self is formed through internal thought processes and conflicts, Meadian sociality emphasises social processes, which are 'outside' the self, as constitutive.

It is often assumed that in order to understand ourselves we need to go back to think about our childhood, since that was the time we learned particular things and experienced particular things. In thinking about childhood, we can see the differences and similarities between psychoanalytic theories and interactionist theories. For both psychoanalytic theory as well as Mead's theory, childhood is important to the self (Crossley 2001, p. 145). However, precisely *how* it is important differs markedly between the two theories.

Mead argues that by social interaction through childhood games and play children learn about society's norms and values (Mead 1934, pp. 368–373) and in this way children learn about the 'generalized other'. Society's norms and values (which are called the 'generalized other' by Mead) are easy to forget since we are continuously using this knowledge automatically. Society's norms about how we conduct ourselves in a café include, for example, the assumption that we will sit on a seat, order a drink or food and talk to people at our table. Childhood learning about the generalized other enables people to pre-empt how others will respond to things. For example, imagine you were to stand up from where you are reading this book, throw the book into the air and start shouting. What would others around you do? We can say with a certain confidence that throwing books and shouting is not a generally accepted social act. Yet if we had been bitten by a wasp, this behaviour might be perfectly understandable. The reaction of those around us would depend on the social situation. If you are in a library or a crowded bus, others will respond with caution. If you are with family or friends they might be less reluctant to question you about why you are behaving in this way.

The fact that we can pre-empt others' behaviour is for Mead evidence that we are able to draw upon our knowledge of the generalized other. For Mead, fantasy or 'abstract thought' is the means through which the generalized other is manifest (Mead 1934, pp. 155–156). In psychoanalytic theory, fantasy symbolises the deeper tension that characterises the self, as we shall see in the following critical discussion. Because of the prominence of psychoanalytic theories of the self in everyday life it is crucial to critique these approaches and examine their differences to the social construction of the self.

Psychoanalytic scholarship about the self represents an established intellectual tradition and one which has been argued to apply to sociological understandings of the self (see, for example, Elliott 2001, 2005). Yet the contrast between the ways in which the self can be examined through Meadian analysis and psychoanalytic theory could not be more marked. Despite the historical emphasis and subsequent proliferation of therapeutic discourse in contemporary life (Furedi 2004) Mead's theoretical tradition better accounts for the ways in which the social work identity is forged. As we shall see, there is some common ground between the two approaches: the prominence of childhood in the formation of the self and the role of language and communication, for example, are central to both approaches.

Psychoanalytic theory influenced much of the theorising about the self until the 1960s social constructionist theory-building shifted the emphasis away from the Freudian self more towards the social self (Jackson & Scott 2010a, p. 9). Although the social self is prominent in scholarly literature, we are most familiar with psychoanalytic notions of identity. For example, in popular culture we uncritically accept the concept of personality—the idea that we can describe particular traits about ourselves—yet this is merely a theoretical concept that has gained popularity in contemporary culture. We explore this further in Chapter 4 in relation to social work theory.

In particular, ideas from psychoanalytic theory have had significant purchase in various disciplines since the 19th century and continue to be embedded in social work theory and practice. The idea that in order to resolve a problem one must engage in therapy or counselling is an example of the underlying assumptions from psychoanalytic theory. The 'therapeutic turn'—or the historically identifiable point at which we elevated therapy as important to our well-being—is not only a process involving individual subjectivities, but is argued to have become a ubiquitous aspect of contemporary social life in western societies (Furedi 2004; Lasch 1979; Reiff 1966).

Evidence for this is the comparatively recent rise in the number of self-help books, television shows and other media which promote the idea that through learning more about ourselves we are free to change things we do not like in us. Yet in this tradition, who we are—or the self—is splintered in that it contains a conscious, socially mediated self as well as an unconscious dimension to identity. Symbols connected to the self such as language, dreams and everyday interactions offer interpretations of this conflict between the unconscious and the conscious. Therefore the psychoanalytic self cannot ever be seen to be conflict-free. Accepting those theories that see desire and the unconscious as being problematically connected in time to stages of development from childhood would seem to mean that the adult self cannot be free from pathology.

The therapeutic application of psychoanalytic theory equates to what has been termed the 'talking therapies'. Here individuals can reflect upon and explore subjective issues. Although the ubiquity of therapeutic practices is utilitarian (Elliott 1996; Elliott & Lemert 2006)—they offer 'individuals a radical purchase on the dilemmas of living in the modern epoch' (Elliott 1996, p. 329)—it is the contribution made by George Herbert Mead that enables a richer and more socially orientated analysis of the self in contemporary times (Jackson 1999; Jackson & Scott 2010a, 2010b).

To understand individuals, one must look at their relationships with others and the broader society in which they are immersed. This idea differs from the focus on the *individual themselves*, an idea which dominates the public sphere due to its fascination with therapeutic discourse (Furedi 2004). In social work, as we shall see in Chapter 4, there has been a dual focus on psychology and sociology which is realised through the differing strands of social work theory.

For Mead, to understand individual action, one must see the action as part of an individual's *interactions*: 'Significance belongs to things in their relations to individuals. It does not lie in mental processes which are enclosed within individuals' (Mead 1922 [2011], p. 69).

Whereas in psychoanalytic theory the mind contains an 'unknowable unconscious' (Jackson 2007, p. 4), for Mead, the mind is only 'knowable' through social processes. Therefore in understanding the individual, one must understand their relationship to others in society and the role these relationships play in determining identity. Specifically, this means that the individual gradually learns how to interact and understand the role of others and the values of society. This learning occurs from birth onwards, with children learning about society's rules and values through interaction. Mead says:

In the process of communication the individual is an other before he [sic] is a self. It is in addressing himself in the role of an other that his self arises in experience. The growth of the organized game out of simple play in the experience of the child, and of organized group activities in human society, placed the individual then in a variety of roles, in so far as these were parts of the social act, and the very organization of these in the whole act gave them a common character in indicating what he had to do. He is able then to become a generalized other in addressing himself in the attitude of the group or the community. In this situation he has become a definite self over against the social whole to which he belongs. (Mead 1925 [2011], p. 199)

In social work it is vital to remain oriented to the role the social dimension plays in influencing human experience. The connection between the individual and the society within which they are embedded is central to social work, as we shall see throughout this book. Let's now consider the role of childhood in relation to the development of the self.

For Mead the period of childhood is of crucial importance to social competence as it enables individuals to learn the dominant norms and attitudes of society—'in the instance of the infant ... effective adjustment to the little society upon which it has so long to depend' (Mead 1934, p. 368). There is a more detailed examination of childhood play in Chapter 2, where it is discussed in relation to human development, but it is important to note the placement of childhood as central to Mead's sociality because for him it is a time when children undertake learning that helps them engage in social exchanges throughout their lives.

For Mead, sociality—which is the engagement in social interactions and processes—is constitutive of selfhood (Mead 1934). Being 'constitutive' of selfhood means that it constitutes, 'makes' or 'produces' the self. Put simply, Mead argues that *we can only become ourselves, and continue to be ourselves, by interacting with others.*

There are many examples of the ways in which our relationships with others reinforce our identity or self. Imagine the way you might greet a person with whom you might be working. A simple 'hello' might result in a particular set of gestures, dialogue and other ways of communicating such as through non-verbal activity. You might, for example, make eye contact with your colleague and smile. You might sit down across from them to begin your discussion. Your posture might be upright and formal. You might be holding on to stationery such as a pen and a pad of paper. Think about the differences between the 'you' in this context and the 'you' in another context. Think about, for example, greeting a family member or close friend in your home. You might not make eye contact with them and might walk past them to get to your chair, briefly saying 'hi' to them. Once you get to your chair you may slump down and watch television or start reading a book. Your friend or family member may not look up from their activity and may simply reply 'hi' back to you. The 'you' in both of these situations are examples of the different roles we play in everyday life. In both these examples, the interaction with others takes different forms. The familiarity which is embedded in the relationship and interaction at home means that the 'you' is reflected differently than in the interaction with the colleague. The tiny changes in mannerisms, bodily postures and movements as well as other forms of communication are all employed differently depending on the context. Both of these are examples of sociality—engagement with other people. In interacting with you, the social interactions reinforce your own identity as 'worker' or 'family member' or 'friend'. In my own research about selfhood I have found that the role that interaction with others plays is crucial to our ongoing identities (Dunk-West 2011). It is therefore crucial to understand the role that sociality plays in the context of people's everyday life worlds.

Yet so far we have been thinking about the self as an individual, and not so much about the broader social setting within which these interactions take place. Although the individual self has been given prominence in Mead's work, it is also important to understand how *society* is theorised in relation to the ways in which selfhood is argued to be produced. In particular, individual behaviour ought to be made sense of in the context within which it takes place. Is society just a collection of individuals? Are we free to choose our actions or are we influenced by other factors? The degree to which one person is able to exercise choice within this context is an historically enduring debate (Handel 2003, p. 133).

The tension between the individual and society is related to the so-called 'agency versus structure' debate. Put another way, this refers to the idea of individual will versus societal pressure. Ending this debate means reconciling the tension between seeing individuals as able to shape their lives through choice and seeing them as constrained by social circumstances and therefore less free to make choices. Are we free to act or are we following a script? There is no easy answer to this question.

Consider what assumptions underpin the idea that we can become 'better'. The notion of working hard to achieve particular means relies upon the idea that individuals are able to change their circumstances. Material wealth, for example, is something that some people strive to achieve. Having agency relates to the freedom to make changes in one's life or circumstances. To have unlimited agency means that everyone has the same opportunities to make changes and choices in their lives, whereas to believe that structure shapes society means supporting the view that individuals are less powerful than social institutions and that although individuals may try to achieve certain goals, their success is ultimately shaped by the influence of social structures.

Mead's approach is to argue that there is little use in making distinctions between individuals and society, since it is individuals who *make* society. A useful starting point to understand how Mead views the dynamic between the individual and the social emerges through the explanation in the following quote:

> The social act is not explained by building it up out of stimulus plus response; it must be taken as a dynamic whole—as something going on—no part of which can be considered or understood by itself—a complex organic process implied by each individual stimulus and response involved in it. (Mead 1934, p. 7)

Sociality is not only constitutive for the formation of the self—that is, social interactions do more than enable people's selves to be produced. Sociality exists through complex, dynamic interactional processes. Therefore the individual is part of a broader 'organic process' (Mead 1934, p. 7) in which other individuals interact. These interactions form what we might call 'society'.

Whilst Mead's conceptualisation of selfhood has achieved a great deal of attention in sociological literature, the ways in which he theorises 'society' have been of lesser interest to scholars (Athens 2005, p. 305). Yet Mead is clear about the relationship between the individual and society:

> Human society as we know it could not exist without minds and selves, since all its most characteristic features presuppose the possession of minds and selves by its individual members; but its individual members would not possess minds and selves if these had not arisen within or emerged out of the human social process. (Mead 1934, p. 227)

Social values relate to what Mead refers to as the 'generalized other' which, as we have seen, is the 'attitude of the community' (Mead 1934, p. 154). These attitudes are internalised to a greater and greater extent through the process of socialisation until individuals have intuitive knowledge of broader society's attitudes (Mead 1934, pp. 155–156) and social interaction becomes so familiar it is routine (Crossley 2001, p. 145). This process occurs from birth onwards, throughout childhood and into adulthood. It is a central question, then, to consider the role of changes in society, given the shifts and changes brought about by the contemporary world.

Scholars interested in late modern social life make links between broader forces such as globalisation and individualisation (see, for example, Giddens 1992) and the ways in which these are manifest in the decisions individuals make in everyday life. For example, the relatively recent trend in which people in committed intimate relationships live apart from one another, so called 'living apart together' (LAT) (see Holmes 2006), can be used as evidence of the increasingly detraditionalised (Giddens 1992, pp. 178–181) environment in which couples negotiate their lifestyles, jobs and relationships. The ways in which these changes in relationships fit with the life course are further discussed in Chapter 2. Detraditionalisation simply means that we have more choices available to us than when our roles were more clearly defined. For example, the traditional roles of 'male bread-winner' and 'wife' meant quite different things in the 1950s to today.

Mead notes the importance of communication in the ongoing interaction between people. In particular, communication is attained in the same manner as all knowledge which is required of social competence: through socialisation. Mead stresses that communicative action is a social process, yet it also links the individual with the means by which to reflect upon his or her self:

> The process of communication simply puts the intelligence of the individual at his [sic] own disposal. But the individual that has this ability is a social individual. He does not develop it by himself and then enter into society on the basis of this capacity. He becomes such a self and gets such control by being a social individual, and it is only in society that he can attain this sort of a self which will make it possible for him to turn back on himself and indicate to himself the different things he can do. (Mead 1934, p. 243)

For Mead, communication is intrinsically connected to the socialising process which, in turn, forms the ongoing social interaction which produces the self (Mead 1934, p. 257). Mead examines other forms of interaction—such as an individual reading a novel or a journalistic text—and demonstrates that although these are varying communicative forms which require knowledge about the generalized other they are forms of communication (Mead 1934, pp. 256–257). Social exchanges in which no personal interaction is required—say that which occurs through engagement in social networking sites or via email or instant messaging—meet the requirements for Mead's depiction of sociality. This is because (i) such exchanges draw from written forms of communication, (ii) they involve more than one person and (iii) they occur as part of existing networks between individuals. Technology both facilitates and replicates interaction that is similar to interaction in the social world (West *et al.* 2011). As Mead says:

> You cannot build up a society out of elements that lie outside of the individual's life-processes. (Mead 1934, p. 257)

In this way, forms of communication which utilise new technologies such as Web 2.0 (see Gauntlett 2007, 2011), including Twitter, Facebook and other social networking sites, can be considered as involving Meadian social interaction. These new forms of communication help to underline the importance we place on interacting with one another in social life (Gauntlett 2011).

THE SELF, REFLEXIVITY AND CONTEMPORARY LIFE

So far we have considered the role of others in helping us make relationships which produce our identities. Also significant is the role of reflexivity and reflexiveness, an area which has been the subject of sociological examinations of the self. In social work, reflexivity means a particular set of processes which help us know who we are as professionals. There is an explanation of the differences between these concepts in the theoretical and applied social sciences in the Glossary at the end of this book. We now consider the role of reflexivity in understanding the processes whereby our selves are 'made' through interaction with other people.

Reflexivity entails engaging in three interrelated processes. Firstly, we think about, or reflect upon, something specific. Secondly, we critically evaluate that activity. Thirdly, we change future relations of actions based on a conscious decision to change the particular activity. For example, I might reflect upon an incident in which I felt I did not get my point across to a colleague. I might think about one particular incident and decide that I was not assertive enough. Based upon my wish to be more assertive and taking into account my perceived failure to be assertive on a previous occasion, the next time I relate to that colleague, I will deliberately work at being more assertive and this will change my behaviour towards them. I might use different words, have different gestures or come across as 'rude'. These changes are brought about as a direct result of my reflexive engagement with my self and the ways in which I see myself (as non-assertive, for example). Reflexivity in social work is not new (see Schon 1983, for example) and relates to the idea that we reflect upon our social work practice to get better and better.

There is an argument in sociology that identity has become an 'ongoing project' (Giddens 1992, p. 30). This means that we are constantly reflecting upon who we are and who we want to be and making changes to realise this idealised version of ourselves. As Giddens (1992, p. 30) says, 'The self today is for everyone a reflexive project—a more or less continuous interrogation of past, present and future'.

Both Bauman (2003) and Giddens (1992) argue that the characteristics of the late modern world, such as globalisation, have 'transformed' ways in which individuals interrelate in personal relationships in their day-to-day lives. For example, because of greater communication across continents, we now have more opportunities to see how others live which may cause us to think about how we live. In western countries, television shows and other forms of technological communication expose us to new alternatives. This new type of 'extended reflexivity' (Adams 2003) means that reflexivity has been increased *because* of globalisation and other large social shifts. However, Giddens' 'extended reflexivity', in which complex social conditions are theorised to have provided new possibilities for self-fashioning, does not address the everyday social and cultural practices within which we are engaged (Adams 2003).

Whilst Giddens' extended reflexivity is viewed as a *product* of contemporary life, Mead argues that what he calls 'reflexiveness' is firmly embedded within social relations. It is not increasing because of new social conditions. Both Giddens and Mead highlight the importance of the social setting from the onset of human life (Adams 2003, p. 232). Mead's reflexiveness is merely a part of his broader theory of the self. It is a feature of the interaction between people. For Giddens, reflexivity is increasing because society is changing.

Mead argues that 'reflexiveness' means being an 'other' to oneself, only through continual interaction with social processes (1934, p. 134). Mead says that (what would be named) 'reflexivity' is not merely a tool for self-fashioning but is required for social functioning (Jackson 2007, p. 8). What people think of as their 'minds' are, in fact, firmly locatable outside their selves (in contrast to psychoanalytic notions of subjectivity which see identity as related to an 'inner' world of individual thoughts and reflections): minds arise only through social interactions. Mead (1934, p. 134) argues that 'reflexiveness, then, is the essential condition, within the social process, for the development of mind'.

The notion of reflexiveness, or reflexivity, is therefore a compulsory condition for sociality, which in turn 'makes' the self. It is a feature of human life and human action (Archer 2007). The term reflexivity has been simplified in both social work and the social sciences because of a failure to recognise the complex processes associated with sociality:

Being reflexive is enormously complex because the actor has to think of many possibilities and many consequences not only for others, but for the constitution of the self. The pressure to select, to choose one of the many lines of action, increases the more you get into the public world... The task of the actor is to continually link and adjust and transform and stabilize the interpersonal and the cultural while maintaining the plausibility of the self. (Gagnon 2011 in Gagnon & Simon 2011 [1973], p. 315)

The process of reflexiveness is central to sociality, which is in turn constitutive of the self and self-making, which is both an aspect of a broader identity and part of a more private sphere. The process of reflexiveness is central to making the social work self. Throughout this text, the exercises are designed to actively engage you in that reflexive process in order to make your social work self. You also do this through engagement with texts, discussions with fellow students and your lecturers as well as through your experiences on placement.

Why is all of this important in social work? It is somewhat of a truism in social work that we are not good at saying who we are or what we do. How do we describe our role to others? How do we distinguish our work from other professions? What value do social workers bring to multidisciplinary work? I believe that although we might not always be able to articulate our work, in practice, social workers develop creative and innovative ways which characterise their practice and identity.

In this book the focus is upon the social work self: how to be a social worker involves understanding one's self and how selfhood is theorised. I argue that the Meadian notion of the self is relevant and helpful to claiming the terrain that social work encompasses. Such a theoretical framework helps in social workers understanding themselves and their professional work. As we shall see, such an understanding relies upon having insights into one's own life experiences and characteristics.

Having a purchase on a theoretical model of selfhood helps social workers to approach knowledge accordingly. The subsequent chapters in this book therefore examine the contexts and material relevant to learning about social work and developing the social work self. Let us now move to consider more fully what this understanding entails.

UNDERSTANDING THE SOCIAL WORK SELF

The centrality of interaction to self-production in the professional context is what drives this book. In other words, becoming a social worker occurs through the intersection of biography, scholarly ideas, imagination and reflexivity: none of these are possible to engage in without human interaction (Mead 1934).

In Table 1.3 some of the key ideas we have examined in this chapter are related directly to social work.

The choice of words and the way we frame social work is influenced by historical, social, cultural and political contexts. The International Federation of Social Workers notes that our definition of social work is always in flux. They offer the following as a way to describe the work of social workers throughout the world:

The social work profession promotes social change, problem solving in human relationships and the empowerment and liberation of people to enhance well-being.

TABLE 1.3 The relation of some of the key ideas in this chapter to social work

General	Specific to social work
The self is not simply a 'personality', it is produced through social interactions	The social work self is dependent on broader social, economic and political contexts
Our experiences are shaped by broader social inequalities and there is a tension between 'agency and structure'	Social workers work with people to change individual behaviour but also to challenge oppressive systems and broader social inequalities
Reflexiveness or reflexivity is important in contemporary life	The social work self is produced through social interactions. Reflexivity is central to social interaction

Utilising theories of human behaviour and social systems, social work intervenes at the points where people interact with their environments. Principles of human rights and social justice are fundamental to social work. (IFSW 2012)

At the end of your studies, and throughout your social work career, it is important to remind yourself what social work means. You will find that your definition will evolve and shift. It is crucial that social workers define their own profession: policy and legislation should never dictate what social work entails. Instead, your social work self will be made through adherence to particular ethical obligations, through understanding the purpose of your work with others and through the ongoing interaction between yourself and those you work with, including your colleagues, employers and clients.

Exercises 1.1 and 1.2 are designed to help you begin to engage with your present understanding of what social work means.

EXERCISE 1.1

Put the following statements in order from most important (1) to least important (10).

Social workers ... need to change the world
Social workers ... need to work hard
Social workers ... are always on duty
Social workers ... should make people do things
Social workers ... are like the police
Social workers ... help people to change
Social workers ... work with communities
Social workers ... should be able to work anywhere in the world
Social workers ... need career goals
Social workers ... should be caring

Think about how you came to believe the statements above and note that we will revisit this activity at the end of the book.

EXERCISE 1.2

Begin to think about the interactions you engage in in your everyday life. For example, think about your interactions at university: has your attendance at university changed the way you view the world? This activity is designed for you to reflect upon who you interact with and how these interactions influence your sense of self. Map these out using the shapes in 1.2. Your self is at the centre and each cloud represents an institution. For example, one cloud may represent university. Draw a line towards your self and write a statement near the line which characterises the strength of its influence on who you are. Another cloud may be your family.

After completing Exercise 1.2 you will see that there are many ways in which you engage in sociality in your everyday life. This is how Mead would say your self is produced or made. Your understanding of the ways in which you come across to others and how you think others perceive you underpins these social exchanges. You learned about appropriate ways to interact with others in childhood and this knowledge is referred to as understanding the generalized other. For example, in lectures, there is an unspoken rule that you sit and listen to the lecturer: you and your fellow students understand that this is expected of you. In noting your relationship to your social work studies in Exercise 1.2, there is a lot of knowledge about relating to others that goes unnoticed. Engaging in these exercises has helped you begin the process of reflexivity in relation to producing your social work self, and you will continue to develop an increased awareness about your emerging social work self throughout this text.

CHAPTER SUMMARY

In this chapter we have explored how the ongoing process of 'making' the social work self requires engagement with formal texts, one's sense of self and interaction with colleagues and class-mates alongside the learning that takes place at university and on placement. We have begun to highlight the significance of this interactionist way of viewing professional self-constitution through understanding how identity is 'made'. This chapter has therefore laid the foundations upon which this book is constructed. The interactionist social work self is one in process. It is the aim of this book to help students *engage* with this process. This can occur through the discussion of the formal learning material which is set out in each chapter alongside creative opportunities to extend such learning.

FURTHER READING

DA SILVA, F. C. (2011) *G. H. Mead: A Reader*. London: Routledge.

GRAY, M., WEBB, S. A. & MIDGLEY, J. O. (eds) (2012) *The Sage Handbook of Social Work*. London: Sage Publications.

MEAD, G. H. (1934) *Mind, Self and Society: From the Standpoint of a Social Behaviorist*. Chicago: University of Chicago Press.

QUINNEY, A. & HAFFORD-LETCHFIELD, T. (2012) *Interprofessional Social Work: Effective Collaborative Approaches*, 2nd edn. Exeter: Learning Matters.

SCHON, D. (1983) *The Reflective Practitioner: How Professionals Think in Action*. London: Temple Smith.

2

Human Development

This chapter:

- Introduces the lifespan approach

- Examines the socio-cultural aspect alongside developmental approaches

- Outlines the key developments in childhood, adulthood and older age

- Invites reflexive engagement with knowledge about the self and others

- Considers the role of social work in the context of human development throughout the lifespan

Piaget - life stages
Erikson - identity
Bowlby - Attachment
Buchanans - Attachment patterns

How old are you? Do you like being your current age, and if so, why? Do you wish you were older, or younger? What would you say is the best age to be? Whenever I have posed these questions to social work students the common answer I get is that the best age is older than adolescence and younger than, say, around 70 years of age. A large percentage of my students over the years have reported that childhood is a 'good age' because of its association with being 'carefree' and a time of little or no worry about those issues associated with adulthood such as career, income and other responsibilities.

Our notions of age and the way we feel about age are somewhat personal but, as we shall see in this chapter, there are common, general experiences that fall within specific age categories. Thus we can make fairly generalised statements about age, and these will hold true for the majority of people. Our favourite age is therefore not only a personal view. It is influenced by a number of forces, including the developmental milestones and socially derived attitudes associated with the age stage in question. How we think about age and the knowledge we have about development are central to our professional work with people in a variety of settings.

In social work we are purposefully developing ongoing relationships with individuals, families, groups and communities. To better understand those with whom we work, knowledge about life stages and human development is crucial. This is because, for example, such knowledge helps us to distinguish between 'normal' development and development that might require additional assistance or assessment. As we shall see in this chapter, knowledge about human development also assists us to help others make sense of their lives. Knowledge about human growth and development is relevant to all areas of social work practice, from the most obvious—working with children—to other areas such as the disabilities field or working with particular age groups such as younger people and older people as well as communities. Understanding broader demographic trends, for example the increasing number of older people as a percentage of the population, helps us plan better for social work services in particular communities.

Generally speaking, there are two main ways of thinking about age. The first—theorised through developmental psychology—relates to the view that our lives are characterised by a series of incremental, developmental stages, each of which brings its own challenges and achievements. The second is more sociological and enables an appreciation of the broader social experiences and the ways in which life stages are produced through social exchange. In this chapter we will examine the lifespan using knowledge from both psychological and sociological theories and research.

Take a look at Figure 2.1 on page 38. What do you notice in this photo of a man, a child and a dog? Is your immediate thought to assume the relationship between these characters? For example, do you see the older man as the grandfather of the younger boy who is there with his pet dog? Let's reflect upon the people in the photograph using the two approaches to human growth and development. Firstly, let's try to think about the ages of the man and the boy. Think about others you may know—these can be people in your family or friendship networks or people in the media—and try to place the subjects in the photograph alongside them. The boy

FIGURE 2.1 What is the relationship between the subjects in this photograph?
© Andrew Dunbar

looks too tall to be a toddler and not quite old enough to be an adolescent. If he were to be between these age ranges—that is, between toddlerhood or early childhood and adolescence—this would place him in the 'middle childhood' age range. The man in the photograph looks much older than the boy. We can see that the older man is wearing a wedding ring, suggesting that he is in a committed intimate relationship. He looks older than, say, someone in their 20s or 30s but not yet in older age. We could assume that the man is aged in his mid to late 50s. Given this information we can surmise that the man could be the boy's father or he could be his grandfather.

It is also important to understand the historical context in which we are viewing this image—this is because societal shifts change the ways in which our day-to-day relationships are lived out. There is clear evidence that in western cultures people are putting off having children until later in life. Couples and individuals who delay the onset of family life have to weigh up both biological and social factors (Stein &

Susser 2000) in a way that previous generations did not. Someone from the 1940s studying the photo would see it in a very different way from yourself, a citizen of the 21st century where older parents are becoming the norm.

In a moment we will begin to explore how these two life stages—middle childhood and adulthood—are theorised in relation to developmental psychology. In these, and other, life stages we can make general assumptions about social, emotional, cognitive and physical changes and milestones associated with each age. Before we discuss these in further detail, let's go back to the subjects in the image and approach how we understand them in a slightly different manner. We have established that the ages of the subjects are approximately late 50s and somewhere in middle childhood, say 7–10 years. If we think about a man in his late 50s then we might assume he is the father of the younger person. Or, we could assume he is his grandfather.

In this chapter we will examine both of these traditions in the context of the human lifespan and its associated development. There is a vast body of knowledge—mostly in the fields of developmental and social psychology—that has provided theories for understanding human development. In particular, childhood has been the subject of a great deal of research and theorising over the past five decades.

The work of Jean Piaget (1964, 1973), for example, draws upon his empirical work with children and has been advanced in recent years by followers of his tradition, called neo-Piagetians. Piaget is often studied in social work because, although criticised for its generalisations, his work continues to remain highly relevant to the ways in which we understand childhood. Piaget's central theory is that cognition—or thoughts—form differently for children than for adults. Based on his experiments with children, he believed that children make sense of the world around them differently than adults. He believed that children think differently than adults. This central tenet can be applied in direct work with parents who often—understandably—think about their children's behaviours in adult terms.

Piaget's reminder that children do not think in the same 'logical' ways adults do can help to more optimistically frame children's behaviour, and his stages are a kind of mapping of childhood cognitive development. Understanding children's behaviour through developmental theories helps social workers to understand the world of the child, and to see the world through their eyes involves a sophisticated application of theory to individual, social and cultural circumstances. As we shall see, Piaget argues that children progress through various stages during childhood in which their cognition, or thinking, changes according to their developmental stage.

In the same way that childhood is thought about in relation to key developmental milestones, so too can the entire lifespan be thought about in this way. The lifespan can be divided into key categories, and these are elucidated upon below.

FIGURE 2.2 Trilby painting: How can theories of development be applied to this scenario?

Figure 2.2 shows a little girl, called Trilby, painting. We can see that she is engaged in the activity and has mastered her hand and eye coordination, which enables her to successfully complete this activity. Trilby is three years old in this photograph. She is able to grasp the paintbrush and will probably have developed a preference for a particular hand by this age. She can move the paintbrush from the paint to the paper and sweep it across the paper with purpose. Though a seemingly mundane activity (by adult standards!), it is important to remember that Trilby was not always able to paint like this. Rather, her ability to successfully engage in this activity is the product of years of achieving specific developmental milestones. Meeting these milestones depended upon her engagement in the world around her and, in particular, her relationship with her caregivers, her environment, as well as her health which includes her physical, cognitive, emotional and social well-being.

In social work we are often interacting with families and developing an understanding of the individuals within the family as well as its functioning as a whole. It is important to understand both the family and the broader world from children's perspectives. This is referred to in social work literature as being 'child-centred' (see Munro 2011). Being able to see the world through a child's eyes requires the use of your imagination as well as an underpinning grasp on child development. Indeed, social workers must have a working knowledge of the key theoretical and empirical debates relating to human growth and development across the entire lifespan, starting with birth and ending with death. We shall now consider some of the key developmental milestones in childhood before moving on to later life stages of adolescence, adulthood and older age.

INFANCY TO TWO YEARS

Birth is the point at which the newborn baby leaves the mother's womb, and it is from this very early life stage that human interaction begins (Peterson 2004, p 98). Babies and their caregivers are able to look at one another and caregivers begin to interpret babies' gestures to better understand their wishes. A gentle stroke of a newborn baby's cheek encourages them to turn towards this touch and open their mouths as they look for the breast in order to feed. This so-called rooting response is one of a number of reflexes demonstrated by the newborn child. Another reflex behaviour central to communication between the newborn and their caregiver(s) is crying. Crying signals to the caregiver that the newborn is hungry, tired or uncomfortable. For example, the child may need his or her nappy changed or a layer of clothing removed to accommodate for a change in temperature.

In Chapter 1 we examined the importance of human interaction to one's identity through looking at the work of George Herbert Mead (1934). Even at this early life stage, human social interaction—specifically between the child and their caregivers—is crucial, not only for the development of the self but for survival. As we shall see, the central importance of social interaction to the development of identity continues throughout the lifespan.

During the time between birth and two years children's physical development progresses rapidly. Newborns are unable to roll or control their head movements, yet by around 12–14 months of age they are able to walk. Thus, the period between birth and one year is a time of rapid physical change, characterised by advances in the ways in which babies move and interact with others, and this continues into their second year of life and beyond. Children's caregivers often report that their child's physical development is a continual source of surprise. The ability to grasp a toy, to wave to others, to sit unaided and crawl: these are all examples of the ways that babies' physical strength and coordination come together to reach new physical milestones.

Given the rapid changes characterising physical development from birth, the perceived failure to achieve these milestones can be a cause of concern for parents and caregivers. Like other stages, there is much variation in the degree to which children fall neatly into achieving them.

Before the age of two, children develop what Piaget termed 'sensorimotor intelligence' (Piaget 1970), which involves behaving in an increasingly purposeful manner. For example, as babies grow from birth to two years, they develop different types of sucking—from the sucking of a dummy to a toy to a particular way of sucking at the breast or bottle to enable the optimum level of milk flow: the sucking behaviour differs, depending on the purpose (Peterson 2004, p. 58). As a child grows from a newborn to a two-year-old, their ability to act in purposeful ways depending on the environment also markedly increases. In the latter stages of sensorimotor development, babies begin to learn about cause and effect as they begin to anticipate the world around them. Piaget might describe a child thinking in the following way: 'If I roll this ball toward my mother, she will roll it back to me'. In this way, the world becomes increasingly predictable for children as they grow.

The interaction between a child and their environment or social setting is central to the theories of Erik Erikson (1968). Erikson is known for his notion of the identity crisis, which is often associated with the middle age life stage. Erikson argues, however, that at each life stage there is a tension between individual needs and the social expectations upon the individual. Erikson was thus concerned with the 'sociocultural environment' (Peterson 2004, p. 55) in which the child is embedded. At each stage, the individual must overcome the 'battle' between two states. These are:

- Basic trust vs mistrust (0–1 years)
- Autonomy vs shame and doubt (1–3 years)
- Initiative vs guilt (4–5 years)
- Industry vs inferiority (6–11 years)
- Identity vs role confusion (12–18 years)
- Intimacy vs isolation (early adulthood)
- Generativity vs self-absorption (middle adulthood)
- Integrity vs despair (older age)

We will discuss each of these at the life stages they occur.

Let's first explore what Erikson means by trust vs mistrust. For Erikson, the role of the caregiver(s) was central to whether the infant could develop trust:

> The quality of the parental care that infants receive during this stage largely determines the balance of trust vs mistrust in their budding psyches. Resolution of unconscious conflict entails finding a realistic compromise between blind faith in the primary caregiver, as the source of total pleasure, and an acceptance of the unavoidable pain of delay and frustration. The outcome of a satisfactory resolution brings babies their first 'psychosocial strength', which Erikson described as hope, and which will form a cornerstone for all manifestations of faith in later life. (Peterson 2004, p. 55)

There have been some theories that are reminiscent of Erikson's notion of trust and mistrust. For example, Giddens' notion of ontological security (Giddens 1992) argues that individuals carry their early experiences of relationships into their future selves, which affects the ways they view the world. Does this mean that individuals who do not have positive experiences in this life stage will then go on to mistrust the world and fail to form positive relationships? In short: no. Erikson's theory allows individuals to complete previously incomplete resolution in future life stages. Further, what we now know from studies in resilience is that some individuals are able to thrive *despite* negative early experiences (Ungar 2008).

Attachment

A great deal has been written about attachment, both in social work and within the discipline of psychology. So ubiquitous is this term that immediately it is recognisable as central to the relationship between a child and their caregiver. The central role played by caregivers in the development of children is a truism on many levels since children require to be fed, clothed, protected from danger and so on. Yet attachment specifically relates to the emotional dimension of human experience, and the foundational role that the caregiver plays in providing emotional stability for an infant.

Attachment theory was developed by John Bowlby and argues that children require 'secure' attachments to their mother in order for them to be 'stable' individuals in later life. A strong attachment is said to be foundational to a child in their first five years of life, thus it is the responsibility of the caregiver, or mother in Bowlby's terms, to give this much-needed stability from the onset of life. A strong attachment during childhood is argued to be central to happiness across the lifespan. This is summarised through the following statement, in which Bowlby famously argued:

> Mother love in infancy and childhood is as important for mental health as are vitamins and proteins for physical health. (Bowlby 1951, p. 182)

Bowlby's work remains important to child development literature and the theoretical notion that children require strong bonds with their caregivers continues to persist in contemporary childcare literature and practice. However, the application of attachment theory to issues in social work requires careful consideration of the ways in which attachment is conceptualised and placed within a clear theoretical and ethical framework. A critical awareness of gender and power and understanding the complex and contextual ways in which caregivers and their children interact are key to such work.

For example, Buchanan's (2008) research into domestic violence and the use of attachment theory in practice found there are specific ways in which practitioners ought to work with women. Practitioners should have 'knowledge about the impact of relationships on infants' attachment patterns' and should be

- experienced and knowledgeable about working with women and infants who have been subjected to domestic violence
- aware of the de-skilling that can affect women, as mothers, in domestic violence situations, and know that attachment may have been adversely affected
- very clear that the violence perpetrated against her and difficulties with attachment are not the fault of the woman. (Buchanan 2008, p. 11)

The historical and continuing role that gender plays in attachment theory has been highlighted as tending to blame women and serving a patriarchal system of power relationships (Bliwise 1999; Franzblau 1999; Morris 2008). Yet the ways in which family roles and daily routines are constructed have shifted dramatically since Bowlby's theory began to take shape 60 years ago.

Whereas in the 1950s women traditionally held the childrearing and caring roles within a family, in contemporary culture there have been a number of key shifts which have had an impact on the ways children are raised. These include:

- The detraditionalisation of gender roles: This relates to the increase of women's participation in the paid workforce from the 1960s onwards (Giddens 1992) and subsequent care arrangements for children, including nursery care, nannies, relative care (such as grandparents) and childminders. There has also been a greater awareness of the important role that fathers, as well as mothers, play.
- The recognition that culture and cultural relativism are relevant to theory-building: Bowlby's work requires a somewhat 'traditional' view of women whereas in contemporary life we have a broader appreciation of differing cultural views on

raising children, such as the central roles that close and extended relatives have in a child's life.

- Recent research into resilience and childhood: This has found no evidence that adults will be at risk of poor mental health if their childhood experiences are traumatic. Rather, research has demonstrated that some children are able to thrive *despite* adversity. This has meant there is a need to understand children in their contexts, for example in their cultural, social, emotional and biographical contexts.

In social work there is a great deal of literature relating to attachment which takes into account the shifts described above. Thus attachment remains a relevant concept which can help us better understand the child's world and the world from the child's perspective. Prescriptive and presumptive application of attachment theory to our clients should always be avoided: it is never appropriate to assume that a person's present behaviour or state of mind is 'because of poor attachment'. This simplistic application of attachment theory does little more than pathologise our clients and undervalue our profession.

TODDLERHOOD (TWO TO FOUR YEARS)

Piaget argued that, between the ages of two and seven years, children enter the 'preoperational stage' of cognition. This means that children:

- Use language and gestures to communicate and name the objects and people around them
- Are able to group objects together
- Continue to think in a way that can be described as 'egocentric'

If you have ever accompanied a child into a setting in which there are a lot of other people, you may have witnessed the effects of a child's egocentric thinking. For example, a two-year-old may begin screaming and crying in a quiet public space such as a church or a library, and may not understand that their behaviour is frowned upon by others who are attempting to keep quiet. For the child the world around them is merely a place in which feelings of, say, frustration or tiredness may be vented. Notoriously referred to as the 'terrible twos', toddlerhood sees egocentrism, a new emotional range, increasing agility, more stable gait and the increasing desire for independence all combining for some potentially difficult times for caregivers, who may struggle to understand the world from the child's perspective. Therefore some forms of child abuse may be more highly associated with this age stage than any other.

When children are learning to exercise their autonomy in this way during the toddler years, it can result in conflicts which can lead to confrontations between children and their caregivers. This can lead to child abuse. There are a number of ways that neglect and child abuse should be responded to in practice, and specialist training about how to work with children and families in statutory settings is contained within social work programmes. By understanding 'normal' development and the key milestones in each life stage, social work students become equipped with the tools to identify when children are not progressing at the pace expected. The impact of neglect, for example, can mean that children do not achieve their developmental milestones, and they are severely harmed as a result of not having their needs met (Minty & Pattinson 1994).

Positive relationships between parents and their children are central to development. Like Piaget, Vygotsky was interested in the ways in which children's development was dependent upon their relationship with others. Vygotsky's emphasis on the socio-cultural context to childhood development meant that communication was central to understanding how children learn. Vygotsky noted that children were sometimes able to complete particular tasks with the help of an adult. The 'zone of proximal development' is 'the distance between the actual developmental level as determined by independent problem solving and the level of potential development as determined through problem solving under adult guidance, or in collaboration with more capable peers' (Vygotsky 1978, p. 86). Again, the role of others in the development of children is highlighted. Being able to achieve a particular task, for example filling a cup with sand—even with the help of an adult—can serve to extend the child's interest into other tasks and help to advance their development.

Language develops during the toddler years. Caregivers often report that during this age it is a relief to begin to hear what the child wants instead of having to interpret their wishes through gestures and behaviours. Language is therefore the important means through which children are able to articulate their needs and place themselves in the world around them (Vygotsky 1978, p. 26). Language also enables better communication and interaction between a child and their caregivers. It is also important to others such as nursery staff and other professionals such as social workers, medical staff and specialist professionals because it can be the means through which the child's view can be better understood.

We now move on to consider the middle childhood life stage.

MIDDLE CHILDHOOD (FIVE TO ELEVEN YEARS)

For Piaget, the period between the ages of seven and eleven years signalled the 'concrete operational stage', which means that children are able to:

- Group objects according to rational 'rules' (for example, grouping all of the small pink beads in one pile and the large pink beads in another pile)

The ability to undertake tasks associated with grouping is argued by Piaget to be possible because children's thinking changes during these ages to accommodate more logical 'rules'.

The major social event to occur during middle childhood is entry into the schooling system. For children who had previously been at home with a caregiver, as well as those who had previously been at nursery, day-care or in the care of relatives or workers, school attendance signals a momentous shift. We have seen in previous life stages that the caregiver has a central role in influencing development. The socio-cultural setting within which the child is immersed has an impact on the ways in which they experience and respond to the world around them:

> According to those who take a sociocultural approach to development, the child should be seen not as a physical scientist seeking 'true' knowledge but as a newcomer to a culture who seeks to become a native by learning how to look at social reality through the lens of that culture. (Rogoff 2000 cited in Smith *et al.* 2003, p. 82)

The culture of the school system is largely institutionalised and regulated through variously structured and identifiable time periods. The emotional impact of school is often noted by parents, who may also feel that this life stage signals the end of the 'baby' years.

Erikson argues that this life stage brings with it the challenge of resolving the tension between 'industry vs inferiority'. Industry, which is the ability to work to complete a task, is embedded within the schooling system. Children are taught and assessed according to their ability to work diligently and achieve particular learning goals. Unlike in other environments such as nursery or the home setting, assessments are competitive processes. In the school setting the system of knowledge acquisition means that children can compare their achievements, or failures, with the other children around them. 'A satisfactory resolution requires the development of cooperation with other people, so that children can freely and successfully exercise their own unique competencies in contribution to a larger productive effort' (Peterson 2004, p. 56).

During this period of time children also learn to socialise together and understand the social rules of self and others. Because of their mastery over their bodily movements, they are able to fully participate in sporting activities and game playing. Engagement in these activities was manifest in Janet Lever's (1978) study into childhood socialisation of gender. Through ethnographic observation of childhood play at school, Lever found that the rules which dominated the boys' and girls' groups were reproduced in relation to gendered occupational 'rules' later in life. The children in her study were grouped according to gender and each group engaged in different games and activities. Additionally, each group learned to resolve conflict in idiosyncratic ways, regardless of individual attributes. Although Lever's study took place more than 30 years ago, the continuation of the dominant group's marked presence in particular professions and positions of power suggests that inequality based on gender and other markers of difference stems from childhood socialisation and still exists today. Thus, there is inherent power in the school environment in relation to learning social norms and rules including gender (as we have just seen) as well as other issues such as disability, culture and other markers of difference.

ADOLESCENCE

Piaget argues that during adolescence, individuals reach the ability to think in the same way as adults. This 'formal operational stage' is the final stage in his theory of child development. Thinking associated with this stage follows on from the previous stage in which cognition based on logic dominates. Additionally, adolescents:

- Can think in abstract terms about things, for example they can hypothesise fantasy scenarios and outcomes
- Are able to conceptualise abstract concepts, theories and notions

For Erikson, the importance of self identification is evident in the conflict between 'identity vs role confusion'. Central to this resolution is being able to negotiate a preferred identity amongst the many that are available:

> The problem is enhanced in contemporary society by the wide range of alternative roles available and by their inconsistency with one another and with the traditions of the past. A satisfactory resolution of the identity conflict entails the development of a coherent sense of self that integrates all the essential features of the individual's past and sets the direction for further personal growth and a productive contribution to society. (Peterson 2004, p. 56)

Social interactions are central to the sense of self (Mead 1934), as we have explored in Chapter 1. Adolescence brings changes through puberty, not only physical ones to sex organs and other areas of the body but also various emotional and social changes. These include:

- Increased self-consciousness
- Shifts in existing relationships, based on gender and sexuality
- Increased interest and/or social expectations around coupling/sexual activity and experimentation
- Increased importance of peer groups and friendships

Sexuality in social work is both a specialist and a general or 'everyday' area of work (see Dunk-West 2011; Dunk-West & Hafford-Letchfield 2011). Often social workers feel ill-equipped to talk to young people about their sexual relationships, but the theories which underpin other practice apply equally to this area of work (Dunk 2007). Listening to young people's needs, understanding their biographies and relationships and working together to address inequality and oppression at the individual and social levels: all of these apply to working with a young person in a sexually active relationship. Let us consider Case Study 2.1.

CASE STUDY 2.1 Seshni Patel

Seshni is 15 years old. Born in a small village in India, at age 5 she moved to London with her parents and brother, Sanjay, aged 2. When Seshni was 14 years old both her mother and father died in a car accident. As no other relatives could be located, Seshni and her brother were placed into care and separated. Seshni did not settle at her foster carers, who were a White British couple aged in their 50s, living in Bath. Seshni ran away from the foster carers and made her way back to London. Once in London, Seshni reunited with her friendship group and her friends gave her money to help her support herself. Seshni told friends that she wanted to find her brother Sanjay but did not know where to begin. Seshni had been 'sleeping rough' for almost three months when she came to the attention of social services after being admitted to hospital, having been found unconscious in a park.

Imagine you are employed by social services as a social worker and you are going to meet with Seshni in the hospital. Think about the following questions:

- How do you think Seshni might be feeling?
- What do you think you could do to support Seshni?
- What is important in the work and why is it important?
- What theories of human development are helpful in understanding this situation?

There are numerous ways you may be able to assist Seshni but they will be dependent upon what Seshni would like to happen and whether you are able to establish a positive working relationship with her. The following is one possible area for social work intervention.

Living arrangements and reuniting Seshni and Sanjay

It is crucial that Seshni receive help with her living arrangements since being homeless places her 'at risk of harm'. Questions to ask include: why were Seshni and Sanjay separated? How was the loss of their parents accommodated for in relation to supports for the siblings? One way to make sense of Seshni's actions is to view her running away as a normal response to the situation. Given her parents died suddenly and she 'lost' her brother and was then removed from her friends and supports in London and accommodated with foster carers, is it surprising that Seshni returned to her community? Given that Seshni has said that she wants to find her brother, it is crucial to work from her 'perspective', to be 'client-centred' (Rogers 1951). Working from the client's perspective involves working with clients in such a way as to help them reach their goals (Egan 2006).

Other questions to ask could include: what are Seshni's needs around her health and education? How have these been met or not met and what can be done to achieve well-being? Are there cultural needs which are not being met? What can be done to respect her cultural background? It is crucial that social workers do not make assumptions about others' cultures but start from the perspective that we all have a culture. Race is a concept which is related to culture. Race refers to 'a set of social relationships which allow individuals and groups to be located, and various attributes of competencies assigned, on the basis of biologically grounded features' (Giddens 2005, p. 696). Culture is a 'historically transmitted pattern of meanings embodied in symbols, a system of inherited conceptions expressed by which men [sic] communicate, perpetuate, and develop their knowledge about and their attitudes towards life' (Geertz 1973, p. 89). Culture is an important kind of knowledge which is embedded in family relationships and practices and relationships and patterns of relating with others. Culture is an important part of identity and enables one to name a collective affinity with a particular group. It is also one of the central tasks of social work to fight oppression and inequality, and reflecting on social work's role in racism and discriminatory practices in day-to-day practice helps the profession maintain accountability towards others as well as towards social work values and ethics.

All of the questions about how the social work role might assist in this situation arise from thinking about Seshni and imagining what it might be like to see the world through her eyes (Lee 1994). Applying developmental theories to her situation helps to raise further questions. For example, what does Piaget say about adolescence? What does Erikson say? Let's briefly look at how these theories might be applied to Seshni. According to Piaget's theory of adolescence, Seshni will be able to think as an adult would—that is, she would be able to engage in thinking about issues more 'deeply' than a person aged, say, in their middle childhood. She would be able to conceptualise complexities. Erikson might say that Seshni is at a time when identity is central, and in particular, it is crucial for Seshni to 'find' her identity. Seshni's culture is an example of an aspect of her identity. Of course, only Seshni would be able to inform you as the social worker about whether these theories are relevant to understanding her current situation, but there are some indications that she feels attached to her peers since she moved back to London to see them. The loss of her parents may also fit with the theme of identity since her entire life has been upturned since their death. We shall consider some of the theories related to grief and loss later in this chapter.

ADULTHOOD

Adulthood is often simply conceptualised as being the period after adolescence and prior to older age. When we think about adulthood, we generally refer to the ages between 18 and 65. This is a large age range and some texts divide adulthood into early, mid and late adulthood. In this book we refer to adulthood to encompass the following general events: work, intimacy, children and separation.

For Erikson, early adulthood is concerned with achieving true intimacy with another person. The conflict between 'intimacy vs isolation' requires successful integration of the self into a loving partnership. Middle adulthood is characterised by an Eriksonian conflict between 'generativity vs self-absorption'. Generativity refers to the sense that one has left a legacy which will thrive in the world beyond one's lifetime. For some people this is a creative product, whilst having children, for some, means that they are contributing to 'future generations' (Peterson 2004, p. 57). Self-absorption is the opposite of generativity in that it means a lack of engagement with the future besides which the self is invested.

Adulthood is popularly associated with finding one's profession or identifying the main source of income generation through work. Yet the negotiation of employment in times of personal and economic hardship can prevent people from experiencing meaningful activity. Unpaid work such as domestic responsibilities and caring for relatives and children can too be unrecognised as legitimate in some countries. For Erikson, work can be associated with generativity which means that it must have some *broader meaning* coded into it by the individual engaging in it.

Shifts in intimacy have meant that the way individuals experience and display their romantic attachments has changed. From the late 1920s, researchers became interested in what was termed 'marital disenchantment' (Pineo 1961, p. 3). This concept captured the ways in which individuals within marriages felt about the marriage at various points. Pineo (1961) noted four stages which characterised research participants' experiences:

marital stages

1. After marriage, people report feeling less happy with being married ('marital disenchantment).
2. The rate of physical intimacy drops.
3. Although there are changes in the marriage dynamic, individuals feel the same.
4. Interaction between people in a marriage changes. Sexual activity decreases. (Pineo 1961, p. 3)

In explaining the above, Pineo says that 'in any situation, such as marriage ... some process of disenchantment is to be expected' (1961, p. 7). For some theorists, the high divorce rates which have characterised the years following such studies into marital disenchantment signal a tendency for 'quick fixes' and a lack of commitment to the institution of marriage over individual desires (Bauman 2003).

Yet people continue to get married and enter into committed intimate partnerships despite the high failure rates of marriage (Giddens 1992). The nature of relationships has certainly changed since the studies into marital disenchantment, but the notion of disenchantment can be useful in capturing couples' experiences post-marriage. Here are some of the key shifts in relationships in contemporary life:

- There have been changes in women's roles through the entry of women into the workforce and changes in the ways in which the household is arranged (Giddens 1992).
- More people are living separately but still are in committed relationships. These couples are referred to in the literature as 'living apart together' (Holmes 2006).
- Same sex couples' friendships can constitute 'family'. This is referred to as 'families of choice' (Weeks *et al.* 2001).
- Shifts in technology and the way we interact with one another have impacted upon how individuals meet and form intimate relationships.

It is important for social work students to understand the shifts in relationships and the centrality of them to adulthood because such knowledge assists in understanding the world from our client's perspective.

OLDER AGE

Societies in the west are made up of increasing numbers of older people as a result of developments in nutrition, lifestyle awareness and medical and other technology. Sometimes referred to as 'grey power', older people are increasingly politically powerful. Erikson argues that, in older age, the task requiring resolution relates to 'integrity vs despair'. The knowledge that one has contributed to society in a positive way and reflecting positively on the life they have led leads to integrity. According to Erikson, people experiencing integrity understand 'that an individual life is the accidental coincidence of but one life cycle with but one segment of history, and that for him [sic] all human integrity stands and falls with the one style of integrity of which he partakes' (Erikson 1968, p. 140 cited in Peterson 2004, p. 57). Erikson's depiction of older age draws upon the assumption that in older age one is looking back at life retrospectively as opposed to looking forward. Yet in developed nations older age has changed, perhaps more rapidly than any other age stage, given technological advances along with increased health determinants.

Older age can signal the end of the employment cycle as people enter a period of retirement or semi-retirement. The age at which retirement occurs is generally around 65, but this will almost certainly increase to adjust for our longer lifespans. Rising costs of childcare alongside lower wages can mean that people entering retirement are engaging in caring roles for grandchildren and others in the family. This is a relatively recent shift which has come about through a combination of factors including longer lifespans, social policies relating to work and childcare provision, and economic conditions.

DEATH

Death, in short, is the end to life. Death is seen as an inevitable part of life and although it is viewed as normative after older age, the impact on loved ones is always great. We will therefore explore grief and loss briefly. It is important to acknowledge the broad scholarship which deals with death and its related issues. Much of the literature in philosophy, ethics, sociology, psychology and disciplines such as health have currency in social work. The application of literature from other disciplines to social work raises important questions. Some of the issues which emerge in other disciplines are summarised below, together with their relevance for social work:

- Issues relating to ethical issues about death. For example, assisted suicide or euthanasia is when a person 'chooses' to end their life. What is the role for social workers in these situations? Should social work as a profession have a view about whether euthanasia is 'right' or 'wrong'?
- Issues relating to ethical and medical issues about death. For example, when is someone classified as dead? Is a person kept 'alive' through technology such as a respirator 'living' or is a coma a state of being 'dead'? Should social workers have a role to play in determining some of the ethical impacts of decisions about these issues? How can social workers support families and others who are affected by these issues?
- Given the role that religion plays in death, for example in relation to the rituals which mark death, how can social workers work with others in a culturally and spiritually sensitive manner?
- How does society understand and deal with death? Is death taboo and if so, why? Should all social workers, irrespective of their practice, understand death and how to respond to others who are grieving?

We explore some of the complexities involved in making ethical decisions in social work in Chapter 5. Although there are no easy answers to the questions raised, there are some key issues which emerge. Highlighting the religious or spiritual beliefs associated with death uncovers the need for social workers to work in a way which invites dialogue about clients' religious beliefs across all work (Crisp 2010). Similarly, starting with the client's viewpoint and wishes and trying to understand how they are feeling about what is happening for them helps people feel supported and understood. This application of empathy is called 'tuning in' and having 'empathic presence' (Egan 2006, p. 49). Egan points out:

> At some of the more dramatic moments of life, simply being with another person is extremely important. If a friend of yours is in the hospital, just your being there can make a difference, even if conversation is impossible. Similarly, being with a friend who has just lost his wife can be very comforting to him, even if little is said. Your empathic presence is comforting, but tuning in is also important in the give-and-take of everyday life. Most people appreciate it when others pay attention to them. They feel respected. By the same token, being ignored is often painful: The averted face is too often a sign of the averted heart. (Egan 2006, p. 49)

In Chapter 3 we discuss some further communication skills which help us in our work with others and in Chapter 4 we explore the theories which underpin our interpersonal practice. In each of these chapters, a clearer social work role emerges. As we have begun to see throughout this chapter, theories about human development and life stages help shape the social work role. We now move on to briefly explore how individual and collective responses to death impact on the grieving process.

Grief and loss

In Shakespeare's *Macbeth*, grief is conceived as a state which can and must move actors to great action, thus the exclamation: 'Give sorrow words. The grief that does not speak whispers the o'er fraught heart, and bids it break'. In this context, grief is portrayed as so powerful and debilitating it can break the heart. The quote gives us some insight into the powerful ways that the emotional context of loss and grief can be so consuming, frightening and completely overwhelming. Grief has many aspects to it, both private and public. Private experiences of grief are tied up with the emotional dimension to human experience, which means that people can be unsure how to respond to loss. Public or socially recognised ways of mourning include funerals, wakes, burials and cremations, celebration of life events as well as various religious-inspired rituals and traditions. Thus, the socio-cultural as well as personal ways that people experience death are important to recognise in social work.

Yet there is also a *relationship between* the personal and the social. When a loss is not socially sanctioned as loss, this can result in the mourner experiencing what is termed as disenfranchised grief (Doka 1989, 2002). Disenfranchised grief is grief which is suppressed by society because of a stigma. For example, in societies where being in a same sex relationship is discriminated against, the same sex partner of someone who has died may not be involved in the deceased person's funeral arrangements, family events or other socially sanctioned rituals associated with death. This sends the message to the bereaved person that they were not as significant as would be an opposite sex partner. Disenfranchised grief means that the mourner, in this case the same sex partner of a deceased person, is personally affected as they are not able to resolve their grief through traditions involving interpersonal relationships and socially sanctioned events and rituals. This means they become isolated and left alone with their grief.

Since death is a part of human existence, social workers must know how to respond to death, grief and loss. Death affects us all and social workers' clients can, themselves, die. This can be difficult for the social worker, quite apart from others who are affected by the loss. In addition people can experience other types of losses throughout their lifespan which can be made sense of using theoretical models from the literature about loss, grief and dying.

GENERATIONS

So far, we have considered age through individuals' experiences which are dependent upon their numerical age. Another way of thinking about the lifespan is to consider the historical epoch within which the individual or group was born. Thus, a 10-year-old today will have a completely different experience than a 10-year-old who was born in 1912. The 10-year-old born 10 years ago will have entered a world with fewer infant mortalities (in developed countries), longer lifespans (in developed countries), internet technology, Web 2.0 and so on. The 10-year-old born in 1912 will have experienced their early years very differently (Plummer 2010). One of the problems with viewing age solely through developmental terms is that we do not get a picture of the broader social events and shifts which make up the landscape into which the person 'fits'. In terms of generations, we refer to each of these groups using terms such as baby boomer, generation X, generation Y and so on. In the historical period we are currently in, for example, a large number of so-called baby boomers are entering retirement. Thus, some general, population-based characteristics may be associated with this generation.

Generation-based ways of viewing the lifespan can assist in a more sociologically informed approach towards making sense of people's experiences. They can also usefully be combined with developmental psychological perspectives which already draw to a considerable degree on a socio-cultural context.

NEGLECT, CHILD ABUSE AND DEVELOPMENTAL THEORIES

Your knowledge of child development is crucial to responding to children in need of care and protection. In understanding normative child development, you will be able to respond to and raise concerns about children whose development is not progressing as expected. Children with undiagnosed disabilities and other difficulties and needs require early intervention. Here are some key points:

- Clearly articulate concerns. Knowledge of child development can assist in social workers understanding children's behaviours including raising concerns when development is 'abnormal' or not progressing as expected.
- Communicate in an age appropriate manner (Miller 2003). This means that your knowledge of child development can help in your work with children and their caregivers: toddlerhood can be a difficult time for parents and conveying information about child development can assist parents in better understanding the world through their child's eyes. Parents can become frustrated with the wilfulness associated with toddlerhood and believe that their child is 'deliberately winding them up' as opposed to understanding the challenging behaviour as a symptom of frustration or thwarted autonomy.
- The ways in which children live through the abuse and neglect they have experienced must be able to be understood through social workers' application of developmental theories, but importantly children must always be protected (Davies 2012).
- Social workers need to have a dual focus in protecting children and being guided by their needs and wishes (Lefebvre 2010). Both protecting children as well as involving them in decisions about their care is important since children do not feel involved enough in decisions about their care, despite this being a policy and practice requirement (for example, see Cleaver *et al.* 2007).

WORKING WITH OTHERS

Because this chapter explores life stages across the entire lifespan, there are many contexts, and professionals, with whom social workers can expect to work in varied environments. The health professions' engagement with the lifespan approach is, generally speaking, a strong one. This is because of the dominance of medical knowledge which is embedded within developmental theories.

Theories in which the lifespan is divided into clearly identifiable stages serve to reinforce the idea that there is a 'normal' way to develop. Since this is the case, there is also an 'abnormal' category within which people's development (or lack thereof) may be categorised. Of course, there is much variance in terms of whether individuals 'fit' with the ages and prescribed stages. There is also variance in relation to professions' engagement in social models of development. It is fair to say that in contemporary practice, the health professions have engaged in social models of health far more than in the past. In Chapter 1 we discussed the impacts of interprofessional working between social work and health and noted that social work's association with social models of health might be incompatible with other professions whose world-views are very different (Bywaters 1986). Yet professional values and priorities and theories are always in flux. Indeed, there is some evidence to suggest that health professionals are moving more towards collaborative working. For example, research which examined general practitioners' (GPs') views about their roles found they felt there had been a shift away from traditional power relationships where medical doctors were at the top of the hierarchy (Jones & Green 2006, p. 936). The authors of the study call this a 'new general practice' in which equal relationships between other professionals promotes a positive work environment which ultimately benefits the client. One respondent in the study, for example, reported that:

> The reason I like my practice so much is this really fluid sort of communication between doctors, nurses, receptionists, everything's sort of on a level, everyone's on first name terms and there aren't any doors that you can't knock on. (Helen, GP locum, in Jones & Green 2006, p. 937)

The study found that this 'new way' of working broke down traditional power relationships between GPs and others and was more in line with a 'patient-centred approach' (Jones & Green 2006, p. 937). Such an approach is, as we shall see in Chapters 3 and 4, compatible with a social work approach in which we work alongside our clients.

Yet how does interaction with other professionals look in relation to the material explored in this chapter? To better examine this, let's consider Case Study 2.2.

CASE STUDY 2.2 Carol Leblanc, Juliette Leblanc and baby Célia Leblanc

Carol is a 43-year-old woman who had recently moved from her native France to London. Carol is Célia's mother. Carol had relocated to be closer to Célia's father but after doing so, just over three years ago, the relationship broke down and they no longer have contact. A few months ago, Carol's sister Juliette, aged 47, came to live with her sister and niece as she was worried about Carol's mental state. Carol and Juliette have a strong, supportive relationship. They were raised in a small flat by their father who had mental health problems as well as a problem with alcohol. Carol and Juliette would often care for their father. Despite some difficulties, Carol and Juliette were able to attend school and go on to complete university studies—the first generation in their family to have done so. Before moving to London, Carol was employed as a journalist for a local newspaper, and Juliette is taking leave from her job as an accountant. Carol has been trying to find freelance writing work but she has not been successful in gaining paid employment. Carol cares for Célia full time.

Célia is aged 2½ and was referred to the local social services by the Health Visitor and GP. Both feel Célia has not met her developmental milestones and, when concerns were raised with her mother, they felt she did not want to accept there would need to be further assessments of Célia. Specifically, there are concerns about Célia's language development, her gross motor skills and her lack of engagement with people around her. Although a happy child, Célia does not talk except to say 'ma ma'. She does not appear interested in communicating with others. Both the GP and the Health Visitor would like Célia to be assessed by a paediatrician.

- What developmental theories are relevant to this case study?
- What do you think ought to happen next?
- Are you concerned for Célia?
- What are the roles of the professionals? Are there any other professionals who could or should be involved?

In any situation where we do not have all of the information, application of theory must be tentative. However, there are some key pieces of information which can be noted at this stage. These are:

- There are concerns about Célia's development. These specifically relate to physical, social and language development.
- There are concerns about Célia's needs not being met.
- Little is known about Carol's mental health, but we do know that her sister, to whom she is reportedly close, has concerns about this.
- There are a number of social factors which provide context such as the recent relocation of the family, and problems with Carol finding paid work.

In relation to working with others, in this scenario the GP and Health Visitor have suggested that because Célia's development falls outside the *normal* range, a more detailed assessment would give a better picture about what is happening for this child. Some of the social issues which are relevant to this context include: exploring the supports for Carol, who is parenting by herself, has moved away from her home and has left her regular workplace to live in a different country; the language context to living outside the family's homeland and how this might affect Célia's presenting difficulties with language and communication; how much social interaction, connectedness and support is available to the family. The latter issues which relate to social support may alter the ways in which developmental theories are applied to the scenario. As noted previously, the application of developmental theory must be tentative and take into account the socio-cultural and broader social issues and contexts within which problems are presented.

CHAPTER SUMMARY

This chapter has explored lifespan development. We have examined the major theoretical traditions associated with this way of thinking and explored how these relate to social work. The socio-cultural context within which development occurs has been considered alongside the important influence of family and caregiver relationships on children and young people.

Using visual prompts, the reader has been invited to reflexively engage with their own reading of lifespan in relation to roles and social expectations or attitudes, as well as their own biographic associations with age. Throughout the chapter the central role of knowledge about human growth and development in social work practice in its many manifestations has been highlighted. In the following chapter we move on to consider how we relate to others, and the communicative skills required to form professional relationships with our clients.

FURTHER READING

BERK, L. (2010) *Exploring Lifespan Development*, 2nd edn. Boston: Allyn & Bacon.

BOYD, D. A. & BEE, H. L. (2011) *Lifespan Development*. Boston: Pearson Education.

GREEN, L. (2010) *Understanding the Life Course: Sociological and Psychological Perspectives*. Cambridge, UK: Polity Press.

LEFEVRE, M. (2010) *Communicating with Children and Young People: Making a Difference*. Bristol: The Policy Press.

PETERSON, C. (2004) *Looking Forward Through the Lifespan*. Frenchs Forest, NSW: Pearson Education.

3

Communication Skills

This chapter:

- Introduces key ideas in communication

- Outlines why communication is central to the social work role

- Describes specific types of communication through the use of examples

- Provides prompts to enable the reader to consider their own communication style

- Outlines how social workers use their communication skills in their work with clients

In social life, our interactions with others are guided by complex rules which, once broken, disrupt the flow of communication between people. Imagine acting as a houseguest in your own home, for example (Garfinkel 1984). How would your behaviours change? We might expect that you would be more polite and less relaxed than you would normally be in the comfort of your usual surroundings. How would the familiar people around you react if you adopted a formal tone in your interactions with them?

Sociologist Harold Garfinkel sought to uncover what would happen when the unwritten rules in everyday life were disrupted or 'breached'. He called upon his students to undertake experiments such as the one detailed above. (Although these experiments enabled new ways of theorising human interaction, experimenting on others without ethics approval is not recommended! See Chapter 7 for more information about ethics and research.) Amongst other key sociological contributions, Garfinkel's work drew attention to the *assumed* knowledge we draw upon when we interact with others. It was in breaking or 'breaching' the codes which rule our behaviour towards others in specific situations that their strength could be understood (Garfinkel 1984). Our knowledge of social rules forms the backdrop of our interactions with others during day-to-day life.

Unless we really think about it, we are unaware of the rules that govern our behaviour. In this chapter we will begin to explore some of the key communicative devices we draw upon in social work. Like social norms or rules of behaviour, some of the concepts relevant to communication such as 'listening' appear commonsense; however, as we shall see, successfully employing a range of verbal and nonverbal techniques helps us to engage well with others—and this is vital to good, competent social work practice.

Given that this chapter draws upon the skills you use in everyday life, exercises are designed to get you thinking about ways in which you currently communicate. As a social work student learning about social work *practice*, it is important to name and understand how particular techniques help us communicate. Practising and devoting time and imagination to understanding communication are key to learning.

How do you know you are being listened to? What happens when you are trying to communicate with another person and you feel they are not hearing what you are saying? In the following section we will consider various forms of communication and ways in which interpersonal interactions take place. As discussed in Chapter 1, interpersonal interaction is the means through which we realise and develop our selves (Mead 1934). Communication is also the central conduit through which we relate to our clients, and developing a reflexive awareness of how we come across to others is vital to our work, particularly as beginning practitioners.

Students out on placement often encounter practitioners who have 'practice-wisdom' and do not seem as reflexive as students of social work. Considering the role of reflexivity in the creation of the social work self, this is not surprising. It is therefore useful to think about reflexive engagement with one's own communication style and methods whilst recognising that with practice, this becomes more intuitive. In relation to this, thinking about types of questions to ask and statements to make in response to role play scenarios can often feel stilted and disingenuous.

Like all beginnings to learning, this phase soon passes as students develop confidence and learn from mistakes and insights from others.

As with all aspects of the social work curriculum, entering into the reflexive arena requires a deliberate engagement with the self. Once the foundational work in the area of communication skills has been achieved, through practice, reflexivity in relation to the social work self becomes more aligned with Mead's notion of 'reflexiveness' (1934) which we explored in Chapter 1.

In a recent study into communication skills learning and subsequent social work practice, for example, one participant reported that learning about communication 'was incredibly helpful in teaching me to routinely reflect my own thoughts, feelings and actions. I think that it is quite easy not to reflect unless you are taught to "get into the habit"' (account from Helen, in Dixon 2012, p. 11). 'Getting into the habit' is what Mead might see as 'routinized' behaviour and it is through practising particular styles of communication that the social work self is constituted.

Before we explore key concepts relating to communication it is important to ask the question: 'what is meant by communication?' Communication entails social interaction. It is a dialogical, spontaneous and complex process. For example, relating to others involves:

- Demonstrating that one is listening and hearing
- Actively communicating through verbal or spoken cues
- Communicating through body language and gestures
- Using external metaphors and tools such as visual art, literature, sculpture, object placement and other creative forms (Morgan 2000)
- Recognising barriers to communication and responding appropriately
- Taking action arising from communication

We now consider differing types of tools for verbal communication.

ⓘ DEMONSTRATING LISTENING

There are many different cues which demonstrate that a person is listening to another. Sitting across from another person and demonstrating listening through non-verbal cues involves what is termed 'attending'. Attending involves recognising that geographical placement of one's self has an impact on communication. Sitting behind a desk or writing as another person is speaking can be off-putting to clients, for example (Nelson-Jones 2012). A social worker who adopts an open stance without barriers between themselves and clients can help the flow of conversation. Generally speaking other non-verbal cues which suggest that listening is occurring include nodding, maintaining eye contact and remaining physically still. Cultural traditions and norms, gender, age and class as well as religion all play a part in the ways in which listening is conveyed.

Techniques which assist in communication can feel artificial when first experimenting with them in role plays and other formal learning opportunities. Communicative techniques are not intended to be used to manipulate or belittle our clients. As with all interactions with clients, asking them for feedback, for example about whether they feel listened to, is the best way to monitor your effectiveness in communication. Above all, being genuinely curious (Rogers 1961; White & Epston 1990) and interested in our clients' selves, biographies and narratives is central to social work interaction which is respectful and responsive to individual needs.

Consider the following exchange:

Interior. Coffee shop. Buzzing with people. A man, Alexandro, aged 40s, and a woman, Nora, also 40s, sit opposite one another at a coffee table. They are siblings in mid conversation.

Nora (*animated, looking at Alexandro*): ... and I mean I could not believe it! (*Alexandro looks around, gaze hovering on people around him.*)
Nora: The cheek of it!
Alexandro (*eyes still on those around him*): Mmmm.
Nora: Are you listening to me?
Alexandro: Huh (*finally looks at Nora quizzically*): What?
Nora: I just told you about what happened to me last time I went in there. Did you even listen?
Alexandro: Just because you had a bad experience once doesn't mean it will happen again.
Nora: I can't even bear the thought of stepping through those doors again. All those other mothers and babies. And the social workers... No, I can't go back. I'll manage.
Alexandro: Ok.
Nora: I mean the depression isn't as bad as last time, right?
Alexandro (*looking off into the distance again*): Did I lock the car?
Nora: Do you know this is the first time I've been out of the house in weeks?
Alexandro (*grabbing at his pocket, miming locking the car*): I'm sure I did this. Did I do this? (*as if talking to himself, nodding*). Yes, I did. I'm sure I did.
Nora: Feels kind of weird to be out. The noise.
(*Alexandro looks at his nails. Silent.*)
Nora: It's weird to be without Jack too, though I'm sure he's fine with Mum. He's just so completely connected to me as I'm his only source of food. It's overwhelming sometimes. (*Looking around the cafe*) So weird to be out. Maybe we should get back...?
Alexandro (*jumping up from his seat*): Ok.

The scene above involves Alexandro and Nora who are in a coffee shop. Did you notice the way that Nora's questions and comments are not answered and not responded to in any empathic way by Alexandro? We have some clues about how these are ignored both in his body language and gaze as well as in what he says and doesn't say. Nora is trying to open up about how she is feeling but the signals she receives from Alexandro does not make this possible. Being able to see an example of when communication does not work can help to understand the importance of good communication skills in the professions. Imagine that Alexandro had followed up on Nora's comments where she is beginning to disclose how she is feeling. We know through these comments that she has a history of depression and was treated or assessed at a mother and baby facility in the past. We also know that she is finding it strange to be out of the house. There is also a lot that we do not know. We don't know, for example, why she has not been out of the house, what age her son Jack is and whether she has other children, a partner or friends and family around her. We will now consider particular techniques which aim to maximise communication between professionals and their clients.

② ASKING QUESTIONS

Asking questions when conversing can help to extend the conversation or end the conversation. We will explore two types of questions which can be used in varying ways when working with clients. Open-ended questions invite a long, explanatory response. Closed-ended questions require shorter answers. Here is an example of an open-ended question from Alexandro.

> Nora: It's weird to be without Jack too, though I'm sure he's fine with Mum. He's just so completely connected to me as I'm his only source of food. It's overwhelming sometimes. (*Looking around the cafe*) So weird to be out. Maybe we should get back...?
>
> Alexandro: Can you tell me more about what you mean by feeling overwhelmed?

In asking this question Alexandro is inviting Nora to tell him more about how she is feeling and the situation she finds herself in. Open-ended questions in this context help to demonstrate to Nora that he is listening to her and that he is interested in hearing more. This is quite a contrast to his earlier response when he stood up to leave. Given that we can assume that Nora is keen to talk about how she is feeling, using an open-ended question in this way is likely to have a positive impact on Nora who has been trying to raise the issue of her feelings since the beginning of the conversation.

③ REFLECTING

Reflecting involves mirroring what the person has just said. Sometimes the same words can be used or they can be *paraphrased*, which means to put the original phrase into other words whilst keeping the original meaning. For example, reflecting meaning in the context above produces the following dialogue:

> Nora: Do you know this is the first time I've been out of the house in weeks?
>
> Alexandro: This is the first time you've been out of the house for weeks.
>
> Nora: Yes! Can you believe it? Time is flying past.

Reflecting feelings involves reflecting back what has already been said in relation to emotions. Here Alexandro reflects the emotion Nora articulates:

> **Nora**: Feels kind of weird to be out. The noise.
> **Alexandro**: It's a weird feeling, being out. Different noises to home.
> **Nora**: Totally different. The house is just so quiet with just me and Jack.

Reflecting in conversation can help when people 'lose' where they are in the narrative. For example, if there is a gap in conversation which is due to the speaker losing their place, it can help to provide a reflective statement. Reflective questions and statements need to be used sparingly. Overusing them can make the conversation stilted or disingenuous.

④ CLARIFYING

Clarifying questions and statements help to 'check in' with clients that they are being understood. In social work, it is vital that we use empathy to imagine what it must be like to view the world through our client's eyes (Lee 1994). Clarifying questions must fit with our client's narrative. For example, using our two characters, here is an example of a clarifying question which is inappropriate:

> **Nora**: Do you know this is the first time I've been out of the house in weeks?
> **Alexandro**: Speaking of your house, did you say that you've been decorating?

It is clear from Alexandro's response that he is not responding to Nora's attempts to discuss her current situation. An example of a more appropriate clarifying question is as follows:

> **Nora**: Do you know this is the first time I've been out of the house in weeks?
> **Alexandro**: Do you mean you haven't been out without Jack, or do you mean you haven't been out by yourself in weeks?

Here Alexandro is asking a clarifying question because he is not sure about whether Nora means that she has not been out with other people or whether she has not been out at all, including with her newborn baby. In clarifying her meaning, he is demonstrating that he is listening and curious about what she is saying, and in better understanding why she has not been out of the house he is attempting to understand 'the problem' from Nora's perspective. Is Nora not getting out of the house related to her depression, for example, or is it more that life is busy with a young baby and she has not had the opportunity to go out? How does Nora feel about not being out of the house? Does she miss social interaction and feel isolated, for example, or is she instead making a comment about how busy she has been?

SUMMARISING

Summarising information from a whole conversation or segments of dialogue serves a few functions. For example, here is a social worker summarising a client interaction: 'Have I got this right? You've come here so that you can get some more support with your disability which leaves you unable to get your children to school on time', or 'You and your partner Sue would like help with your relationship'. Summarising helps to narrow down the specifics of why someone requires assistance. It also helps to demonstrate listening skills. It is important in summarising that we are tentative about our assessment of the issues. If we were to summarise the dialogue between Nora and Alexandro we would need to note the following issues:

- Nora and Alexandro are siblings, both in their 40s
- Nora has a young baby named Jack
- Nora is feeling 'weird' being out in public
- Nora has a history of depression and thinks perhaps that although she might be depressed she is 'not as bad' as in the past

Being able to summarise often complex information is a central task in social work. Although we might like to draw some preliminary assessments about Nora and Alexandro's relationship, this process is more of an analysis than a summary. Analysis involves synthesising information and knowledge and is the means through which social workers make assessments (we explore assessments in Chapter 6 which looks at placement and organisational settings).

PROBING

Probing invites people to comment more fully or in more detail about a particular issue or emotion. For example, probing questions ask things such as 'What effect has that had on you?' (Morgan 2000) or 'Can you tell me more about what that meant in terms of your previous relationship?' Probing requires attention to the whole of a person's narrative as it can involve bridging two or more themes together. For example, if someone has talked about 'anger issues' at the beginning of the session then towards the end of your meeting they tell you about a history of property damage, probing might entail asking more about 'anger' in those contexts. Note that probing is merely an interest in looking further or more deeply at our client's issues. It is not meant to be a confronting or obtrusive challenging. Probing is an invitation for clients to talk more about issues. In our example, probing might consist of asking Nora to talk more about her feelings of depression and checking with her about isolation and support. These issues are directed through our understanding of what Nora has told us about so far but are also drawn from our knowledge about human growth and development (see Chapter 2), social work theory (see Chapter 4) and mental health and postnatal depression. Here is an example of a probing question:

Nora: Do you know this is the first time I've been out of the house in weeks?
Alexandro: That sounds really difficult.
Nora: Yeah, it has been really hard. Some days I just don't feel like getting out of bed in the morning.
Alexandro: **Do you think depression is making you feel like this?**
Nora: I think it might be. Last time I got really depressed I had trouble getting out of bed. That, to me, is a bit of a sign.

FRAMING ACTION

It is important that the contact between a social worker and their client is *purposeful* (Compton & Galaway 1999). In hearing a narrative from a client, for example, it is a mutual expectation that this contact will produce positive change. Since social workers have various roles and functions which depend on their organisational context, the 'outcomes' from contact with a social worker will differ. Two of the roles that social workers fulfil are:

- Counsellor: in this case the client's interaction with the social worker may occur in order to produce insight and re-frame 'problems' (Morgan 2000).
- Specialist social worker: for example, Nora might require assistance from children and families or mental health organisations in government or non-government. Social workers in this role might respond to her needs through advocacy, referring her on to more appropriate services, linking her in with supports such as local groups and services, agreeing on a contract for direct work together, and so on.

Framing action often occurs at the beginning or ending of sessions with clients. For example, imagine that Nora presented to a social worker in a children and families non-government organisation. Nora and the social worker would have discussed her experiences and subsequent needs in their initial meeting. At the end of the session the social worker may frame action through identifying things that they have agreed upon. The social worker may say something like this: 'So Nora, I have agreed to find out what the waiting list is like for the postnatal group at the hospital. I will call you tomorrow around 3pm when Jack might be asleep to see how you are. And you said you are okay with thinking more about what we might be able to do to help you feel less isolated and that you had a good GP with whom you will make an appointment tomorrow. Does that sound okay? Have I left anything out?' This process of agreeing and framing action is known as *contracting* (Cournoyer 2010). Contracting occurs at the beginning of interaction with clients, but should also occur at various points during each contact with our clients.

WRITTEN COMMUNICATION

Many students are competent at writing assignments, essays and exams, and in social work practice those academic writing skills are essential to extend into good practice. Examples of written tasks social workers undertake are:

- Written assessments, case summaries, timelines, case reviews
- Case notes
- Letters of referral to other organisations/professionals/teams
- Court reports
- Online content, for example contributing to the organisation's website
- Refereed journal articles and media copy
- Research proposals, summaries, reports
- Grant applications and tenders
- Annual reports

With competent writing skills being so central to social work, it is crucial for students to work on any gaps in knowledge about writing. For example, if grammatical errors are due to confusion about the 'rules' of grammar, universities often provide academic writing courses, workshops and one to one sessions which would be worth considering. These help with general issues such as how to construct an essay, tips on building an argument successfully, how to write critically as well as some foundational skills in writing such as structure, content, referencing, sentence construction and so on. Similarly, there are many social work books dedicated to written skill development (Healy & Mulholland 2007) and free online learning activities which help participants learn about correct use of apostrophes, for example, and other grammatical rules. Attending to writing skills early on saves problems in later study and helps to build the skills required in social work.

Each type of writing activity requires a slightly different focus, but here are some general writing tips which apply across both academic and practice contexts:

- Re-read your work and make sure it makes sense.
- Think about the purpose of your written piece of work: is it to provide a critical argument? Is it to create a record of a meeting with a client? Knowing the purpose of your writing is central when reading back your work. Ask yourself: have I achieved the requirements of the task? Is it clear why I have written what I have?
- Stick to the 'facts'. Unless the piece requires reflection (you will likely have to use references in reflective accounts), it is important to present information as objectively as possible. In case notes, for example, say: 'Daniel told me: "I want Mum to leave me alone"' rather than: 'Daniel wants to be left alone by his mother'. This helps to identify where different types of information have originated and differentiate fact from opinion.

THE SELF, REFLEXIVITY AND EMPATHY

In Chapter 1 we explored what we mean by the 'self'. Mead's interactionist self requires social interaction and identity is formed not through internal traits but through unique biographical events (Mead 1934). How we communicate to others is of concern in social work. Being able to reflexively engage in how we come across to others is therefore important, as is the ability to empathise. All of these require us to 'know' or understand ourselves in relation to others. Rather than seeing your self through therapeutic discourse as fixed and unchanging (Furedi 2004), think about how different situations bring out different ways of expressing or 'being' your-self. Complete Exercise 3.1, thinking about how you might be talking, gesturing, relating to others. Would you be confident? In your comfort zone? Would you be playful or serious? Would you be able to relate easily to others in that environment?

EXERCISE 3.1

If I was in a temple, I would be...
If I was at home I would be...
If I was in a school I would be...
If I was at work at a restaurant I would be...
If I was at university I would be...
If I was in the library I would be...
If I was at a game of football I would be...
If I was at the beach I would be...

Although it is the same 'you' in all of the places suggested, these differing locations would have provoked varying anticipated behaviours and attitudes. These might have depended on your own previous experiences of similar or the same places, or how you might imagine the people and surrounding culture of the place in question. Knowing that you respond differently to different social and cultural contexts is important in social work. This is because different emotions and experiences come together to influence the ways in which you interact with others. Imagining yourself at a football match may be one person's idea of pure joy while for someone else such an environment may be experienced as extremely challenging. In differing contexts our behaviours change and how we appear to others also changes. Being interpreted by others as aggressive or rude, for example, may occur because of a lack of understanding about how one comes across to others. When you engage in role plays at university, other students and tutors can often offer helpful, critical yet sensitive insights into how others interpret your tone, manner, gestures and communication styles. It is important to be aware of these and to experiment through play in learning activities: this is key to learning (West *et al.* 2011).

Through using imagination and play, children learn about how to take the perspective of others (Mead 1934). Similarly, in adulthood, we use this skill to under-stand others (Mead 1934). Therefore empathy requires both emotional literacy and imaginative action which enables one to imagine the perspective of others. The statements in Exercise 3.2 represent accounts from various different people. Practise your empathic imagination by thinking about how the person making the statement is feeling.

EXERCISE 3.2

I'd met this girl and we stayed at hers. In the morning I was running for the bus when they got me. Everyone knows they are racists. I was in their turf. I should have known better.

EMOTION: _Anger → feels he is streated unequally_
REGRET

They hurt me. I can still feel their hands on me. It was my fault.

EMOTION: _pain/responsibility_
FEAR

When he was born he was exactly the same. I loved him then and I still love him. He's my son and yeah he's got a disability but stop discriminating against him. He was determined then and he's determined now. I couldn't ask for a better son.

EMOTION: _proud → fuelled by judgement_

It's like I'm two people. When I've got the smack I'm loved up, you know. When I'm without it I'm so alone and scared. I love it but I hate it too.

EMOTION: _fear → not in control_

Some of the emotions you may have thought about when reading the different statements may have included, for example (in order of the accounts in Exercise 3.2), feeling regret, fear and terror, horror, pride and conflicted or torn. When we considered Nora's account earlier in the chapter we explored different ways we could better understand her views and experiences through using differing communicative devices. Understanding how someone feels requires empathy which requires imagination and knowledge about the world around us. It is important when discussing emotions with our clients not to assume or generalise about emotions. As ever, tentative and careful discussion about emotions helps people find their own words to describe and understand their experiences and the world around them.

Your own biography or life events will have exposed you to different experiences than your fellow students. Direct experiences of the impacts of discrimination, oppression and injustice, or an interest in social issues such as addiction, violence, abuse and ill health, often prompt people's interest in studying social work. Using one's own experiences of oppression or inequality can help in engaging in imaginative accounts whereby the task is to understand the world from another person's perspective.

Sometimes students feel they do not 'bring enough experience' to their social work studies. There are numerous ways students can engage with developing empathy besides first-hand experience. Being able to imagine others' perspectives and associated emotions is the key task in the arts. Watching films, reading fiction and non-fiction books, listening to music and looking at visual art all help to develop empathic understanding. Engaging in reading about theories can also assist in this process, as we shall see in Chapter 5 when we explore ethics and values.

USE OF SELF

In this book we have begun to explore how to 'be' a social worker through engagement in key social work ideas including theories. In order to become a social worker, one must work to encourage the ongoing development of the social work self. This occurs through interaction between formal and informal learning. Such learning can occur in both structured and less structured environments, the former, for example, occurring in the university setting and the latter on placement.

In scholarship relating to therapeutic interactions, particularly in counselling, the emergence of the 'professional' has conceptualised identity in a compartmentalised way (Dunk-West 2011). The self we are at home, for example, is meant to differ from the self we are at work. Aspects of the 'personal' self, for example, might be used in 'professional' work: is one's sense of humour to be used in professional life? There are no easy answers in the literature as the question of the 'use of self' in practice has continued to be debated in social work scholarship (Heydt & Sherman 2005; Mandell 2008; McTighe 2011; Reupert 2006, 2007, 2009; Urdang 2010).

Although the questions and theories which make up the 'use of self' literature have their roots in psychoanalytic theory (Mandell 2008, p. 236), some of the ideas from this area of scholarship are relevant to our discussions in this book. Yet it is important to see the distinction between the idea of the 'use of self' and the way this book conceptualises the self.

The theoretical foundation of this book is that Mead's theoretical work, in which the self is produced through social interactions (Mead 1934), is relevant to social work. This means that the self we are at work and the self we are at home *are* different—but this is not because we are holding back or deliberately forcing a persona, but rather because our surrounding environment and subsequent *interactions produce the self.*

The way we reflect upon our selves is relevant to this chapter because we are exploring communication and communicative techniques which help us engage with those around us in the professional setting. Therefore the literature which examines the 'use of self' can be used—albeit with a critical lens—to assist in making the connections between our methods of communication and the ways in which we have communicated with others in the past, in different contexts, and those in our emerging social work role. Mandell articulates this in the following way:

> When countertransference approaches to the use of self are trapped by their failure to address power, while anti-oppression approaches are reductive to oppressor/ oppressed relations, a gap is created. Neither the traditional use of self literature nor the developing work on critical reflection seems to adequately capture a process of combining insight into one's own personhood—comprising individual

developmental history and multiple social identities in the context of personal experience, education, socialization and political milieus—with a critical analysis of one's role as a social worker in the relations of power that constitute our practice. This kind of multi-layered process is ... what we should be aiming for. (Mandell 2008, p. 237)

Therefore it is vital that we focus on communication skills and practices as one level of social work interaction. These must be combined with a critical appreciation of the world around us and some of the 'bigger' systems within which we operate in our day-to-day lives. These bigger systems include organisations and institutions as well as social norms, attitudes and practices.

Before we move on to consider working with others, take some time to complete the five questions in Exercise 3.3 in light of the material covered in this chapter.

EXERCISE 3.3

1. I communicate verbally by (for example, use of hands to gesture, using animated facial expressions, sitting close to the person you are speaking to):

   eye contact, nodding - cue, facial expressions, small comments

2. In terms of effective interpersonal communication, I think I am (choose which statement fits, you can choose more than one option):
   a. good at getting my point across
   b. not so great at getting my point across
   c. sometimes good at getting my point across; how I communicate depends on the context
   d. always effective at getting my point across

3. I am good at 'reading' people (choose which answer fits).
   a. True
   b. False
   c. Sometimes true/false

4. It is better that social workers do not force particular types of communicative devices (such as reflective questions and the like) because it patronises the people with whom we work.
   a. True
   b. False
   c. Somewhat true/false

5. It is always important to consider power and power inequality and how it has a bearing on communication between social workers and the people with whom they work. This awareness of power can be addressed through (suggest ways that you will address this in your work as a social work student and in your social work career):

   empathise, make client feel comfortable take an interest in whats being said - show I am interested

WORKING WITH OTHERS

Making the link between broader theories of inequality and person-to-person inter-action enables social workers to communicate in ways that help to address power imbalances and inequalities. Therefore, the way in which we communicate as social workers is immensely powerful in itself. Addressing broader inequalities in 'micro' or person-to-person interaction has been highlighted in Jan Fook's theoretical work (Fook 1993, 2002; Hugman 2005, p. 1142). Equally it is important how we communi-cate with other professions, since this is the means through which we convey to others who we are as social workers and what social work means.

Working with other professionals requires high level communication skills. It can be difficult to articulate the underlying values and theoretical foundation upon which social work is built, particularly if other professions come from very different perspectives. We have discussed in previous chapters some of the tensions which can occur in multidisciplinary settings, but this quote from a participant involved in research into interprofessional identity sums up why it is important to connect with others on a 'human' level:

> Whether it's a manager of a ward or social services or a day centre, treat us as individuals, it doesn't matter whether you're a manic depressive, schizophrenic, got personality disorder ... or mental condition let's say, or whatever, or severely depressed, you're an individual, you're a human being with problems and address that person as an individual and not as a condition. (Reynolds 2007, p. 451)

Similarly, other professionals can help to increase our knowledge about the profes-sion itself. Using effective communication can assist social workers in having their views heard by other professions and help to foster positive working relationships.

CHAPTER SUMMARY

This chapter has introduced communication in social work. We have examined some of the key ways in which verbal communication can be used to elicit client narratives, in particular: demonstrating listening; asking questions; reflecting; clarifying; summarising; probing and framing action. Written communication was also explored, with some key tips on how to develop written skills in the academic and practice contexts. Finally, we considered the use of self and working with others in relation to communicating as a social worker.

FURTHER READING

COURNOYER, B. R. (2010) *The Social Work Skills Workbook*, 6th edn. Florence: Cengage Learning Inc.
HEALY, K. (2012) *Social Work Methods and Skills: The Essential Foundations of Practice*. Basingstoke: Palgrave Macmillan.

HEALY, K. & MULHOLLAND, J. (2012) *Writing Skills for Social Workers*, 2nd edn. London: Sage Publications.

LISHMAN, J. (2009) *Communication in Social Work*, 2nd edn. Basingstoke: Palgrave Macmillan.

NELSON-JONES, R. (2012) *Basic Counselling Skills*. London: Sage Publications.

THOMPSON, N. (2011) *Effective Communication: A Guide for the People Professions*, 2nd edn. Basingstoke: Palgrave Macmillan.

TREVITHICK, P. (2012) *Social Work Skills and Knowledge: A Practice Handbook*, 3rd edn. Maidenhead: Open University Press.

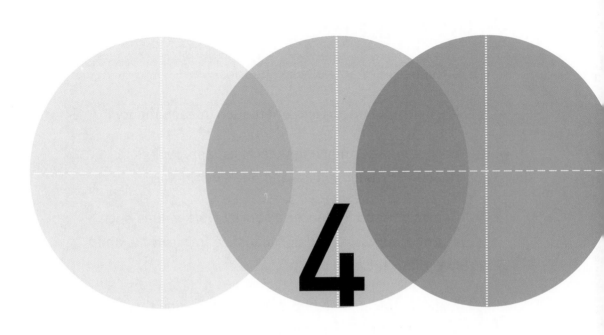

4

Social Work Theory

This chapter:

- Introduces key social work theories

- Identifies the underlying orientation in each theory

- Encourages scrutinising theoretical approaches in relation to values, ethics and one's world-view

- Considers broadly conceived social work values such as anti-oppressive and social justice frameworks and how these apply to practice

- Explores the tension between the public and the private worlds of experience and how these apply to social work

cognitive behavioural therapy
Humanistic approach
Empowerment approach
Ecological perspective
feminist theory
Structural approach
Sociological social work
individual : culture
: social

Dear Dr Agony Aunt,

I am a woman in my late 30s and am at my wits' end, as I can never seem to find the right guy. I have had two significant relationships which both ended with them saying that they found me emotionally distant and more like a friend than a girlfriend. These comments at the time really hurt me but I know that they were true as I didn't like to kiss and cuddle very often. The guys were lovely people and I feel I really lost out when they dumped me.

Generally I find it hard to open up to people as I'm really shy which, as I said, has meant that I have only had a few long-term relationships. My friends are all so sexually confident but I find that I wear clothes to cover my body and don't go out as a result of feeling like I don't fit in. I want to be more like them but can't seem to feel comfortable with myself. I see television shows and read magazines like yours and find myself comparing—not so favourably—myself to others. I am successful in my work and have some really great friends whom I have confided in, though I am sure they don't realise the extent to which this gets me down. How can I find a partner for life when I'm so unhappy with the way I am? Will I ever be confident and self-assured?

Feeling Lonely, via email

...

Dear Feeling Lonely,

You have taken the first step in dealing with your problems. In reaching out for help, you have shown that you are willing to examine where these issues arise from and how you might be able to fix them. I will offer you some general advice and hope that you will seek out the expert help, which will assist you in your journey towards greater self-acceptance. It appears to me that your issues seem to stem from your inability to really confide in and connect with others—which you say is down to your shyness. Whilst people with introverted personalities do tend to find it difficult to act in an extroverted way, I don't feel that your problems with intimacy are because of your shyness. Consider instead why you might have subconsciously sabotaged your previous relationships. What is it that is scary about intimacy and closeness? In answering these questions you may wish to further understand how your childhood learning about relationships might have impacted upon the ways in which you behave in relationships. I recommend that you get in touch with a registered counsellor to help you resolve these issues.

Best of luck,
Dr Agony Aunt

The correspondence above, though fictionalised, represents similar columns which appear in newspapers and magazines throughout the world on a daily basis. As we saw in Chapter 1, the way in which we think about ourselves has been so shaped by psychological theories of the self that the tendency is to uncritically accept them.

Consider, for example, the response above from the 'expert'. The advice given is that the letter-writer seek professional help. Peppered through the response are important clues as to which sets of theories or discourses the expert is utilising. The mention of the subconscious, for example, presupposes that such a thing actually exists. Similarly, the elevation of childhood as an indicator of present behaviour is presupposed. As we saw in Chapter 1, such notions of childhood can be seen in psychoanalytic theories and have become a central part of the ways in which we understand the self in contemporary popular culture. Finally, the role of the expert is assumed to be beneficial if not *crucial* in helping the individual overcome their personal problems. Inherent in the account is the presumption that the following are real and objectively true:

psychological (handwritten margin note)

- Personality
- The subconscious
- Childhood as a predictor of adult interactions
- That experts and therapy are required to 'fix' individual pathologies

Yet all of these assumptions need to be critically understood: whilst all are presupposed to be 'true' in contemporary western culture (Furedi 2004) it is only through examination of the theoretical world-view held by differing theories that social workers can be of better assistance to their clients. The uncritical acceptance of these notions does little to assist our clients. Consider, for example, that the person writing the letter may not require therapy or any assistance from professionals in order to overcome her articulated concerns. In their everyday work, social workers come into contact with individuals experiencing problems or wanting change so it can become second nature to assume that in order for change to occur, individuals require the assistance of experts. However, as we shall see, such a position does little to account for agency, which is the ability to bring about change in one's life. It is crucial that social workers reflect upon their understanding of the expert, and social work theories make this explicit.

The purpose of this chapter is to outline some of the key theories which underpin social work practice. Through a brief but critical discussion of differing approaches, we will better understand the underlying assumptions and challenge the role of the expert.

SOCIAL WORK THEORY: DIFFERING ORIENTATIONS

Figure 4.1 represents the ways in which social workers work to effect change through intervention at various levels. Social work theories examine how to assist others in making change which involves a shift in:

- Individual behaviours
- Thoughts or cognition
- Social interactions
- Social structures, systems, policies and institutional practices

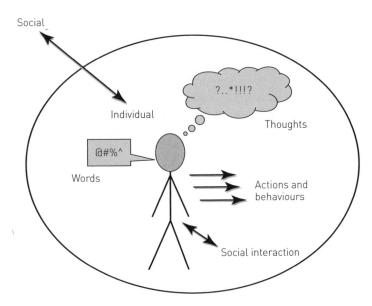

FIGURE 4.1 Different social work theories focus on different areas of human experience, action, thoughts and social structure

While many theories focus on changing individual patterns of behaviour or ways of thinking, others theorise that individual change does little to address broader social problems in which inequality is produced. Such approaches instead argue that social workers ought to focus on changing broader systems or structures (Mullaly 1997).

For example, if a client working with a social worker was experiencing poverty through unemployment the social worker's intervention could vary, depending on which theoretical perspective is informing their social work practice. Using theories in which change is individualised, the social worker might try to help the client gain employment, which would address the problem of poverty. The social work intervention might entail looking at individual 'blocks' to employment such as lack of experience or skills desired by employers. Assisting the client through referring them to community groups and services designed to help people into employment might be a course of action when taking an 'individual' approach. Yet this course of action relies upon the notion that employment is available to people who are willing to undergo personal transformation to get them 'work ready'. A more structural approach involves taking a broader view of the problem. Though the individual client's issue relates to poverty due to unemployment, a structural approach would entail understanding the client's problem in the context of their broader socio-cultural environment and arrangement of societal institutions, practices, policies and legislation. For example, the client may live in an area that is characterised by high unemployment and poverty. They may be ineligible for unemployment benefits or the benefits themselves may be inadequate to meet the rising costs of living, including food, housing, clothing, fuel costs such as electricity and gas, and costs associated with communication such as the internet and mobile telephone accounts.

The social worker using a structural approach may work with the individual along with other individuals in the community to lobby political figures to address the inequalities evident in their community such as the lack of access to employment. In this way, the social worker is assisting the client to form relationships with others with a view to bringing about change, not through a focus on the individual's circumstances, but through a focus on the shared experiences which are due to external factors such as lack of jobs. The social worker may try to raise public awareness about the issues facing people in the area and may do so through public education, writing letters to key community leaders, policy-makers and legislators.

Although each of the tasks relating to the individual and structural approaches differs, often in practice social workers will work towards *both* assisting others in making individual changes in their lives to increase well-being *and* promoting principles such as social justice through challenging oppressive social structures. Indeed it is vital that social work continues to assist in addressing problems identified by individuals, and that it distinguishes itself as a profession that is committed to bringing about social change (Fook 1991). We shall explore some of the key theoretical approaches used in social work. As we consider them it is important to distinguish between those which advocate for individual change and those advocating for social change.

In social work this tension between the individual and structural levels of disadvantage requires constant reflection and analysis on behalf of the social worker but it also requires personal commitment. Not only must social workers decide whether they intervene through individual or social action, they must also account for their own personal values and beliefs. For example, can a person be a competent social worker if they are abusive in their private lives? To believe in social justice requires a clear professional and personal value-base, and we will explore this further in Chapter 5 when we explore ethics. It is crucial to recognise and engage in this tension. Social work has long been concerned with the coming together of the ways in which individual experiences feed into broader society:

> The triangular discourse about the extent to which and the ways in which social work is personal, political or professional have always been present in social work. I have interpreted them as being about the struggle to achieve social work's claim of bringing together the interpersonal and the social. (Payne 2005, p. 186)

Despite the different foundations upon which theories are built, in social work across differing practice settings and differentiated theoretical applications, the process whereby we implement theories is very similar. The 'social work process' (Compton & Galaway 1989) involving the assessment of the 'problem', intervention and review requires collaboration, clearly defined timeframes and a belief that people are able to successfully 'address the challenges they face' (Healy 2012, pp. 56–57). We will now examine some of the key theoretical models which frame contemporary social work practice.

COGNITIVE BEHAVIOURAL THERAPY

Cognitive behavioural therapy (CBT) (Figure 4.2) is an approach that argues that in changing an individual's thoughts, or cognition, their behaviour will change. There is much empirical evidence to suggest that CBT is an effective intervention to address a range of issues such as anxiety and phobias, or substance misuse (Vasilaki *et al.* 2006; Witkiewitz & Marlatt 2004) for example. Because CBT has a high success rate and is a relatively inexpensive way to treat individual problems, it is increasingly used in practice, particularly in mental health settings. Internationally, CBT is practised by psychologists as well as social workers, and in social work the idea that thoughts affect behaviours is broadly accepted. The specific ways in which CBT can be utilised in social work are far reaching. The benefit of CBT to social work is that underpinning this approach is the belief that the self is able to shift and change previously unhelpful ways of thinking and acting (Ronen 1997, p. 204) without recourse to constraining notions such as personality 'types'. Using this broad conceptualisation of the self helps to frame individual pathology in terms of change. In this way:

> CBT ... is neither a strict implementation of learning theory, nor is it merely a collection of effectual techniques. Rather, CBT constitutes a holistic way of life, a way of thinking and perceiving human functioning and needs, and a way of operating within the environment in order to achieve the most effective means of accomplishing one's aims. (Ronen 1997, p. 202)

FIGURE 4.2 Cognitive behavioural therapy relates to thoughts and behaviours

HUMANISTIC APPROACHES

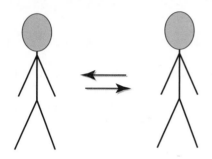

FIGURE 4.3 Humanistic approaches focus on individuals and the helping relationship

Humanistic approaches (Figure 4.3) emphasise the quality of the relationship between the client and the professional and it is therefore the interaction between the social worker and their client that is central to bringing about positive change. The key theorist in the application of humanistic approaches to social work is Carl Rogers (1951, 1961). Rogers argues that in order for the therapeutic relationship in counselling to be successful, the counsellor must have particular abilities. These include: empathy or the ability to understand the world from another's perspective, 'unconditional positive regard' which is the ability to think positively about people no matter what their circumstances, and to be congruent which means that there is a real connection between the values and beliefs of one's profession and those of one's true self (see Rogers 1951, 1961). Research consistently demonstrates, particularly in counselling, that the relationship, or *interaction*, between the professional and the client is crucial to successful outcomes for the client (Lambert & Barley 2001; Ribner & Knei-Paz 2002). Such findings underline that the relationship between social workers and their clients is of central importance in working together successfully. Using a humanistic approach entails interacting in a genuine, truthful and empathic manner, and social workers using such an approach thus need to be aware of their language, their communication style and the way in which they come across to others. More importantly, however, they need to build a relationship in which clients feel able to disclose information and work together towards a common goal. A Rogerian approach is often thought about in relation to counselling work, but in contemporary social work practice the underpinning values of this framework are just as important in casework or community work as they are in one-to-one interactions.

Motivational interviewing is a type of intervention used in social work, particularly in the substance use field, which similarly emphasises the Rogerian importance of the relationship between the social worker and the client. Rogers advocates for an approach which is led by the client: it is up to the client to direct the issues discussed, for example. In motivational interviewing the professional is a facilitator who helps their client 'examine and resolve ambivalence. The specific strategies of motivational interviewing are designed to elicit, clarify, and resolve ambivalence in a client-centred and respectful atmosphere' (Nelson 2011, p. 111).

mixed feelings

STRENGTHS PERSPECTIVE/EMPOWERMENT APPROACH

Rather than seeing people in relation to what is going 'wrong' in their lives, the strengths perspective and empowerment approach instead takes a more positive angle in that the social worker's motivation is to work towards encouraging and

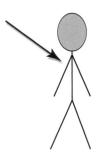

FIGURE 4.4 Strengths perspectives are interested in individual strengths

helping to facilitate change through the unconditional support of their client's capabilities (Figure 4.4). Such approaches are more interested in the future than in the past (Healy 2012, p. 14) and can therefore be seen as a counter to psychoanalytic approaches in which problems in childhood, for example, can be viewed as a barrier to current functioning (as discussed in Chapter 1). The strengths perspective argues that individuals have particular skills and strategies for coping with adversity and it is vital for social workers to work 'with' and 'for' client strengths (see Saleeby 1992, 1996, 2006). There are some similarities with other approaches such as solution-focused, problem-solving (Perlman 1957) and narrative approaches (Morgan 2000; White & Epston 1990) in that these all share an interest in separating the 'person from the problem' (Healy 2012, p. 71). Similarly, alongside the privileging of client strengths in social work practice, the notion of empowerment is often cited as being important. It is crucial to note however that social workers do not 'empower' individuals.

Rather, social workers work to assist in individuals' empowerment through working *alongside* their clients, consistently working to understand clients' struggles and challenges, advocating against constraining social structures and sharing information that assists in promoting change. Central to empowerment approaches is the understanding that there is unequal distribution of power which results in disempowered individuals. Social workers from this perspective must therefore work alongside clients in collaboration: 'we are partners against oppression, but in this dance, leading and following may be fluid and interchangeable. The concept of coteaching implies that clients and workers teach each other what they know about the presenting problem and about the oppression(s) faced' (Lee 1994, p. 29).

Both of these theoretical positions are useful in the problem-saturated landscape within which social work can take place because 'our focus on problems and work with disadvantaged populations creates the occupational hazard that workers will focus too much on client weakness and problems and fail to identify strengths' (Compton & Galaway 1989, p. 223).

SYSTEMS THEORY/ECOLOGICAL PERSPECTIVE

Systems theory and the ecological perspective or ecosystem approach argue that the individual is best understood only in relation to their environment (Figure 4.5). Although there are various traditions arguing that clients must be understood through analysis of their setting, they share some common ideas. Interactions in the world around us, including its people, geographical places, organisations and institutions, make up our ecology. Systems theory can be used with groups (Balgopal & Vassil 1983) and individuals (Rose 1962).

For example, social workers working with a young person having problems living at home with their family would be interested in the ways the young person

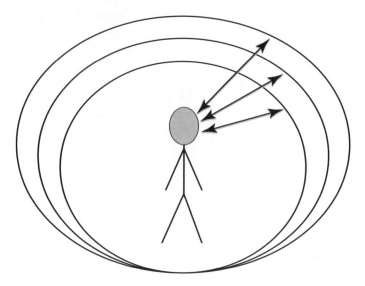

FIGURE 4.5 Systems approaches highlight the external environment and the individual's place within

is interacting in the broader family or family 'system' and the role they play within such a system. This is because 'the family as a larger system relies on each individual member to play his or her part if it is to function successfully as an entity in the community' and the family is connected to the community in varying ways (Compton & Galaway 1989, p. 120). In this way, individuals are connected to others through varying 'systems'. Social workers using these theories to underpin their practice must work to understand their client's ecological setting and which interactions become stressors (Germain & Gitterman, 1980).

Although this group of theories is rich in 'technical terminology' (Payne 2005, p. 157), historically social work has long been concerned with understanding the person in relation to their environment (Healy 2012, p. 13). In Chapter 1 we considered the role of psychological discourses in shaping the way we currently think about ourselves. Ecological perspectives tend to shift the focus away from the individual and are more concerned with how individuals' attempts to *interact* with particular systems or organisations become problematic. A social worker's role is to assist people in resolving problems in these interactions as well as to link people with others who may further assist in successfully realising their aspirations (Pincus & Minahan 1973, p. 9).

FEMINIST SOCIAL WORK THEORY

Feminist social work theory involves the critical analysis of power in relation to gender and understands it both in the context of broader social structures and through individual experiences in day-to-day life (Figure 4.6). The relatively recent

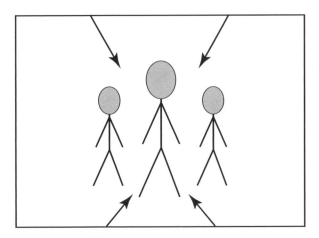

FIGURE 4.6 Feminist social work highlights broader social inequalities

shift in women's social roles has been the result of increased labour participation outside the family home and changes in traditional gender expectations due to contraceptives allowing women to choose when and whether to have children (Giddens 1992). Yet despite these changes, women continue to experience gendered oppression in contemporary social life. For example, women are more often diagnosed with depression than men. Further, 'racialized, "minoritorized" and immigrant women are more likely than British-born white women to enter the statistics of those experiencing mental illnesses' (Bondi & Burman 2001, p. 9). Women are subject to higher rates of sexual violence than their male counterparts. Domestic violence is overwhelmingly perpetrated by men towards women. All of these social issues, and more, are important to the ways in which social workers work with both women and men, adults and children:

> Women have been at the centre of the struggle to define the appropriate role for social work in rapidly changing societies. Although crucial policies and legislation are formulated by men, women undertake the bulk of the caring tasks carried out within the home, and dominate the basic grades of paid professions doing such work. Thus, arguments about the purpose of social work are intricately wound up with disputes over women's position in the social order. (Dominelli 2002, p. 17)

In social work it is vital to understand the sociological analysis of gender. The implications for practice are varied. Understanding differential power through the lens of gender means that social issues such as child sexual abuse in the family, for example, can be better theorised and responded to in practice (see Dominelli 1989).

CRITICAL SOCIAL WORK AND STRUCTURAL APPROACHES

Like feminist social work approaches, critical and structural approaches to social work practice entail awareness of and action towards the *external* causes of individual problems (Figure 4.7). At the beginning of this chapter we explored the issue of poverty and unemployment from both an individual perspective and a social perspective. The social perspective entailed understanding how external factors such as a community's high rate of unemployment or lack of jobs made it difficult for labour force participation. Thus, a social work focus on individual factors contributing to unemployment from a critical perspective does little to acknowledge

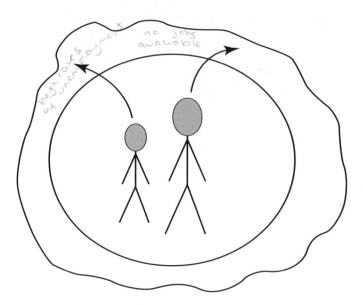

FIGURE 4.7 Critical approaches are interested in change at the structural level

or address the wider issues at stake. In this way, individual problems are always framed as being part of a broader community or social setting which constrains or oppresses individuals. Such an approach requires social workers' reflexive engagement with oppression:

> Critical social work demands that social workers reflect upon the ways in which social disadvantage and oppression shape our sense of purpose as practitioners. This perspective demands that a social worker should, at the very least, have a critical understanding of social disadvantage and how to respond to individuals living in oppressed or difficult circumstances ... it is often necessary for social workers to critically reflect on the broader societal attitudes that contribute to the discrimination and oppression experienced by service users. (Healy 2012, p. 12)

In Chapter 3 we examined the ways in which social workers develop the necessary skills to listen, empathise and act upon our clients' needs, and these skills are as central for structural work as they are for interpersonal work. Advocating on behalf of clients to external organisations, for example, requires many of the same communicative skills used in interpersonal exchanges. In Chapter 6 we will consider the organisational contexts in which social work intervention takes place. Social workers are required to challenge the ways in which institutions discriminate against others on the basis of gender, sexual identity, race, disability, class and other areas of difference (Mullaly 1997, p. 104). While it may seem intuitive that social workers challenge oppression, in practice this can feel risky. For example, a social worker in a statutory setting in which they work with young people may know that the closure of a local service for young people who are survivors of sexual assault will further oppress young women. The social worker's attempts to bring about structural change in their own organisation can be met with resistance and result in the worker feeling that their structural social work is curtailed by hierarchy and organisational culture. Yet it is also important to recognise the role that social work plays in the maintenance of oppressive systems, and ultimately social workers from this perspective are urged to take action:

> Social workers need to understand the nature of state power and the role of social work as an element of state control and oppression, and to construct an approach to practice which is underpinned by this understanding. Such practice must be directed at challenging and changing structures which oppress. (Davis 1991, p. 70 cited in Mullaly 1997)

SOCIOLOGICAL SOCIAL WORK

In Chapter 1 we examined our professional identity, through examining the theory of self developed by George Herbert Mead. In Chapter 2 we also saw the ways in which social models of self have influenced developmental psychology, for example, in relation to highlighting the importance of the social and cultural settings in which the individual develops. Historically, sociological theory has heavily influenced social work theory (see Forte 2004a, 2004b). The notion of sociological social work (Figure 4.8) is the means through which a broad application of sociological

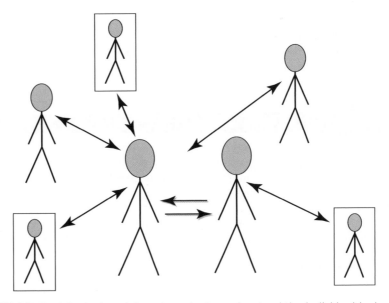

FIGURE 4.8 Sociological social work seeks to understand the individual by looking at social and individual contexts

theory can be translated into social work practice (Dominelli 2004), and sociological social work helps social workers respond to the challenges of contemporary life (Dunk-West & Verity, forthcoming). Since interactions are central to Mead's self-making, it follows that social work ought to be interested in the relationships between people. The meaning of one's environment and relationships within that environment are constitutive of selfhood: social work must always therefore originate from this understanding. In all of the theoretical traditions discussed in this chapter, the importance of the social environment is clear. Although social work theories can feel distinct from one another, in reality they share the same axis of understanding about people as being understood in relation to their environment (social, cultural settings) and relationships with others.

Similarly, a sociological lens helps social workers understand the broader patterns of inequality and oppression which are experienced by particular groups (Dominelli 2004; Cunningham & Cunningham 2008). Discrimination on the basis of gender, age, culture, race, disability, sexual identity, gender identity, socio-economic status, health status and other difference continues to occur in contemporary life. Institutions discriminate as well as individuals, and social workers must take responsibility for practising in a way that counters inequality and actively advocates for and with people who are discriminated against. Anti-discriminatory approaches (Thompson 1993) and anti-oppressive practice, pursuing social justice: these are *foundational to all social work* interventions. The sociological analysis of power and broader patterns of inequality are at the core of competent social work practice and are threaded through all social work theories and methods. It is vital that social work students engage in understanding power and its (unequal) distribution in society. This involves understanding how social workers and their organisational settings contribute to inequality. Developing an ethical framework for oneself (see Chapter 5) helps to direct social work practice appropriately, with inequality actively addressed in social work interventions.

Now take some time to complete Exercise 4.1, a reflexive exercise designed to engage you with the material we have covered in this chapter.

EXERCISE 4.1

Think about a personal issue you have had in the past. Reflect on what the issues were and whether others in your family, community or society have experienced similar issues. What social work approaches help you in understanding this issue? What are your favourite social work theoretical approaches? Do you think social workers should use theories that help them understand social problems and injustices or individual problems and injustices? Your answers to these questions will be personal to you, but are worth noting at this stage and comparing at various points in your academic study as well as into your social work career.

Map out how you see social work theory informing your practice. You can do this visually using a diagram with arrows and shapes, or you could draw a picture. For example, in the picture a river or stream could represent your work with clients and the terrain beside could represent the foundations upon which such work is built. Stones set on the terrain may represent your three preferred social work theories. In particular, while you are completing this exercise, think about an issue using your sociological imagination. What are the implications for individuals and what does the issue mean in the broader historical and social context? Highlight which theories you think will assist you in your future role as a social worker. How do these theories differ from the perspectives of other professionals?

CHAPTER SUMMARY

As we have seen, different social work theories emphasise different things. As you continue your reading and social work studies, you will begin to develop a preference for certain theoretical frameworks, but you will probably have some preference already. In this chapter we have briefly examined some theories which argue that social workers ought to focus on the individual and others which argue it is more important to fight against oppressive structures and systems. Yet other approaches argue that individuals are best understood as relating to the world and people around them and social workers should aim to help individuals overcome difficulties in these interactions with systems. What makes social work distinctive is its concern with both the personal and the social.

Social work theories ought to be approached with a 'sociological imagination' (Mills 1959). Regardless of the theoretical orientation underpinning practice, social workers need to develop this imagination through the dual focus upon the individual and the social setting (Schwartz 1974). Understanding a person requires being curious about their lives, their biography as well as the society in which they are embedded:

> The sociological imagination enables its possessor to understand the larger historical scene in terms of its meaning for the inner life and the external career of a variety of individuals. (Mills 1959, p. 5)

In our challenging social and economic landscape the tension between the public and the private, or the macro and the micro, is more important to resolve than ever. Social work needs to continue to highlight the dual focus on the individual and the environment if we are to realise our desire to effect positive and long-lasting change. At the beginning of the chapter we considered poverty and unemployment; to return to this issue, here is what C. Wright Mills—the scholar who invented the term 'sociological imagination'—had to say about it:

> When, in a city of 100,000, only one man [sic] is unemployed, that is his personal trouble, and for its relief we properly look to the character of the man, his skills, and his immediate opportunities. But when in a nation of 50 million employees, 15 million men are unemployed, that is an issue, and we may not hope to find its solution within the range of opportunities open to any one individual. (Mills 1959, p. 9)

FURTHER READING

ADAMS, R., DOMINELLI, L. & PAYNE, M. (2005) *Social Work Futures: Crossing Boundaries, Transforming Practice*. Basingstoke: Palgrave Macmillan.

BECKETT, C. (2006) *Essential Theory for Social Work Practice*. London: Sage Publications.

COMPTON, B. R. & GALAWAY, B. (1989) *Social Work Processes*. Belmont: Brooks/Cole Publishing Company.

HEALY, K. (2012) *Social Work Methods and Skills: The Essential Foundations of Practice*. Basingstoke: Palgrave Macmillan.

HOWE, D. (2009) *A Brief Introduction to Social Work Theory*. Basingstoke: Palgrave Macmillan.

MILLS, C. W. (1959) *The Sociological Imagination*. New York: Oxford University Press.

PAYNE, M. (2005) *Modern Social Work Theory*, 3rd edn. Basingstoke: Palgrave Macmillan.

5

Everyday Ethics

This chapter:

- Explores personal and professional values and how these relate to social work

- Explains the importance of ethics in underpinning social work practice and theory

- Outlines the key ethical theories which inform social work

- Examines the ethical dimension in relation to particular scenarios

- Highlights ethical dilemmas within organisational contexts and professional roles

Ethics: moral principles that govern a persons behaviour

utilitarianism
kantianism
virtue based

In our contemporary, everyday life we are faced with a number of ethics-related dilemmas each day (Singer 1993, 2004, 2009). Consider, for example, the myriad of product choices available in western cultures. Whether choosing from 12 different types of potatoes or selecting the best supplier for a service, it can be difficult to make choices about goods and services. Specifically, how much thought should go in to buying a product? Is it better to buy cruelty-free and organic? Should we buy food in glass containers which can be recycled or the cheaper, plastic version? Should we worry about giving our custom to companies whose ethics towards its employees are dubious? Should we buy products that have been tested on animals, subjecting them to suffering? Should we participate in meat eating or become vegetarian or vegan in order to help the environment and avoid species' mass production, suffering and slaughter? Should we select locally grown and sourced food to reduce our 'carbon footprint'? Such questions may have come up in your purchasing of products in everyday life. Broader questions about how to live include: should we care for others or look after ourselves? Should children have 'rights'? Are social workers ever 'off duty'? In this chapter we will begin to examine the relationship between our personal and emerging professional self regarding ethics. We consider how to make ethical decisions and what is required in order to justify such decisions. The chapter concludes with an examination of some of the ethical issues in organisations.

Ethical decision-making involves 'the systematic exploration of questions about how we should act in relation to others' (Rhodes 1986, p. 21). Our values influence how we go about our everyday activities. Values are important in social work. There is even a suggestion that successful work between a social worker and their client is promoted when they have some shared values (Loewenberg *et al.* 2000). To begin to think about your own values, complete Exercise 5.1. This has been designed to help you firstly, notice where you stand on a particular issue and secondly, begin to reflexively engage with your values.

EXERCISE 5.1

Read the statements below. Mark a point on the spectrum that represents where you 'stand' on a particular issue. Try to answer honestly rather than putting down what you think are the 'right' answers.

The best place to raise children is within a family

Agree |_____/_____ Disagree

All children need a mother and a father

Agree |_____0_____/_____/ Disagree

Euthanasia (choosing to die) is wrong

Agree _____/_____|Disagree

Abortion should be freely available

Agree _____|_____/_____ Disagree

Everyone should have access to education

Agree _____Disagree

If you work hard, you deserve wealth

Agree _____Disagree

Women and men are equal

Agree _____Disagree

Plastic surgery is wrong

Agree _____Disagree

Everyone should eat healthy food

Agree _____Disagree

Cultural diversity means tolerating difference

Agree _____Disagree

People living in England should know how to speak English

Agree _____Disagree

People who get good grades at university are clever

Agree _____Disagree

Women should not wear revealing clothing

Agree _____Disagree

Sexual behaviour should only commence once someone is married

Agree _____Disagree

ADHD is over-diagnosed

Agree _____Disagree

Older people are nice

Agree _____Disagree

Technology is important to young people

Agree _____Disagree

Life is riskier now than when my grandparents were young

Agree _____Disagree

Multinational companies are bad

Agree _____Disagree

Unemployed people need to get a job

Agree _____Disagree

People with a disability need special help with things

Agree _____Disagree

Monogamy (being faithful to one sexual partner) is not natural

Agree _____ Disagree

It is healthy to have hobbies

Agree _____ Disagree

Community is important to young people today

Agree _____ Disagree

Social workers are powerful

Agree _____ Disagree

Did you find you answered the questions in Exercise 5.1 quickly and were you surprised by any of your answers? Do you foresee that any of your values will get in the way of your development as a social worker? One person's personal values can clash with another's. Having completed this exercise, it is important to note that people's values are constantly changing. This means that your responses today may differ markedly from your responses to the same questions after you have completed your course and, again, in subsequent years. This is because our personal values are influenced by external factors which include, for example, those around us, our education, background and culture, and our life experiences. Your social work studies will likely change your values as well as the way you see the world around you.

Our values influence the ways in which we interact with our clients and those around us in everyday life. When we meet with clients, we must not only be aware of power and inequality, but also understand how our values can affect the service we provide (Shardlow 1995, p. 65). Values come together in practice in complex ways because:

> Social workers are not autonomous professionals whose guiding ethical principles are solely about respecting and promoting the self-determination of service users. They are employed by agencies, who work within the constraints of legal and procedural rules and must also work to promote the public good or the well-being of society in general. (Banks 2012, p. 31)

An example of how personal values come into our practice is when you believe something that a client has done is either 'wrong' or 'right'. This is not to be avoided; rather, acknowledging our personal values is an important process which should emerge during reflexive practice, and may be articulated in supervision, for example. Social work students often report that their values have changed throughout the course without them consciously trying to. It is fair to say that while it is important to 'notice' one's values, being open to new ways of thinking and being able to unravel values are perhaps most central to social work learning.

So far we have thought about values as they relate to ourselves, as influenced through our biography and broader socio-cultural context. In social work there are also professional values that we need to understand and integrate into our practice. In practice, our professional values can clash with one another. More specifically, this relates to what we call in social work an 'ethical dilemma'. As we shall see, an ethical dilemma occurs when there is a clash of ethical principles. Here Richard Hugman explains:

> [T]here are ... times when the professional ought to give conscious attention to the reasons why one choice seems better or worse than another, whether about the way in which something is done or about the objective that is being sought. In these circumstances the person is engaging with ethics. Ethics, in this sense, is the 'conscious reflection on our moral beliefs'. (Hinman 2003, p. 5 cited in Hugman 2005, p. 1)

In your everyday life you will have encountered ethical dilemmas. For example, imagine that you have first-hand evidence that your close friend's partner is cheating on them. As far as you are aware, they are in a monogamous relationship. Do you:

(a) Tell your friend.
(b) Say nothing.
(c) Tell the friend's partner that you know in the hope that they will 'come clean'.
(d) Tell another friend.
(e) ....

There are many options for how you might respond to that situation, and the choice you make will depend on what you think is important. For example, if you chose to tell your friend, you may have thought things such as:

- They have a right to know
- It's my responsibility as their friend to be honest
- Not being honest will hurt my friend
- Once they know all the facts then they can make the decision for themselves about how they respond
- It's the right thing to do

If you thought that saying nothing was the best option, then you may have felt this was justified for the following reasons:

- It's not my business as a relationship is private
- My friend may not believe me and I will lose them as a friend
- The information will hurt my friend
- It's not my responsibility to act since I wasn't the one who cheated
- It's the right thing to do

When we make decisions relating to ethical dilemmas we are weighing up the conflicting sides of the debate in question. Ethical decision-making requires us to understand the ethical principles underlying the situation and the responsibilities we have towards others.

In social work we encounter ethical dilemmas on a daily basis. Without the language and conceptual frameworks to make sense of these, we quickly lose our way.

In the following sections, we consider the ways in which social workers are expected to engage in their professional conduct with others through examining key ethical theoretical traditions. Yet ethics are not straightforward in social work, and merely learning about differing traditions is only half way to becoming an ethical practitioner. Your task in your practice as a social work student and throughout your career is to make your own decision in response to ethical dilemmas. Your decision must have its foundations in ethical scholarship and you must be able to clearly use these theoretical ideas to justify your chosen course of action. Examples of questions that emerge in social work practice include:

- What is the right thing to do?
- Should I go against my client's wishes?
- Should I obey the law?
- How should I respond to another worker whose practice is below acceptable standards?
- Should I breach my client's trust?

There are many disciplines interested in the pursuit of ethics. These include 'pure' disciplines such as philosophy and sociology (see, for example, Morris 2012) but also applied disciplines such as social work, medicine, nursing and other allied health professions. We now move on to consider the central traditions which are concerned with the question of ethical conduct.

UTILITARIANISM

There are many differing philosophers, such as Bentham and Mill, and subsequent philosophical traditions associated with utilitarianism. Broadly speaking, in utilitarianism the outcome of an action is considered in relation to its benefit, or utility, for the greatest number of people. Doing the 'greatest good for the greatest number' involves bringing about happiness and well-being for the majority of people. Dilemmas are therefore resolved through understanding that 'the right action is that which produces the greatest balance of good over evil' (Banks 2012, p. 50). Therefore the focus is upon the *outcome* of actions.

To give an example of the application of utilitarianism, consider the dilemma shown in Figure 5.1 on page 98.

Imagine the scenario. There are many people on a bridge which is about to fall down. There is one person standing under the bridge. Both the person under the bridge and the people on top of the bridge are in mortal danger. You can only send out a warning to either the person under the bridge or the people on the bridge. Do you warn:

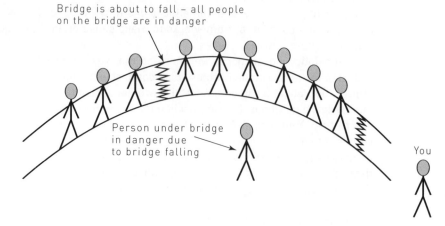

Who do you warn?

Bridge is about to fall – all people on the bridge are in danger

Person under bridge in danger due to bridge falling

You

FIGURE 5.1 The bridge dilemma: What would you do?

- The people on the bridge *or*
- The person under the bridge?

A utilitarian approach would consider the dilemma in relation to outcomes. The people on the bridge are at risk of death and injury due to the falling bridge and the person under the bridge is at risk of death and injury due to the bridge falling on top of them. Applying the notion of the 'greatest good for the greatest number' to the scenario would mean that the warning would go out to the people on the bridge because there are more of them than the one person under the bridge.

There are many ways in which utilitarianism is applicable to everyday social work practice. For example, how does an organisation decide on whether to provide social work services to one client or to groups of clients? Providing the outcomes were equally beneficial to both an individual and a group, a utilitarian response to this question would argue for 'the greatest good for the greatest number'. Since a social worker can see more clients in a group setting than individually, the decision to run more groups than individual sessions would be made using this perspective.

KANTIANISM

Unlike utilitarianism's focus on outcomes, a Kantian approach to an ethical dilemma highlights one's *duty* towards others. Immanuel Kant, a philosopher from the 18th century, argued that there are moral principles that apply to everyone. He 'thought that a system he called the "categorical imperative" could produce rules for any situation. In its simplest form the categorical imperative says that each of us should always act in such a way that our actions could become a rule for everyone without creating a contradiction' (Bowles *et al.* 2006, p. 57). 'Respect for persons' is central to Kantian philosophy (Banks 2012, p. 51).

Consider the example of the ethical dilemma posed in Figure 5.1. A Kantian perspective would argue that failing to warn *everyone*, both the people on the bridge and the person below it, fails to respect everyone and would set an unworkable rule for future relations between people. Without the understanding that people have a duty to warn others of dangers, trust would be diminished. Without trust, relationships between others become strained.

Here is another example of the Kantian categorical imperative in action. Imagine that a client asked their social worker if they were planning on working for the organisation in the longer term. Imagine that the social worker does not like working at the organisation and is actively applying for jobs so that they can leave. The social worker has a choice about how to respond. Should they lie or tell the truth? If they tell the truth to their client will this undermine the service? If they lie, from a Kantian perspective they would be setting an undesirable precedent. Note in particular the way that lying is examined through the Kantian perspective in which rationality is central:

> ... if you want to lie in a particular situation you should assume that if you lie then everyone else will start lying too. But if this happened, then lying itself would be impossible because lying depends on trust. If everyone lied then no one would ever believe what anyone said and lying would not work. Successful lying requires other people to keep telling the truth. It involves the liar treating themselves as an exception, which violates what Kant thought of as a fundamental obligation, to treat all people as morally equal, a principle that social workers adopt under the banner of equal dignity and worth. (Bowles *et al.* 2006, p. 57)

Thus if they were to use this perspective the social worker may decide to be tactful but ultimately truthful in the likelihood of them being at the organisation long-term.

VIRTUE-BASED ETHICS

Virtue-based approaches argue that acting ethically requires a virtuous self. Virtues include temperance, courage, justice and being truthful (Cohen & Cohen 1999). The philosopher Aristotle is associated with this perspective:

> As defined by Aristotle ... moral virtues are states of character concerned with rational control and direction of emotions. Moreover, such states of character are ... habits acquired from repeatedly performing virtuous actions. A person who has acquired a habit of confronting life situations without being deterred by undue or irrational fears possesses the virtue of courage; and a person who has acquired a habit of rationally indulging—neither overdoing nor underdoing—bodily desires such as for food or sex possesses the virtue of temperance. (Cohen & Cohen 1999, p. 19)

Whereas other approaches highlight consequences of actions and rules for the way we ought to behave, a virtue-based ethical standpoint requires the individual to *become* virtuous. Being virtuous is particularly appropriate to professional roles such as social work (Rhodes 1986), where congruence is central to the helping relationship (Rogers 1961) and reflexive development is ongoing. Thus, using this approach would mean that as a social work student, when you reflect upon your work with clients, you would also consider your virtuousness. Thus, you might ask questions such as: did I promote justice in that exchange with my client? Was I honest with all concerned in my recent exchange with my clients? Have I shown courage to stand up to inequalities and oppression? These questions are important to prompt reflexive thinking and subsequent action. They would help not only in relation to one's ever-evolving social work practice, also with one's development as a virtuous professional (Cohen & Cohen 1999). As we shall see, there are some similarities between virtue-based ethics and ethics of care.

ETHICS OF CARE

Ethics of care, also referred to as care ethics, 'links morality to the concrete situation ... [and] perceives morality in terms of concrete interpersonal relationships that can be understood only by people who have compassion and empathy for the predicaments of other people' (Cohen & Cohen 1999, p. 14).

Since, in general, ethics is concerned with decisions about situations where there is some ambiguity about what is best, theories of moral development have been drawn upon to understand this process. Crucially, previously accepted theories of moral development have been legitimately challenged through the work of Carol Gilligan (1982). Whereas historically moral development had become associated with rational decision-making, Gilligan argues that the 'male oriented system of morality ... does not take account of approaches to ethics which tend to be adopted by women' (Banks 2001, p. 47). Gilligan's (1982) work emphasises the complex interaction between the individual, the situation and the context as well as highlighting the importance of the nature of an individual's relationship with others. Ethical conduct from a care ethics perspective therefore requires asking 'What rights and responsibilities accompany the caring relationship?'

BIOETHICS

Bioethics outlines a clear set of ethical principles which underpin the helping relationship. These can be applied to professions working with people, including the medical profession and allied health professionals including social workers. Each of the principles should be embedded in professional practice as they are foundational to the ways we respond in our work with others. The following is derived from Beauchamp & Childress (1989), who argue there are four principles important to medical ethics (and applicable to social work) as well as certain qualities which must characterise the relationship between a professional and their client(s).

Principles

1. Nonmalificence: avoiding harming people
2. Beneficence: doing good
3. Self-determination: promoting and respecting others' autonomy
4. Justice: those in need are provided for fairly, professionals understand power relations and act accordingly

Qualities for the professional's relationship with their client(s)

1. Veracity: being honest, telling the truth
2. Confidentiality and privacy: respecting clients' right to privacy, and to not disclose their information and biographies to others
3. Fidelity: being faithful to professional promises

Bioethical approaches are practical and clearly applicable to the helping relationship, yet this is also a source of criticism, as we shall see in our consideration of human rights approaches.

HUMAN RIGHTS APPROACH

In contemporary life a human rights discourse has become synonymous with concerns which broadly relate to people's rights and freedoms (Ife 2008, p. 4). The Universal Declaration of Human Rights was formally recognised by the United Nations Assembly in 1948. This declaration outlines the rights of citizens in relation to their governments, and came about because of the government-sanctioned abuses which took place during the Second World War. Since this time, the declaration has been applied to many international contexts. Although the ethical stance inherent to the declaration is focused on the rights of peoples as *citizens*, often people will refer to human rights as being relevant to a range of contexts including institutional and interpersonal interactions. As we shall see, there is a strong case that a human rights approach can inform both social work ethics as well as practice, theory and education (Ife 2008, p. 160).

Ife argues that a human rights approach in social work involves understanding that people ought to be treated with respect and dignity *as a fellow individual*. So often in social work clients' issues are externalised: the term 'service user', for example, identifies people who are clients as somehow different from social workers, as though social workers do not use services themselves! What makes social workers any different from others in our societies? Further, a human rights perspective rejects the notion that oppression and inequality due to differences in race, class and gender is best addressed in social work through specifically defined types of intervention. Social justice is still vital to social work (Ife 2001, p. 4) but awareness of and action to address oppression and inequality should be embedded in every approach to each individual, couple, family, community, group and society. Underpinning all interactions in social work with others ought to be recognition of a *shared humanity*:

A human rights discourse ... is concerned with ideas of what it means to be human—what is the nature of our shared humanity that transcends culture, race, gender, age, class... From this perspective, moral principles for a social work based on human rights might be expressed simply this way:
- Act so as to always affirm and realise the human rights of all people.
- Do nothing to restrict, deny or violate the human rights of anyone. (Ife, 2001, p. 129)

The use of universal rights, which apply to everyone, is an 'alternative framing' of the individualised ethical frameworks usually applied in social work (Ife 2001, p. 121). When ethical dilemmas emerge in social work practice, a human rights approach enables the clients to be actively engaged in resolving the issues at stake. This is a radical departure from other ethical theoretical models in which the social worker has the power to resolve the dilemma (Ife 2001, p. 122) through their own action or inaction.

CODES OF PRACTICE, CODES OF ETHICS AND OTHER INSTITUTIONALISED ETHICAL RULES

Codes of ethics outline ethical conduct for professionals. Internationally, there are various codes of conduct/codes of ethics and other documents in social work which outline the core values for the profession and give some clarity about the ways in which professional conduct is expected to take place. Social workers must abide by their code of ethics and may face serious consequences if these are breached, from receiving formal warnings to being 'struck off' and prevented from practising again. Professional associations of social workers have committees who investigate and take action regarding breaches of ethics or professional conduct. Codes of ethics and ethics audits can be used in organisational settings to manage ethical concerns using a 'risk management' framework (Reamer 2001).

Some codes also offer general advice about what to do in the event of an ethical dilemma. In social work codes of ethics have a long history and have served as 'a public declaration of one's commitment and obligation to its rule over one's conduct' (Siporin 1972, p. 91).

Yet codes of ethics can also be criticised because they may be seen to detract from an individual's responsibility or obligation towards others, to reinforce professionals as powerful since the code 'belongs' to them, and to diminish the importance that everyday interactions have on the society as a whole (Bauman 1993; Ife 2001). Yet despite these criticisms, codes of ethics can be important in social work. As Ife argues, 'it is the morality of social work and social workers' actions that is at issue; ethical codes are merely a yardstick by which that morality can be measured and evaluated' (Ife 2001, p. 110).

It is vital to view codes of ethics through a critical lens. Take a look at your code of ethics, which you will be able to access through your professional association. Note what words or terms will be more important or less important in future years. Note also that ethical frameworks differ from legislative frameworks: at times in history social workers have played a role in implementing policies which are now viewed as abhorrent. For example, the systematic removal of Indigenous children from their families in Australia on the basis that white culture was preferable to Indigenous Australian culture created what is referred to as the 'stolen generations'. Although perfectly legal, there is no justification for such action using the application of various ethical theoretical standpoints. It is important to analyse the ethical dimension to your own social work practice in contemporary times, as we shall see in the next section.

Finally, rapidly increasing technological advances changing the ways everyday life is lived (Lash 2001) mean social work will take differing forms in the future. Virtual services, online counselling and support, and shifts in the ways we assess individuals' identities will need to be accommodated (Dunk-West 2011): all of these affect the ways we imagine and articulate the ethics of the work. The important issue relating to ethics and social work is to understand, articulate and justify your actions using an ethical theory base.

ETHICAL DILEMMAS IN SOCIAL WORK: WHAT TO DO?

In social work, whether as a student or as a qualified worker, there are daily dilemmas which one must contend with and bring to resolution. Ethical dilemmas involve making 'a choice between two equally unwelcome alternatives' (Banks 2001, p. 163). Students often report that being 'inside' an ethical dilemma feels confusing and although they may know what they want to do, they are unclear what the ethical justification is for their course of action. It can feel so jumbled that, represented visually, it looks like Figure 5.2.

There are frameworks which can help social workers and social work students resolve ethical dilemmas (Reamer 1990). Common approaches entail 'breaking down' the problem or dilemma into differing compartmentalised areas. The process of gaining clarity about an ethical dilemma is represented in Figure 5.3 on page 104.

Although at first the dilemma can be seen as messy and without shape or form, in breaking it up into the key areas which are relevant to ethical decision-making it is easier to understand the key ethical principles which are in conflict. For example, consider the friend whose partner is cheating on them. Moving through the process of gaining clarity we can ask, and answer, the following questions. This is one suggested course of action:

Who is involved? What do they want to happen? Myself, my friend and her partner. To a lesser extent, the person who the partner was with. My friend's partner does not want me to say anything. I can only guess what my friend wants, but I would assume that she would want to know.

FIGURE 5.2 Ethical dilemmas can be messy, complex and confusing

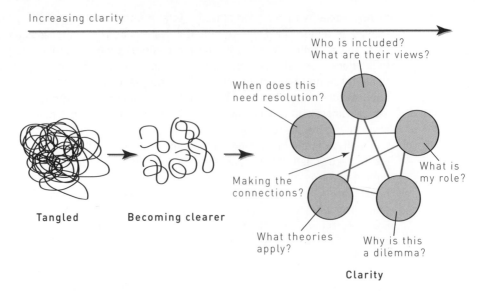

Increasing clarity

Who is included?
What are their views?

When does this
need resolution?

What is
my role?

Making the
connections?

Tangled   Becoming clearer

What theories
apply?

Why is this
a dilemma?

Clarity

FIGURE 5.3 Asking pertinent questions can help to unravel an ethical dilemma

What is my role?   Friend.

Why is this a dilemma?   If I tell my friend, it may cause her upset/harm. It may also mean the end of the relationship. If I don't tell my friend, then I will feel that I am not being honest or truthful with her. Is it doing good to cause harm? Is it worth causing harm for the sake of veracity (telling the truth)?

When does this need resolution?   As soon as possible.

What theories apply?   Any theoretical perspective could apply but I will choose care ethics to make sense of this dilemma because I feel that the relationship between myself and my friend is important. We have been friends since we were children and we have been through so much together. We have a mutual obligation towards one another to be honest and I feel very confident that my friend would want me to tell them.

The resolution/decision: To tell my friend. The harm caused by telling my friend is outweighed by my obligation as their friend to be honest and tell the truth.

ORGANISATIONAL ETHICAL ISSUES

In this chapter so far we have explored ethics in relation to the ways we choose to live as well as the ways we behave and respond to our clients in social work. In this section, we consider some of the key ethical issues which emerge out of working in an organisational context. Although ethical theory is more usually focused on clients in social work, complaints about ethical conduct are also often made by professionals about their colleagues' conduct (Loewenberg *et al.* 2000, p. 174).

As noted in our discussion of ethical theories, the manner in which power is exercised ought to be an enduring concern in social work practice. It is important to understand the ethical implications of the organisational context in which social work is practised.

In some countries such as England, for example, government employers of social workers arrange services based on client groups. Children and families statutory social work (services that are provided because of legislation and state funding), for example, caters for the care needs of children and their families. This organisation has a legislative mandate to use specific legal Acts to remove children from their families and place them into the care of others (including foster care, relative care, approved carers, residential care and adoptive families): social workers play a central role in this statutory action. Having a legal mandate, social workers removing children from their homes also need to have a clear *ethical* justification for their actions. Consider the following situation:

CASE STUDY

Mary and Veronica are aged 5 and 7 respectively. Their parents, Anika and Roberto, are heroin users and currently unemployed. Anika and Roberto have successfully managed to coordinate the care of their children, despite the challenges brought about by the recession which meant they lost their jobs. Recently there have been some highly concerning developments regarding the well-being of the children. With the recent scrutiny of welfare payments, Anika and Roberto have had their benefits cut as they were unable to provide enough evidence of their job search efforts. This has meant that Anika and Roberto have resorted to leaving the children home alone at night while they engage in criminal activity such as theft. When recently charged by police for burglary offences, it emerged that the children had been left all night alone. The parents do not wish to work with social workers.

Do you think the situation requires removal of the children from their home? Without adequate additional information such as the perspectives of the children, how the parents view the situation and an analysis of the issues at stake, it may be difficult to justify a particular type of intervention. What is clear, however, is that it is unsafe to leave a seven- and a five-year-old by themselves in the house overnight. The ethical dimension of social work intervention in this situation involves the following: the children's safety and well-being versus the autonomy of the family and parents. Promoting the autonomy of the parents places the children at risk of harm and promoting the safety and well-being of the children reduces the autonomy of the parents. Social workers in statutory roles such as this one make *paternalistic* decisions. Such decisions involve overriding another person's autonomy—the parents in this case—in order to prevent harm occurring to others—in this case, the children.

The scenario above has been created for the purposes of this book but illustrates some key themes relating to child protection and children and families work.

Working in this field can include encountering any or all of the following: poverty, oppression and disadvantage, substance misuse, violence including domestic violence, physical, sexual and emotional abuse and exploitation of children. Student social workers can often be reluctant to engage in this kind of work because it may not feel 'right' to remove children from their homes, for example, or they may believe that social work should only be involved with people who voluntarily engage in the services. The reality is that in working in children and families organisations, a great deal of other work aside from the removal of children takes place, such as preventing family breakdown, promoting and encouraging parenting, and direct work with children, young people and their parents and carers. Another ethical issue which can arise when working in this field is the sometimes limited way in which social workers and social work students feel they can undertake structural social work. Lobbying government as a government employee can be frowned upon by the organisation, which can provoke an ethical problem. Similarly, in adults work in England personalisation policies have assumed too much autonomy in some people who may require more assistance than is provided, and social workers may not wish to work in such ways. All of these concerns relate to what is referred to as the 'care or control' aspects of social work. Do we care for our clients or do we control them? Can we do both? What happens when our values conflict with those of our organisation? These are questions which social workers and social work students on placement must think through and come to some sort of resolution regarding.

The other major cause of ethical problems in organisational settings relates to workers who are either impaired or engaging in unethical practice.

THE IMPAIRED WORKER

In ethics literature 'the impaired social worker' (Reamer 1992) relates to social workers who are unable to carry out their normal responsibilities due to an identifiable reason:

> Impairment is '...interference in professional functioning that is reflected in one or more of the following ways: (a) an inability and/or unwillingness to acquire and integrate professional standards into one's repertoire of professional behaviour; (b) an inability to acquire professional skills in order to reach an acceptable level of competency; (c) an inability to control professional stress, psychological dysfunction, and/or excessive emotional reactions that interfere with professional functioning'. (Lamb *et al.* 1987, p. 598 cited in Reamer 1992, p. 166)

When working in an organisational context, it is important to recognise the potential for harm towards clients which can occur through worker impairment. Focusing on the needs of clients can help to disentangle competing obligations towards clients and colleagues, as we have seen earlier in the chapter. Yet speaking out against one's colleague or 'whistleblowing' brings with it various ethical and professional issues and much can be at stake. It is also important to recognise that working with particular client groups or contexts can provoke differing coping mechanisms for social workers. Recognising when one's own behaviours have the potential to cause unintended harm to clients is central to ethical practice. Literature which discusses issues of 'burnout' or vicarious traumatisation can be helpful in embedding policies into the organisation which assist in reducing the effects of difficult or emotive work on workers (Women's Health Statewide: www.whs.sa.gov.au/pub/draft_VT_polic_1.pdf).

DUAL ROLE RELATIONSHIPS

Dual role relationships refer to the assuming of another role with clients in addition to the helper role:

> When a professional assumes at least one additional professional or personal role with respect to the same client, the relationship thus formed is termed a dual-role or multiple role relationship. (Cohen & Cohen 1999, p. 137)

Why are dual role relationships problematic in social work? The existence of roles subsequent to the helping role can prevent the worker from carrying out their duties in a professional manner. Further, social workers are in positions of power and should not abuse the trust of their clients. Here are some of the clearest examples of dual role relationships:

- Entering into sexual relationships with clients
- Entering into friendships with clients
- Personally accepting large gifts or money from clients
- Engaging in business relationships with clients
- Providing social work services to friends and family

There are some areas which are less clear however. For example, imagine you have been working with a man who has recently been diagnosed with a life threatening illness. Your role has entailed assessing his needs and providing him with information about relevant services for him and his family. At your final meeting, he brings in a handmade card and a pot plant for your office. Whether you accept this gift depends on the meaning and context of the gift being given. Organisations sometimes have a formal record of all gifts given as well as the context in which they are given, so that a transparent account is made regarding the circumstances surrounding the gift. Similarly, social work students often give a token gift to their placement supervisors or assessors to mark the end of their placement. Giving the gift after the final report is written separates the two processes—assessment and endings—which means ethical conflicts are lessened. What is important in these situations is that the application of ethical ideas is clearly stated to explain or justify a particular decision or set of decisions.

WORKING WITH OTHERS

The ethical perspectives discussed in this chapter demonstrate the breadth of this area of intellectual and professional debate and scholarship. The definition of social work from the International Federation of Social Workers, which we explored in Chapter 1 of this book, outlined the ethical dimension to our profession: 'social work addresses the barriers, inequities and injustices that exist in society. It responds to crises and emergencies as well as to everyday personal and social problems'. The consideration of 'barriers, inequities and injustices' is central to the concept of social justice. Social justice holds particular currency in our profession, and is a common theme in social work codes of ethics from many countries.

We have discussed the bioethical approach advanced by Beauchamp & Childress (1989). We shall now consider this again in the context of working with other professionals. In particular, read through the principles and qualities with the following questions in mind:

- Do these 'fit' for GPs?
- Do these apply to social work in all areas of practice?
- Can you imagine these would be useful for allied health professions such as physiotherapists, occupational therapists, dieticians and speech therapists?

Principles (Beauchamp & Childress 1989)

1. Nonmalificence: avoiding harming people
2. Beneficence: doing good
3. Self-determination: promoting and respecting others' autonomy
4. Justice: those in need are provided for fairly, professionals understand power relations and act accordingly

Qualities for the professional's relationship with their client(s) (Beauchamp & Childress 1989)

1. Veracity: being honest, telling the truth
2. Confidentiality and privacy: respecting clients' right to privacy, and to not disclose their information and biographies to others
3. Fidelity: being faithful to professional promises

Because of the generalised and applied nature of bioethics, the principles can be applied to a number of professions. What we have seen throughout this chapter is that the large scope of ethical approaches offers the potential to assist the social work student and practitioner to come to a decision or act in a particular way. Being able to take a particular perspective and think 'how would this perspective view the problem or situation?' is useful in coming to a resolution or offering a framework for analysing one's practice. Yet how does this relate to new collaborations in social work which might be different to the historical alignment with health?

[handwritten margin note: result occurs because of joint professional work]

Bronstein argues that 'interdisciplinary collaboration is an effective interpersonal process that facilitates the achievement of goals that cannot be reached when individual professionals act on their own (Bruner 1991)' (Bronstein 2003, p. 299). If we think about the interdisciplinary context within which social work is situated, using Bronstein's definition of such work means there are new ethical goals to be reached in social work. For example, some of the environmental issues which have surfaced in recent years, such as climate change, have impacts on social life (Lever-Tracy 2010). As the ways in which people live their day-to-day lives change because of these shifts, ethical issues related to 'climate justice' (Star 2008) will emerge. Interdisciplinary work in this area might therefore see social workers alongside environmental scientists, sociologists, biologists, urban planners and geographers, to name but a few. Each of these groups brings with them their theoretical orientations as well as their ethical perspectives. It is therefore plausible that social workers may be increasingly thinking about the following:

- What are the ethical considerations which relate to housing for people who have experienced extreme weather events?
- In the future, what kinds of social work services will people be entitled to?
- What is social work's ethical obligation to the environment?
- How can social work be sustainable?

There are many more questions which relate to this area and additional ones that will only become evident as we know more about our changing world and subsequent needs. Recent research identifies the need for social work to rise to meet the challenges being brought about by 'climate change ... [which is] widely recognised as one of the greatest threats facing society' (Evans *et al.* 2012, p. 746). The authors also note that 'the risks that climate change poses for the most vulnerable people in society in particular' have been addressed in government policy in England but ought to be central to social work more generally (Evans *et al.* 2012, p. 746).

CHAPTER SUMMARY

This chapter has explored personal and professional values and ethics. We have looked at some scenarios in which ethical dilemmas may surface. These include through direct social work practice with our clients as well as within the organisational setting. We have examined some of the key ethical theoretical perspectives in order to better understand the ways in which our actions can be applied to ethical theory and ethical theory can be applied to our actions. Ethics are central to any kind of social work practice, regardless of the setting. As social workers and social work students, we must always be able to articulate the ethical justification for our work with others. It is only through relationships with the people we work with and an ethical foundation for our practice that we can be accountable and help to promote individual and social change. This chapter has set out some of the key ideas which require consideration and adaptation to one's own practice and worldview.

FURTHER READING

BANKS, S. (2012) *Ethics and Values in Social Work*, 4th edn. Basingstoke: Palgrave Macmillan.

BEAUCHAMP, T. L. & CHILDRESS, J. F. (1989) *Principles of Biomedical Ethics*. New York: Oxford University Press.

COHEN, E. D. & COHEN, G. S. (1999) *The Virtuous Therapist: Ethical Practice of Counselling and Psychotherapy*. Belmont: Wadsworth Publishing Company.

HUGMAN, R. & SMITH, D. (eds) (2005) *Ethical Issues in Social Work*. Abingdon: Routledge.

IFE, J. (2008) *Human Rights and Social Work: Towards Rights-based Practice*, 2nd edn. Cambridge, UK: Cambridge University Press.

REAMER, F. (2006) *Social Work Values and Ethics*. New York: Columbia University Press.

6

Practice Learning in Organisational Settings

This chapter:

- Examines how practice learning fits with social work education

- Explores the ways the social work role is situated in its organisational setting

- Outlines suggestions about how to start on placement

- Highlights how social work skills, such as those used in assessing, are central to advancing practice learning

- Looks at the role supervision plays in developing the social work self on placement

Conversation, writing, talking, communicating and engaging with others: all of these skills that we use in our everyday life are the 'nuts and bolts' of activities in placement settings. Yet often these everyday actions become infused with meaning and cause trepidation when students are on their social work placement. This chapter outlines the knowledge and skills required for successful learning experiences in practice settings. It starts by exploring the spontaneous and complex world of social work practice through the lens of learning. Exploring learning in the practice context requires understanding the position of social work in its organisational context. Assessment in the context of client work across organisational specialisms is then examined. Reflexivity is discussed in relation to student learning. The chapter concludes with a discussion of supervision.

LEARNING AND PLACEMENTS

As noted in Chapter 1 in our discussion of identity, participation in social relationships and the external social environment are crucial to the ways in which we experience ourselves and develop our self (Mead 1934). The central idea in this book—which follows from this—is that through social interaction the professional self is constituted. In Chapter 1, Mead's foundational idea of the self as theorised through an interactionist tradition was explored. We have returned to this theme throughout our consideration of the key academic subjects social work students encounter during their studies. In this chapter the importance of relationships formed through professional practice is highlighted, and seen as foundational to successful practice learning experiences.

Often the social work placement is viewed differently than 'academic' subjects or modules. While there is a crucial difference between theory-rich topics and the experiential aspect to placement education, the interactionist notion of the production of the professional self is equally applicable to both types of knowledge acquisition. Placement is enormously important in the development of the professional self. In fact the movement of social work students into practice learning settings is the ultimate way in which the professional self is constituted.

In this sense, there is a difference between being in the 'field' and being in a controlled university environment. The physical relocation of students into the organisational setting exposes students to new and varied learning experiences which arise from interaction with clients, staff, volunteers, other professionals and fellow students. Learning how to combine the knowledge gained through immersion and reaction in the spontaneous, dynamic setting of the placement with the knowledge attained through engagement in academic modules is the task of the social work student.

Based upon previous experiences within educational settings you may be aware of the ways in which you like to learn. For example, some people prefer to learn through others' experiences, while for another person reading is a more effective way to gain knowledge. Here are just some examples of various types of learning activities which are relevant to 'academic' knowledge:

- Reading books, journal articles, non-fiction, online content and other text
- Hearing others' stories
- Audio listening to lectures
- Listening to lectures, watching lecturers and writing notes
- Revisiting lecture material online after physically attending a lecture
- Talking to other students about theories
- Engaging in conversation through facilitated classes such as seminars, work-shops and tutorials
- Watching a documentary, film or other visual clip
- Writing notes about a particular topic after reading a book, attending a lecture or engaging in a learning activity
- Applying a theory to a practical situation through being presented with a problem (for example, a case study with questions about how you would act)
- Observing or listening to a debate or expert panel discussion

It is worth reflecting upon how you like to learn in these contexts. Your course is structured around providing various types of the above activities, as educators recognise that people learn in differing ways. Now think about a practical activity that you have learned that is connected with transport. This could involve thinking about how you learned to drive a car, roller skate, ride a scooter, ride a bike and so on. Reflect upon the following questions: Did you...

- Observe the mode of transport being used by others before attempting to try it yourself?
- Study the mode of transport, looking at the wheels and body, and understanding how it was powered before beginning to control the apparatus?
- Experiment through trying different techniques, making mistakes and learning along the way?
- Ask someone else to instruct you to help you learn through their instruction and feedback?

Unlike academic forms of learning, the knowledge required to operate a type of transport requires skills. The two types of learning differ: in the transport example, the practicality and physicality of the learning activity is evident. Moving away from the classroom into a new environment as a student social worker requires a level of reflexive knowledge, and it is helpful if students are aware of their preferred conditions of learning as well as the way they like to learn. Some students, for example, like to read about an organisation and understand the client and community needs, the organisational philosophy and mandate and get to know the staff before they begin to work with clients. Other students feel better experimenting from the beginning, for example, engaging with client work very early on and reflecting on this work together with the organisational setting as they go along.

There is no 'right or wrong' way to learn, but it is important to recognise that 'all students, irrespective of their experiences or cultural backgrounds, come to their first field placement with some trepidation, anxiety and excitement about this new learning challenge' (Cooper & Briggs 2000, p. 4). Practice teachers or supervisors therefore have a central role to play in facilitating a positive learning experience (we explore this later in the chapter). First, let's consider the organisational setting within which placements take place.

SOCIAL WORK AND THE ORGANISATIONAL SETTING

Amongst the professions, social work is uniquely suited to enormously varied contexts which can range from health settings to community development to policy, research and direct practice with either voluntary or involuntary clients. Internationally, social work's identity varies in that social work may have more of a presence in particular fields of practice. For example, in Australia, New Zealand and the USA it is common for social workers to have a clinical or therapeutic focus. Social policies, professional associations and social shifts all impact on employment opportunities for social workers as well as how social work is situated in broader culture. Social work students are often aware of how social workers are portrayed in the media—this is particularly the case for workers in, say, child protection. It is often only when students begin their course that they become aware of the vast opportunities for social work in traditional settings (such as in child protection, aged care, working with people with disabilities and so on) as well as in newer settings such as schools, doctors' surgeries and health practice settings. Social workers can also work in community settings such as in community development, population-based interventions and international settings. Table 1.1, on page 14, listed just some of the areas social workers are employed in throughout the world. Take some time to look through this table and note a few which you think would be of interest to you. Note areas in which you know you would *not* like to work. Finally, note which fields of practice you are open to learning more about.

Although there is a great deal of diversity in terms what social workers do in their organisational settings, all social work students on placement need to orient themselves to their particular settings. This is where Table 1.1 can be helpful. Choosing a 'box' in which to put the organisation can help at the beginning to compartmentalise the work.

Thinking about the organisational context helps to demarcate the work of the setting from other types of social work services. It can be helpful to begin to understand the organisational context through varying resources. Staff descriptions of the work undertaken can help social work students to orient themselves to the organisation. Similarly, policy documents and other written material can also assist in understanding the scope of the service. Usually when students are on placement, at the beginning it can feel as though there is too much information. Given time, however, students develop a sophisticated understanding of the organisational setting including the culture and history of the service. The following are suggestions about how to begin as a social work student on placement:

1. Develop a positive working relationship with your supervisor *as well as* with other colleagues. Other colleagues can help you gain a varied perspective on

the work and represent diverse practice experiences which can help broaden your knowledge and strengthen your developing practice.

2. Read policy, funding and other documents and study organisational charts. Attend organisational meetings. These activities will help you understand the scope of the work and the broader organisational culture.

3. Become both 'inward' facing as well as 'outward' facing. Engage in thinking or conversations to try to understand the organisation from clients' perspectives. Visit other organisations in the region to get a picture of the community needs the organisation fulfils. Ask: what are the tensions between the needs of clients and the provision of services? What is the role of social work? How do these contribute to the work I will undertake?

4. Connect with other students on placement. Compare your experiences. It is vital to continue to engage with your university through seminars, tutorials, visits from the university and other activities. Your informal networks with other students are equally crucial in helping to support your learning.

5. Record your learning (Cleak & Wilson 2004, p. 27). Through documenting your knowledge acquisition you can create a clear picture of the development of your professional self. Include pictures, clippings from articles, notes to yourself, drawings and other media.

6. With the support and knowledge of your supervisor, take risks. Try using a different theory, for example, and get feedback from clients about how they experienced your work with them. Push yourself to try new things and fully develop your social work self.

THE PROFESSIONAL SELF

As we have noted, there are 'boundaries' in the ways social workers relate to people and these are marked out depending on the nature of one's relationship. A social worker's *purpose* (Compton & Galaway 1999) informs *how* they relate to others in a professional setting. The ways we relate to others differ, depending on the context and nature of our relationships. As discussed in Chapter 3 when we examined communication skills, Garfinkel's research (Garfinkel 1984) found that we rely on unspoken 'rules' which dictate the way we conduct ourselves with others. In particular, Garfinkel argues that the *way* we interact depends on *with whom* the interaction takes place.

It is the task of the student social worker to develop newer ways of relating to others in the professional context of the placement. The 'discovery of "self"' through interaction with others on placement is often recorded in student journals as being a major achievement in their learning (Lam *et al.* 2007).

At first, interactions of the student social worker in their professional role can feel awkward. For example, students can think: is it okay to laugh with clients? Is it unprofessional to disclose personal information to my supervisor? Students on placement develop the professional self through engagement with their own learning in terms of theory and practice, supervision with their practice teacher and reflection about their emerging professional self. This can be depicted as a gradual coming together of the 'personal' along with the 'professional' self (Figure 6.1).

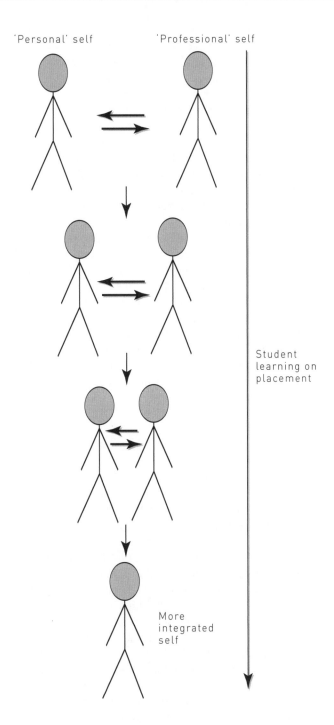

FIGURE 6.1 Making the connections between the everyday self and the professional self helps the professional to emerge

Developing the professional self in social work education includes learning through university-based topics as well as through placement experiences. During this process students gradually 'grow' their professional selves. Figure 6.1 illustrates the ways the existing self interacts with the professional self until a kind of integration occurs. This is because our actions, behaviours and communication change from a professional context to a personal context, as we examined in Chapter 3. As a refresher to the differing manifestations of self in varying contexts, imagine that a woman in her mid 30s says 'Yusef has left me'. How you respond to this depends on the relationship you have with the speaker. As her social worker, your response will be guided by your ethical and theoretical frameworks and the purpose of your role. You might say, for example, 'Are you okay?' or 'Do you want to tell me about that?' or even 'That must be awful!'. Your responses will depend on a number of factors, including your history with the client(s) and the purpose of your role and organisational setting which will define the scope of your work. Now imagine that your friend tells you 'Yusef has left me'. Like your professional response, your answer to your friend's disclosure will depend on the circumstances, but the difference will be that you can probably give advice, give her your opinion and communicate in a far less formal or structured way. Although there are similarities in the ways we respond to clients and to friends, there are marked differences because of the professional nature of social work. The professional self is therefore developed through interaction: placement is crucial to testing out and developing this self. The ways in which people make sense of this process are as unique as our selves, and reflection helps us notice and engage with the process.

ASSESSMENT

Despite the differing organisational contexts in which social work takes place internationally and nationally, the process and function of assessment is universally important to social work practice. Put simply, an assessment identifies need. Once need is identified, services and professional intervention can be matched (Taylor 2011, p. 2). Whether this process is undertaken formally through particular formats such as assessment proformas or informally through conversation with clients and groups, skills in assessment are vital to social work generally (Milner & O'Byrne 2002). Assessment skills are learned during placement. The process of assessment offers practitioners opportunities for identifying and responding immediately to need which can 'go beyond' traditional assessment (Mantle et al. 2008, p. 440). Although the issue of how social workers capture their identity is somewhat problematic (Dunk-West 2011), the process whereby social work students begin to understand the needs of their clients, groups and/or communities remains important to their developing skills and knowledge.

Exercise 6.1 is provided to help you develop your assessment skills with individuals, families, groups and communities. These 'levels' of assessment help to frame broader issues within the communities you may be working with in your placement setting and relate to the structural social work we discussed in Chapter 4.

EXERCISE 6.1

Case study: Jennifer Scanlon

Jennifer reminds you that she's 'fifteen and a half' and perfectly able to negotiate sexual activity with her boyfriend Daniel (who is 16 years old). You are a social worker in the Adolescent Team in a non-government organisation (NGO). Yesterday you were given referral details about Jennifer, a young woman who attends the local high school who had disclosed to a teacher that she was 'slapped across the face' by her mother. Social services are carrying out a mandated assessment. Your role is to work with Jennifer to support her and you are in close contact with the social worker from social services with Jennifer's consent. Jennifer tells you in an interview today that her mother hit her two nights ago due to finding out about Daniel and Jennifer's sexual relationship. Jennifer tells you that in her culture, bringing shame on the family is taken very seriously and if her father finds out she'll 'be dead'. Jennifer also says that her parents are 'behind the times' and, as they left India when Jennifer was a baby, she 'feels more British than Asian'.

Developing your assessment skills

1. What is your assessment of Jennifer? In one sentence, what is/are her need(s)? How might your role assist in meeting this/these need(s)?
2. What is your assessment of the family? In one sentence, what is/are the family's need(s)? How might your role assist in meeting this/these need(s)?
3. What is your assessment of the community? Imagine Jennifer's scenario was similar to others presenting at your placement setting. What would be the needs of the community? How might your role assist in meeting this/these need(s)?

Finally, reflect on the role of assessment in your organisational setting. Is assessment the means through which services are allocated? Who assesses and where does the information go? Identify your learning needs in relation to assessment and make a plan for addressing these needs during the course of your placement and beyond. Being able to understand the links between clients' needs, your own role and the organisational setting and broader community is central to sociological social work (Dunk-West & Verity, forthcoming) and structural social work as discussed in Chapter 4.

Although people's responses to the needs in the scenario in Exercise 6.1 will vary slightly, generally speaking there are some 'themes' which are present in Jennifer's situation. These are:

- Safety and family
- Relationships and cultural expectations
- Sexuality and 'shame'
- Cultures and organisations (school, social services and the NGO)
- Family relationships and differing expectations

This case study has enabled some thinking in relation to Jennifer's circumstances. It should be noted that in placement, the communication skills we discussed in Chapter 3 are required in order to successfully engage with clients for the purpose of assessment. We now move on to examine student learning on placement and how this is facilitated through reflexive engagement.

WHAT ABOUT REFLEXIVITY ON PLACEMENT?

Being reflective involves recalling prior events or sensations. Reflexivity is the active decision to act differently as a result of the analysis of the reflection. As we have discussed in Chapters 1 and 3, reflexivity is of interest to the social sciences (see Lash 2003) and there is some evidence that we are, in western cultures, becoming increasingly reflexive in our everyday lives (Beck & Beck-Gernsheim 2002) and relationships (Giddens 1992). In social work, reflexivity and reflective practice are well conceptualised and historically embedded within our profession (see, for example, Hamilton 1954). In placement settings, engaging in reflexive activities helps to conceptualise the learning and bring theories encountered within the university setting 'alive' in the spontaneous setting of the social work organisation.

Being reflexive in relation to placement experiences involves engaging in recalling one's practice and analysing the practice with a view to *changing future activity* based upon the analysis. One helpful model suggests that this process entails: **retrieval** (the social work student remembers the interaction, aided by activities such as a process recording or written summary) ➜ **reflection** (thinking the issue through, aided by supervisor) ➜ **linkage** (the student articulates the theories informing action and interaction) ➜ **professional response** (anticipating future events through activities such as role plays and future client engagement) (Bogo & Vayda 1987, p. 71).

The spontaneous and sustained immersion in the placement experience (Kolb 1984) makes it possible for reflection-in-action to take place, yet tools must be utilised to make the connection between theory and practice (Argyris & Schon 1974). Many tools will be found in students' academic requirements for placement learning such as the activities contained within their portfolio or workbook. Exercise 6.2 is designed to reflexively engage with organisational and practice contexts alongside students' understandings of power (Fook 1999), inequality and the role of social work.

EXERCISE 6.2

For this activity, study the items shown opposite, which include a feather, a closed door, a rock, a winding road, a ring, a handshake and so on. Think about what these mean *to you*. Now look at each of the diagrams representing the client, the organisation, you and broader society. Select three of the items and draw these in the empty spaces labelled 1, 2 and 3. You can use an object for more than one person or organisation. For example, you might select a feather for both the client and broader

The client

You
the social work student

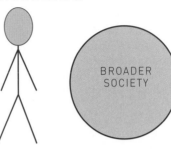

THE ORGANISATION

BROADER SOCIETY

1. _____   1. _____   1. _____   1. _____

2. _____   2. _____   2. _____   2. _____

3. _____   3. _____   3. _____   3. _____

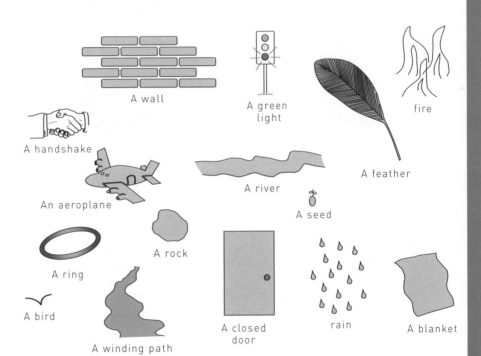

A wall

A green light

A feather

fire

A handshake

An aeroplane

A river

A seed

A ring

A rock

A closed door

rain

A blanket

A bird

A winding path

society. Think carefully about your choice of object/item. The purpose of choosing a particular object is that it sums up your view about a particular issue. For example, if you chose a ring, a rock and a handshake as metaphors for the organisation you may explain this by saying that the ring represents fidelity or relationships and these are central to the organisation. The rock represents a solid history as the organisation has been in operation for over 30 years. It may also have been chosen because it is 'solid' and in your view, the organisation could do more to be receptive to change. The handshake may represent a move towards including clients and external organisations in the everyday running of the service. This is just one explanation for a choice of objects: your own choices are only limited to your imagination and your perceptions.

Once you have selected objects for each of the pictures, have a look at each of these. Reflect upon your meanings for the objects and the overall depiction of each given the three objects. Do you notice any patterns? Are you, for example, optimistic and generally positive about the organisation and broader society and negative or pessimistic about yourself as a social work student and the client? Or are you positive about the client and negative about the organisation? Think about power and inequality. Where are the tensions and symbioses? Are there some who have more 'powerful' objects and others are less powerful? What does this say about the distribution of power and manifestation of inequality? Take the time to really think these issues through: this activity can be a tool for supervision or discussion with your fellow students. Comparing your responses with others and discussing reasons for these can produce additional insights and reflection.

Finally, given your analysis of the client, the organisation, yourself as a social work student and broader society, what can you do to impact positively on each of these? If you have identified structural oppression with affects the ways in which your clients experience your service, what can you do to counteract this? Write three suggestions about ways *that you can change your practice* by being more aware of power, inequality and the social work role.

Engagement in this exercise and your changed views, insights, perceptions and behaviours as a result of it: this is social work reflexivity in action.

SUPERVISION

It can be particularly challenging for social work students to be on placement within an organisation where there is no social worker. Having supervision through an external supervisor who is a social worker helps to frame activity within a social work knowledge-base. Whilst some students can feel that being in a non-traditional setting is counter to their learning, the benefits of such a placement are varied. Shifts in the employment opportunities for graduates alongside increasing levels of multidisciplinary working reflect the creative opportunities available through non-traditional placements. As Bellinger notes:

> Placements are opportunities to develop new possibilities for practice in response to changing social conditions as increased regulation reduces opportunities for creative responses. Patterns of qualified social work

employment continue to change and services are increasingly provided by multidisciplinary teams and non-statutory agencies under contract. (Bellinger 2010, p. 2462)

Supervision is the means through which reflexive engagement with one's professional self and practice—as well as related issues—takes place. It serves a number of functions (Kadushin 1976) and has a particular meaning in social work. As Wilson explains:

> Supervision is both a series of *events*—regular formal meetings between a student and agency staff member—and a *process* of enabling students to learn and to deliver an appropriate standard of service to the client group. Students are expected to be taught experientially, learning by observing others, participating in the agency's work and reflecting on their own work. They learn about the practice context; about deriving knowledge to understand situations and create opportunities for advancement. Importantly, this learning is about themselves and their orientation to practice. (Wilson 2000, p. 26 (italics in original))

In the practice setting, social work supervision can make the difference between a student who feels overwhelmed by and unclear about the work and setting and a student who feels supported in a learning environment. Students often report feeling 'tired' and 'overwhelmed', particularly in the first few weeks of placement. This is often because they are absorbing a great deal of new information in an unfamiliar setting. Supervisors have a central role to play in mediating this environment with the processes through which social work students constitute their social work selves.

The differing ways that supervision takes place are often dictated by the organisational setting. For example, universities may need to appoint an external social work supervisor if the organisation does not employ social workers. Student engagement with the on-site supervisor can help to open up new opportunities for learning (Cleak *et al.* 2000, p. 165) since social work might be an allied profession in the organisational context, for example. Similarly, group supervision, whereby one supervisory session is held with a number of social work students, can also open up new opportunities for learning (Cleak *et al.* 2000; Maywald 2000). Supervision enables students to practise their emerging social work self as well as reflect upon this self. Thus supervision is an important place to consider the constitution of the professional self.

WORKING WITH OTHERS

Working with others in differing professions while on placement can be overwhelming, particularly at first. This can be partly due to the challenges of engaging in a new environment, including gaining an understanding of policy and of the nature of service provision. Additionally, students on placement can feel unsure about what a

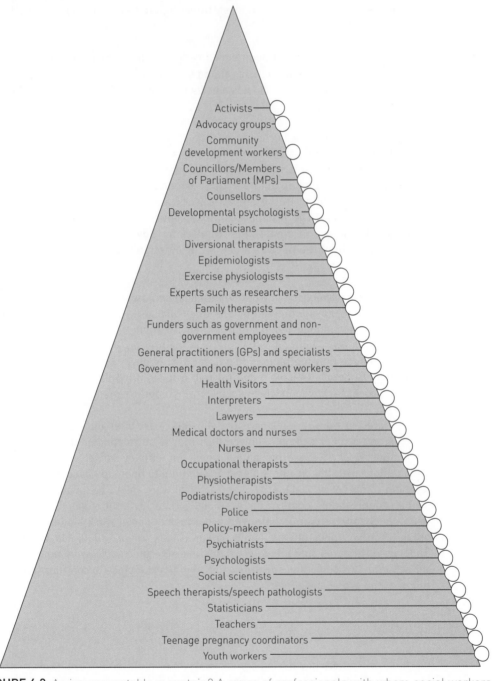

Activists
Advocacy groups
Community development workers
Councillors/Members of Parliament (MPs)
Counsellors
Developmental psychologists
Dieticians
Diversional therapists
Epidemiologists
Exercise physiologists
Experts such as researchers
Family therapists
Funders such as government and non-government employees
General practitioners (GPs) and specialists
Government and non-government workers
Health Visitors
Interpreters
Lawyers
Medical doctors and nurses
Nurses
Occupational therapists
Physiotherapists
Podiatrists/chiropodists
Police
Policy-makers
Psychiatrists
Psychologists
Social scientists
Speech therapists/speech pathologists
Statisticians
Teachers
Teenage pregnancy coordinators
Youth workers

FIGURE 6.2 An insurmountable mountain? A range of professionals with whom social workers work

particular profession 'does' and how it differs, or is similar to, social work. Figure 6.2 captures in a visual way this seemingly insurmountable 'mountain'.

Conduct an audit of your knowledge about the professions shown in Figure 6.2. Next to each of them, note how much you know about the group/profession by assigning an icon as follows:

☺ I feel confident that I know enough about the work of this group
☺ I feel confident that I know a little about the work of this group
☹ I do not feel confident that I know about the work of this group

In evaluating existing knowledge, think about how you know about the profession. How has your knowledge originated? Did you have ideas about the professional grouping which have subsequently changed? If so, why did your ideas change? Have you had positive experiences? What connections are there to social work? What are the differences? It is highly likely that you have come into contact with many of these groups in your everyday life. You may have been a client or people you know such as relatives and friends may have told you about experiences they have had with a particular professional.

Entering an organisation in which individuals from varying professions are represented is an opportune time to broaden knowledge. Induction and orientation meetings with other staff, for example, can be excellent opportunities to ask of others: can you tell me about your profession? Such conversations can also be opportunities to reflect upon social work differences and similarities, and possibilities for collaboration. Like many aspects of practice, working interprofessionally requires confidence in one's own ability to make it work as well as trusting and positive relationships in the working environment (Quinney & Hafford-Letchfield 2012, p. 25). Thus it can be useful to see the placement setting as an opportunity to practise working interprofessionally.

CHAPTER SUMMARY

This chapter has explored learning in the practice context. I have argued that the social work self is constituted through interaction (Mead 1934) on placement. The organisational setting of social work placement learning was explored, and it was argued that despite the differing contexts for social work nationally and internationally, the core skill of assessment helps to frame initial work in placement. Reflexivity was explored as the means through which professional practice occurs. The chapter concluded with a short exploration of supervision and the various forms it can take, and a brief look at the nuances of the interprofessional landscapes in practice settings.

FURTHER READING

CHENOWETH, L. & MCAULIFFE, D. (2005) *The Road to Social Work and Human Service Provision: An Introductory Text.* Southbank: Thomson.

CLEAK, H. & WILSON, J. (2004) *Making the Most of Field Placement*. Sydney: Cengage Learning Australia Pty Limited.

DOEL, M. (2010) *Social Work Placements: A Traveller's Guide*. Abingdon: Routledge.

LOMAX, C., JONES, K., LEIGH, S. & GAY, C. (2010) *Surviving your Social Work Placement*. Basingstoke: Palgrave Macmillan.

7

Research in
Social Work

This chapter:

- Demonstrates the ways in which research is relevant to the social work role

- Encourages research mindedness

- Outlines epistemology, research design and methodology, and explores some of the key methods employed in social work research

- Examines literature reviews, sampling, data analysis and dissemination

- Outlines how social work values and ethics can be applied to social work research

Research often makes it into media headlines. For example, print copy such as 'new study shows…' and 'researchers found…' or a statement of fact such as 'young people twice as likely to be at risk of sexual violence' pushes research into the public sphere through sharing researchers' findings with the broader public. News stories appear so definitive in the reporting of research findings that it becomes difficult to weigh up competing studies such as those with differing findings.

Yet there is little research that can be said to be categorically 'true', particularly from the perspective of social work in which we understand social issues as complex, subjective and historically grounded. If we take the final claim above relating to young people and sexual violence, can we assume that this figure is true? In order to assess the veracity of the claim we need to consider a number of questions, such as:

- How many people were involved in the research, or what was the research population?
- How was the research undertaken in terms of methods? For example, were people interviewed or were statistics such as the number of sexual assaults collated and matched alongside age? How were these 'data' collated to come to the findings?
- What definition of sexual violence was used?
- What about victims of sexual violence who do not report the crime to the authorities? How were these accounted for in the data?
- What was the profession of the researcher or research team?
- Why was the research undertaken?
- Who funded the research?
- Was the research ethical? For example, did people involved in the research give their consent?
- How do the findings compare with existing studies?
- Where was the research undertaken?

The answers to all these questions will help us to better understand the study's findings. The questions above relate to the research population and research design, ethical considerations, data analysis and findings in relation to existing knowledge. We shall explore all these concepts in this chapter. Despite research often being seen as 'marginal' to social work (MacIntyre & Paul 2012), empirical work, which is research in which the researcher 'does' research with others, has a clear application in this area. Research can both inform as well as reflect practice and theory, and can also help organisations understand and respond appropriately to the needs of the communities they serve. In addition research helps to bring previously individualised issues to the attention of others, including the general public, policy-makers and organisations.

In this chapter we begin to consider research by examining the process of research, from its design to the choice of methods to the ways in which research findings are communicated with others.

RESEARCH MINDEDNESS

In previous chapters we have considered the approach to understanding social and individual problems through the exercising of what C. Wright Mills (1959) calls the *sociological imagination*. In understanding and developing a passion for research, a similar imaginative sensibility is required.

Research mindedness is the ability to extend the curiosity about the world around us towards empirical ends. Research mindedness is central to social work— indeed, it is argued by some to be so compatible with social work itself that research and practice go hand-in-hand (Everitt *et al.* 1992; McLaughlin 2012, p. 11). The following account provides an example of the ways in which research and practice influence one another:

> I was working in a very deprived area and in my work with individuals and communities I was struck by the level of resilience to hardship these people demonstrated. In my work I had only come across research that talked about problems: problems of poverty, problems of relationships, poor health outcomes and so on. Though these problems were very real, there were also a lot of counters to all the negativity. My clients used to tell me that they didn't want me to see them as victims and although they needed some assistance in one area of their lives or relationships, this did not mean that they were not coping in other areas of day to day life. I firmly believe that requiring social work intervention is no different to medical intervention: it should not be seen as a sign of weakness but I didn't feel that this view was represented in the literature I had read. This prompted an interest in resilience and I discovered that quite a bit of research was going on to investigate resilience in individuals. Community based approaches such as the notion of capacity building helped frame a more positive way forward in my work with the communities. These emerging theories were examined in the social research at the time: luckily I stumbled upon the library that my organisation ran. Reading about research and new theory in journals and books changed my approach in my everyday practice. For example, when I worked with individuals, I shared the recent research about a particular issue, including research that said different things. Sharing this knowledge at appropriate times seemed to work well. I also wanted to know more about the community so I developed some questionnaires for clients of the service. These helped me further understand the issues relevant to the community which had been framed in their own words. This process also led me on to research non-problematic communities in my future work as an academic.

Other examples of the connection between practice and research are growing since many social workers go on to undertake research themselves to justify programmes or demonstrate social work effectiveness. Examples of social work research include:

- Finding out what the community needs are via questionnaires
- Evaluating programmes to see whether they are effective. This might entail running focus groups or interviews to understand how programmes are perceived and experienced by others
- Research specific to a client group, such as older people, young people, children or families, people with disabilities

Social work students sometimes find it difficult to see the relationship between their own everyday life, their social work identity and the world of research. Imagination and curiosity are vital to understanding research.

Research mindedness is developed through a genuine curiosity about the world. For example, think about the meaning behind the everyday activity of 'catching up' with friends or family members. 'Catching up' is the concept of getting together and communicating with someone you know. Indeed this notion of 'catching up'—which might entail going for a hot drink such as coffee or tea or going to a pub to drink alcohol—has no currency to people in varying cultures. There are also various types of 'catching up': from the conversations you might have with your fellow students after the summer break or placement to meetings with prospective employers or mentors. At first glance it would seem that 'catching up' is a social activity, shared between two or more people, and is a feature of contemporary life in developed nations. Curiosity about this social event might lead to ask questions such as:

- What purpose does 'catching up' have?
- Are the methods of 'catching up' similar across different
  - age groups, or
  - cultures, or
  - genders, or
  - sexual identities, or
  - classes?
- Do problems emerge from these events and if so, how are they managed?
- What are the experiences of people who do not drink alcohol during 'catching up' activities at drinking venues?
- Why does 'catching up' involve food and/or drink?
- Does 'catching up' fulfil the need for social interaction?

These are just a few questions that might be asked when reflecting upon the everyday activity of 'catching up', and reading these may have prompted you to think of further questions. Questions emerge when curiosity is focused on the notion of 'catching up', which generates more and more questions. When beginning to exercise your research mindedness, try not to let yourself be too sure of the answers to the questions. If you feel unsure how to generate questions, it can be useful to imagine that you are explaining a concept, situation or social issue to someone who has no knowledge of it. For example, explaining homelessness might entail describing differing types of homelessness, how people become homeless, what can be done to help people who are homeless, how to prevent it and so on. These aspects to the issue of homelessness require curiosity and imagination which can lead to the generation of questions. These questions can then be narrowed down in a more focused manner in preparation for the empirical work ahead.

The task for the researcher, then, is to narrow down the questions and decide on usually just one aspect of them. It is important to avoid trying to 'solve' a particular issue through one piece of research. We shall explore this in the next section when we consider how to develop a research question.

RESEARCH QUESTIONS, AIMS AND SCOPE

There are various discrete stages or steps in research, and many researchers adopt a project management approach to the process. The stages include choosing a topic, deciding on methodology and methods, undertaking the research and analysing subsequent data and finally, disseminating the research findings (Sarantakos 2013, p. 104).

The first step in research involves opening up areas of inquiry using the imagination and curiosity, as we saw with our consideration of homelessness. The next stage is to narrow the focus, and devising a research question facilitates this process. Imagine a funnel into which all of your ideas about a particular issue are being poured (Figure 7.1). This process involves 'letting go' of some topics or areas that might be of interest.

Research questions relate to the specific focus of the intended research. In this sense, it is useful to remember that 'research is about answering questions' (D'Cruz & Jones 2004, p. 15). In thinking about the research question and research design, the researcher will need to decide who the research is interested in, what the research will consist of, why the research is important and how the research will be carried out. All of these variables require careful consideration. Although it may appear that choices about the research are limitless, the choice of research question may also be affected by such factors as budgetary restrictions and availability of research participants (Sarantakos 2005, p. 131).

Once the research question has been formulated, it is time to consider how to go about answering it. In the following section we will examine the choices relating to methods, and what influences these choices.

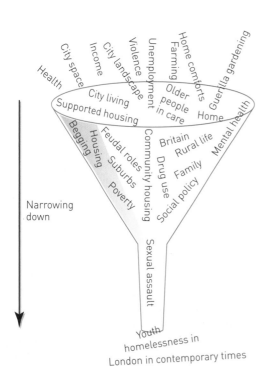

FIGURE 7.1 Narrowing down topics is an important step in research

EPISTEMOLOGY

When you begin to think about your research, you may already have ideas about methods, for example interviews, focus groups and so on. Preferences for certain types of research reveal something about one's world-view. This is because your ideas about research are connected with your world-view or epistemology (Crotty 2007; Liamputtong & Ezzy 2006; Sarantakos 2013).

Epistemology relates to the way in which we approach knowledge. Crotty defines epistemology as 'the theory of knowledge embedded in the theoretical perspective and thereby in the methodology' (2007, p. 3). He argues that the epistemology affects the theoretical perspective employed which, in turn, influences the methodology and subsequent research methods (Crotty 2007).

For example, if you have a preference for large scale studies in which many participants are consulted using a traditional, scientific study design then you will likely believe that things can be proved or disproved. This kind of research is influenced by the belief that one can make general, *objective* assumptions about others. This perspective is referred to as objectivism, and positivistic research is connected to this theoretical tradition (see Crotty 2007, pp. 18–41). On the other hand, some people believe that statistics and research which claim that things are universally 'true' have little credibility because we all 'interpret the world' or *construct* in our subjective/unique ways (see Berger & Luckmann 1973; Crotty 2007, pp. 42–65; Mead 1934). This perspective is referred to as constructionism or subjectivism, and interpretivistic research is connected to this theoretical tradition. It is useful to think of these two competing views, objectivism and constructionism, as being at opposite ends of a spectrum. Many researchers would see themselves along the spectrum at particular points. Do you have a preference for objectivism or constructionism? Place a mark along the following spectrum to indicate your own preference.

OBJECTIVISM  CONSTRUCTIONISM

There are many theoretical traditions associated with both objectivism and constructionism. For the beginning researcher, it is useful to think about research relating to objectivism as being in the quantitative tradition and research relating to constructionism as being in the qualitative tradition. We now move on to consider research methodology and methods.

RESEARCH METHODOLOGY AND METHODS

In distinguishing between methodology and methods, it is useful to think about research methods as describing specifically *how* the research is *done*. The methodology includes the broader perspective which outlines the general approach in the research as well as the choice of research methods (Sarantakos 2005, p. 30). An example of a methodology is phenomenology. Phenomenology is a range of theoretical positions which are interested in the meanings individuals attach to particular situations, events and phenomena encountered in the course of everyday life (Schutz 1967). Schutzian (1954) phenomenology, for example, highlights individual meaning-making processes as important to understand through the research process. In understanding individual meanings, societal meanings—or 'social reality' (Schutz 1954, p. 492)—is discovered.

When considering research methods the most important thing is to make sure that the method 'fits' with the research question being answered, rather than choosing the method based on researcher preference (Stanley & Wise 1983, p. 724 cited in Letherby 2003, p. 86).

As a beginning researcher, it is helpful to have a sense of the scope of research methods available. The following are examples of some of the key research methods used in social research, but are by no means exhaustive. New research methods continue to emerge and researchers often use a combination of approaches, also called 'mixed methods', or they adapt a method to suit their research question. When considering the methods listed below, it may be helpful to think about them in relation to a particular issue you consider worthy of further research. This will assist in thinking through how a particular method might fit in with the research question being asked.

INTERVIEWS

Interviews are a very popular research method (Holstein & Gubrium 2011, p. 150; Silverman 2007, p. 39) and often preferred by social workers who are used to relating to others using dialogue (D'Cruz & Jones 2004, p. 111). There are various ways in which interviews can be designed to suit the overall research design. A key question to think about when designing research which uses interviews relates to the level of researcher involvement. For example, interviews can range from being highly structured with lots of predetermined questions, to more 'open-ended' or unstructured where the direction of the conversation between the researcher and the interviewee is free-flowing and spontaneous. Open-ended interviews are often preferred by researchers in the social sciences because they allow for the interviewer to check with the interviewee that they have understood them:

> ... data are valid when a deep mutual understanding has been achieved between interviewer and respondent. The practical consequence is that most interactionists reject prescheduled standardized interviews in favour of open-ended interviews. The latter allow respondents to use their own particular way of defining the world [and] assume that no fixed sequence of questions is suitable to all respondents. (Fielding 1996, p. 151)

In order to conduct interviews, it is necessary for the researcher to build a good relationship with the interviewee. Your social work skills in communication are vital in conducting this type of research (Hardwick & Worsley 2011, p. 77). As a researcher using interviews, you are asking that someone disclose or describe their experiences and life events. This can be challenging as the rapport necessary to achieve this has to be built at the beginning of the interview in a short space of time (Hardwick & Worsley 2011, p. 77).

Interviews enable 'sensitive' topics to be addressed on a one to one basis (Denzin 1978; Fielding 1996; Silverman 1985; Strauss & Corbin 1990). It is important to think about gender when designing research. For example, women are traditionally socialised to discuss matters through conversation rather than through action (see, for example, Lever's 1978 study about childhood socialisation). Calls for participant interviews may therefore be taken up more readily by women, who may have little opportunity for their experiences or voices to be heard (Reinharz & Chase 2002), and therefore take up the opportunity to be interviewed more enthusiastically than men (Dunk-West 2011).

FOCUS GROUPS

Like interviews, focus groups are very popular with social researchers. Focus groups are groups of people who are brought together by the researcher with the aim of discussing issues as a group. Henn *et al.* (2009) argue that the focus group's intention is to:

> ... stimulate discussion among people and bring to the surface responses that otherwise might lay dormant. Such discussions may enable participants to clarify their views and opinion positions or, on the basis of engaging with others, to articulate more clearly than they otherwise might. The interactive dynamic is therefore considered to be a crucial element of the focus group approach. (p. 190)

Given the dynamism of focus groups, it is vital for the researcher to facilitate the process whereby information is elicited. Again, social work skills are useful to the social work researcher. The researcher facilitating focus groups must understand group dynamics, be able to elicit the views of people whose voices might be less represented because of issues such as gender, class, disability, culture, sexual identity, age and so on and have the confidence to skilfully address these issues.

QUESTIONNAIRES

Most people reading this book will have come across an invitation to complete a questionnaire, whether you have been contacted directly by a researcher, through a site visited on the internet or by a telephone caller working for a market research company. Questionnaires can help researchers gain an overall view about a particular issue.

When designing your questionnaire, it is important to think very carefully about your wording: 'questionnaire construction is a very demanding task which requires not only methodological competence but also extensive experience with research in general and questioning techniques in particular' (Sarantakos 2013, p. 241). Ambiguous questions or those that lack specifics are likely to result in respondents becoming confused and filling out the questionnaire incorrectly (Neumann 2006, pp. 315–316). This will affect the outcome of your research because you may not be asking what you think you are asking. This phenomenon is known as *skewed data* and to avoid this it is important to think carefully about what you are asking and how it relates to your overall research question.

For example, imagine you are conducting research which critically examines the following: what do clients want in a social worker? Imagine you have decided that questionnaires will generate data to assist you to answer your question.

For one of the questions in your questionnaire, imagine you want to find out what clients think about their social worker. You will need to think about what kind of question or questions will elicit this information. If you ask 'Do you like your social worker?' the answer might be 'yes' or 'no' or 'maybe'. Is it important to understand 'maybe' or the reasons for selecting a particular response? If so, you may need a follow up question. You might think about re-framing the question because asking 'Do you like your social worker?' might elicit a different response than 'Do you think your social worker is competent?' Again, it is vital to think about what overall research question you are trying to answer. It may, for example, be better to give respondents a space to fill out their response to the following question:

> 'What do you think about your social worker?' Please use the space below to respond:
>
> ....
> ....
> ....
> ....

Whereas the question above generates qualitative data, that is, information that is descriptive, questionnaires can also measure using numbers. This means that they can be designed using quantitative approaches. For example, another way to measure how a client feels about their social worker is to provide a Likert scale (Sarantakos 2005, p. 250):

> When thinking about my relationship with my social worker, I feel:
>
> | | |
> |---|---|
> | Very positive | 5 |
> | Positive | 4 |
> | Neutral | 3 |
> | Negative | 2 |
> | Very negative | 1 |
>
> (Adapted from Sarantakos 2005, p. 250)

The answers to these interval levels of measurement would then be calculated and therefore measured.

OBSERVATION/ETHNOGRAPHY

There is a strong tradition of ethnography in the social sciences, particularly within sociology and anthropology. Ethnography is 'study through the observation of insti-tutions, cultures and customs' (Henn *et al.* 2009, p. 196) and requires the researcher to be *immersed* in the culture or social setting. Ethnography is a research method-ology (see Crotty 2007, p. 5) and its methods might include observation, participa-tion and interviews, for example. Being immersed in a setting requires a clear decision by the researcher about whether they will be strictly observing the 'action' around them or whether they will be participating and observing. For example, if a researcher wanted to understand the organisational culture of statutory social work in London, an ethnographic method might be used. The researcher would need to think about whether they would engage in the 'action' of the organisation they were immersed in. Would they, for example, answer the telephone if staff were unable to attend to this task? Would they speak to clients of the organisation if they were accompanying a social worker on a home visit? (For an interesting ethnographic analysis about practitioners in child protection, see Harry Ferguson's (2011) book *Child Protection Practice.*)

In ethnographic studies where observation is occurring, it is important to think about how observations will be captured by the researcher. There are various ways to capture data, including:

- Recording interviews, conversations and/or the researchers' thoughts using a recording device
- Completing field notes at regular intervals (at the end of each day, or at various points during the day, for example)
- Keeping mental notes of the events/conversations which are then written down at a later date

The other issue related to this type of research is choosing which kinds of events of, in our example, organisational life are captured. For example, is it important to record the non-verbal communication between colleagues or clients and social workers or is it more important to focus on the events that occur within the setting? (see Sarantakos 2013, p. 229).

Internet ethnography is another means through which particular issues can be researched and 'in some cases the openness and flexibility of design that are hall-marks of ethnographic research can arguably be better achieved by conducting the research on-line' (Aull Davies 2008, p. 151). As with all research, it is vital to gain the consent of the research participant; in internet research this can be an area of uncertainty because of the publicly available information internet technology facili-tates. As we shall see in the next section, all types of research involving others require careful consideration of ethical responsibilities.

Generally speaking, the ethical principles used in social work that we discussed in Chapter 5 are transferable to the research context.

Gaining ethical approval for any research involving others is crucial because it allows critical assessment of whether the proposed research conforms to ethical standards. Ethics committees are a common feature in organisational settings, government and non-government organisations, universities and the like. Such bodies require the researcher to submit a clearly articulated plan for their proposed research which will then be scrutinised and assessed for its suitability. Sometimes researchers are required to adjust their approach according to the judgement made by an ethics committee.

The guiding tenet in all research ought to be to 'do no harm'. This notion, also known in ethics literature as avoiding harm or 'non-maleficence', is a principle underpinning contemporary medical and social sciences research (for example, see Beauchamp & Childress' 1979 text on bioethics). Some researchers believe that research should do more than avoid harm and should, in fact, 'do good' which is the ethical principle of beneficence. Such research is called emancipatory research and has particular appeal to social workers. Researchers hold positions of power (Bloom 1998, pp. 34–36) and emancipatory research attempts to share that power more equally with others such as those being 'researched'.

Emancipatory research seeks to empower those with limited opportunities to exercise power because of, for example, gendered inequality (Letherby 2003, p. 114). Here is a basic example of emancipatory research:

- Research question: How does youth homelessness impact on relationships with their peers?
- Epistemology: Constructionism.
- Methodology: Phenomenology.
- Method: Interviews with 10 young people who are currently homeless, five men and five women.
- Specifics: The lead researcher will recruit three young people who are or have been homeless. They will be paid to be trained in qualitative research and will be employed as research assistants. These young people will conduct interviews with the research population (outlined above), lead in the design and analysis of data and take a key role in disseminating the research through publications and conference presentations/seminars. Interview participants will be paid for their time, invited to assist in the research design and dissemination and will be provided with access to housing or specialised agencies if appropriate/wanted.

The research described above seeks *to empower* others through providing:

- Training and skills acquisition for the research assistants recruited
- Financial and other support/resources for the research population

Confidentiality is an ethical concept and legal principle and is crucial to consider in any research involving others. Just as with social work practice, it is important that participants in studies understand the role of the researcher and the nature of involvement. Researchers often write a short summary of the research—a participant information sheet—in which the key aims of the study are laid out, and including how the information obtained from respondents will be used. It is important that people involved in research are able to withdraw their consent to take part in the study at any point.

SAMPLING

Sampling relates to the question: 'how many people should be involved in the research?' For example, if we decide that we would like to interview people to better understand the impacts of welfare cuts in England, how many people should we interview? In addition, who should we interview? Should we select a random section of the population or should we interview a small number of people who are affected by the government cuts to the public sector? How will we find our sample population? These are all questions which relate to sampling. In short, sampling refers to:

• Who is included in the research
• How many people are included in the research
• How participants will be found and selected

Generally speaking, research uses samples that are either representative or non-representative. Research which claims to have significance for the broader population is said to be *generalisable*. Generalisability means that based on the findings of a piece of research, general assumptions can be made about others who were not included in the study. If five hundred people from a range of *variables* such as class, gender, age, educational attainment and socio-economic status were surveyed about their attitudes towards the 2012 London Olympics, researchers may be able to generalise their findings to the rest of the population. This is because the researchers have included particular features in their research design which allow for them to see their participants as representing the general public.

A number of sampling methods can be used to recruit participants for research. For example, snowball sampling (Biernacki & Waldorf 1981) enables potential interviewees to hear about the study via word of mouth, for example via a forwarded email or in person from someone who was aware of the study. They can then tell others about the study and the sample increases or 'snowballs' in this way. This is similar to opportunistic sampling which utilises existing networks and spontaneous opportunities to meet others who may be interested in being part of research (Liamputtong & Ezzy 2006, p. 48). These kinds of sampling methods are suited to research which is non-representative, that is, it does not claim to represent the broader population. Like representative samples, non-representative samples can make a valuable contribution to existing theory and knowledge.

DATA ANALYSIS

Data analysis is required for the researcher to conclude the findings of the study. Data are the products of whichever research method has been used. For example, the narratives or dialogue from interviews or focus groups are data. Completed questionnaires contain data. Broadly speaking, there are two differing processes for data analysis, and these are dependent on whether research is quantitative or qualitative. We will now briefly consider each of these.

QUANTITATIVE DATA ANALYSIS

The ways in which surveys are collated in quantitative research enables numerical assessments to be made. For example, it is possible to add up and calculate differing aspects of data collected for the purposes of *measurement*. Measures include mode, median and mean.

> **Mode**: this is the highest frequency. For example, in the following list of measures, the number 3 appears the most, so 3 would be the mode.
>
> 1   3   3   5   8   9   10   11
>
> **Median**: the median is the middle score, and in this set of numbers is 6.5. When there is an odd number of scores the median is easy to identify, as being the middle score in the set. When there is an even number of scores the median is calculated by adding the two middle scores and dividing by 2. In this case the middle scores are 5 and 8. Adding those and dividing by 2 gives the median score.
>
> 1   3   3   5   8   9   10   11
>
> **Mean**: this is the average of the scores. Adding the scores and dividing them by the total number of scores gives the mean or average.
>
> 1   3   3   5   8   9   10   11
>
> In this case the calculation would be
>
> $$1 + 3 + 3 + 5 + 8 + 9 + 10 + 11 = 50 \div 8 = 6.25$$

Certain types of measurement are better suited to mean, median and mode respectively. As we can see above, the same set of numbers can have differing mean, median and mode scores. Imagine that almost all respondents to a question in a questionnaire said they ranked their social worker as number 5 which is the top category in a Likert scale from extremely unsatisfied to extremely satisfied. Some respondents, however, ticked the lower end of the scale, at number 1, which suggested they were extremely unsatisfied. When scoring the questionnaire and reporting on the findings, using median, mode or mean could each suggest different things.

Various statistical techniques can be applied to quantitative data. Standard deviation, for example, measures the distance a score is from the average, or mean, of scores in the study. Relationships between particular variables can also be measured. Data can be arranged into visual descriptors such as scatterplots, histograms and bar and pie charts, for example, and there are various computer programs that assist in both creating and computing statistics (for example SPSS). Now that we have introduced some of the ways in which quantitative data are analysed, let's move on to consider qualitative analysis.

QUALITATIVE DATA ANALYSIS

Qualitative data generated from focus groups and interviews, for example, can be analysed using various techniques. Depending on the research methodology used, analysis can vary from narrative analysis to discourse analysis to case studies. Many studies using qualitative data require transcription of verbal dialogue between the researcher and participants.

Here are some data generated through my research into everyday sexuality. In this research project I was interested in how people reflected upon and made sense of their sexualities. This involved interviewing 15 men and 15 women aged between 30 and 65 years. A constructionist epistemology, combined with a phenomenological methodology, influenced the ways in which data were analysed. I began the research by asking: 'can you tell me about your sexuality?' Here is what one respondent said in our interview:

> Ruth:
> It's difficult isn't it? Because I know like when I first um got that email I thought I wonder what it is, you know, what sort of... you're looking to explore and I thought... 'oh god... I don't know' (laugh). Um... I don't know ... I don't know if it's how you sort of think of yourself some people sort of certainly define their selves with their sexuality quite strongly. I've got a couple of friends who are very much like that. And then there are other people who maybe don't cause it much thought. And I probably sit in that category of not necessarily causing it much thought. Um. But I do think that there are... I mean there are elements of... I guess in my role um and where I've been and what I've done um, some of the, you know, whether it's power balance issues as... Having started out quite young in, um, in fairly senior positions.
>
> Ruth, 39-year-old CEO

How do we make sense of these kinds of accounts? The answer lies with the methodology being used. In some cases narrative or life story approaches help to frame people's stories with life events and the ways that they make sense of the world. Broadly speaking, a phenomenological approach, for example, is interested in the meaning people ascribe to particular phenomena.

In looking at the account from Ruth (not her real name), and comparing it to other accounts from the study, we can begin to separate out what are themes. This is called coding. Coding relates to themes which emerge from data and it is vital that the researcher immerse themselves in their data in order to find these. Often researchers will read, re-read and listen to their data. They can also check back with participants during this process, as a kind of triangulation to make sure they have understood the account in the way the interviewee, or group, for example, intended. Data analysis is a broad term which is used to mean many processes (Wolcott 1994). 'Analysis' suggests that this can be a straightforward, time-limited process. In some research designs, analysis occurs while data are being gathered whereas for other studies, analysis is a process whose boundaries are dictated by the timescale of the project. In any case, analysis in qualitative research involves being familiar with data, comparing data, drawing out themes or making some generalisations such as findings and thinking about the significance of the outcomes in relation to existing knowledge and research.

Qualitative researchers must also decide how much they are informed by their data. Do they, for example, privilege people's stories over theories? Or should people's accounts inform theory? Again, the chosen research methodology needs to fit with decisions made about such matters.

Like quantitative packages, computer programs such as NVIVO help to arrange qualitative data.

DISSEMINATION

Dissemination in relation to research concerns itself with how the research findings are shared with others. There are many ways for researchers to share their findings. The method used will reflect the purpose of the research, for example whether it was commissioned by a particular organisation to review a programme or whether the research was conducted by the government (for example, Censuses are large scale studies). Possible methods of dissemination include:

- Presenting the findings at a conference
- Writing a report which is given to organisations and others
- Issuing a media release
- Using social media such as Twitter, Facebook and other networking sites
- Writing a dissertation (for Honours, Masters or Doctor of Philosophy degrees, for example)
- Publishing the findings in peer reviewed journals
- Writing copy for publication in newspapers, magazines and other relevant print media
- Speaking on television, radio and/or digital media about the issue you researched
- Writing a book chapter for an edited book or a book
- Presenting findings to the community through seminars or workshops

LITERATURE REVIEWS

Literature reviews are written accounts which firstly, name relevant literature such as studies or theoretical contributions to the field being studied. Secondly, literature reviews enable the author to argue that their research fits and is important in this broader context of scholarly contributions. A well-written literature review details all of the important research and scholarship about a particular area, highlights what is missing and locates the present study or argument in this context. Considering how much information is contained within a literature review, they are surprisingly brief. It is therefore essential to be succinct and arrange information in a clear format when drafting a literature review.

Literature reviewing is a skill that takes time to develop because the task is to synthesise existing literature. With the current emphasis on evidence-based practice, being able to consult literature through finding and reading appropriate journal articles is a vital skill to social workers. When writing a literature review, it can be helpful to group articles into themes. These themes can be things such as dates, countries where research originates, particular types of theories, similar methodologies and methods used in studies or a myriad of other possibilities. Being able to read a large number of articles and summarise them all by grouping together those that have something in common is a skill well worth developing.

Social work students are required to write many assignments during their studies and it is helpful to learn how to access literature through database searching, using key terms to narrow the search. When reading journal articles, you will notice that they have a similar format. Journal articles in the social sciences usually have an introduction, a literature review, a methodology/method section, a findings section and discussion followed by a conclusion. When reading the literature review from a journal article, notice how the authors summarise existing studies and argue that theirs is important.

In summary, here are some techniques that can assist in writing a literature review for a dissertation:

- Group all your articles according to themes. These could be based on anything from the country where the studies originated, to the method being studied to any other criteria you notice while reading.
- Make notes on your paper copy of articles and summarise in dot points the three key points in the top right-hand corner of the article. This helps when you have a large number of articles.
- Begin writing. Edit, edit, edit. Experiment with moving text around to make your argument stronger.
- Read your work and ask: what is my argument? Is it clear?
- At the beginning of your literature review state what you are going to do. For example: 'The ways in which depression has been responded to in the past decade have shifted. This dissertation argues that depression has been medicalised which has marginalised the social model. In making this argument, the dissertation commences by providing a critical appraisal of the ways in

which the medicalisation of depression has occurred in relation to pharmaco-logical intervention in England.'

- Avoid summarising literature, instead, critically appraise it: say what is good about it and what is neglected.
- Show others your work and ask them to summarise your argument. This helps to check if you have stated your argument clearly enough.
- Use signposting and summarising such as 'this chapter argues...', 'this chapter has...'. This makes it less likely that your examiner will be confused by your discussion.

HOW TO USE RESEARCH IN SOCIAL WORK: WORKING WITH OTHERS

Social workers in organisational settings who wish to do research sometimes work alongside institutions that specialise in research. For example, universities, government workers and people in private research consultancy may be brought in to an organisation to help it undertake primary research. This means that social workers can work with statisticians, qualitative researchers and analysts who may have qualifications in economics, sociology, history, mathematics, or more applied areas such as epidemiology, psychology and social work as well as many, many other disciplines. Social workers in the organisational setting who undertake such work need to clearly articulate what it is they would like to find out in the research. Some organisations have a great deal of input into the research design and execution while others commission the research and have little involvement aside from receiving the final report.

Once research is undertaken, how is it used in an organisational context? The answer is that it depends on the purpose of the research. Often, organisations providing social work services like to have evidence of the efficacy of particular programmes or interventions. This can help with funding, for example, because being able to demonstrate that a particular approach works can highlight its need. Similarly, being able to show tangible outcomes can help services choose which types of intervention are cost effective, meet the needs of clients and are effective. Findings of research that is commissioned is conveyed to the funding organisation through meetings, formal presentations and reports. Written reports usually summarise the literature in the area through a literature review in which the central research problem is contextualised. A summary of findings helps to break down the findings of the research into clearly worded, brief statements. When on placement, students often find themselves reading policy documents and may also read research reports which have been completed 'in house', that is, internal to the organisation, or externally.

Similarly, organisations may base their policies upon other research, such as research reported by the World Health Organisation which found that every six seconds someone around the world dies from tobacco smoking or exposure to second-hand smoke (www.who.int/research/en/). These kinds of statistics help to frame global problems and inform thinking about services for local communities and individuals. How might social work in a community organisation respond to this

being brought to an end

statistic? One possible response is to offer low cost or free smoking cessation classes and supports. Another response is to use advocacy and lobbying approaches to argue that legislators and policy-makers need to protect their citizens against this public health issue. These suggestions are based on existing public health approaches to address smoking in England, Australia and other nations. Social work in this context would aim to address such a 'problem' through understanding it in research terms and adopting a helping service according to the need of its clients and broader community.

Let us now consider other ways that research is used in social work practice by looking at a more individual situation (Case Study 7.1).

CASE STUDY 7.1 The Oscar family

Bob Oscar is 52 years old and lives with his two children, Ruby Oscar, aged 15, and Christopher Oscar, aged 13. Ruby and Christopher have a good relationship and are very close. They both attend the local school. The Oscar family live in private rental accommodation in central London. Bob is White British and Ruby and Christopher describe themselves as mixed race. The children's mother, Jane, died from a heroin overdose when both children were under the age of five years. Jane was from Zimbabwe and moved to London as a teenager. Bob is a housepainter and has a good reputation locally, but in the past few years the work has become less and less frequent. Things have become difficult financially and Bob visits the organisation you work for to see if they can help. He meets with you and tells you some more about his family.

Bob tells you that Ruby is a 'bright girl' but recently she has had health problems and has been having anxiety attacks at school which has made her want to avoid school altogether. Both Ruby and Christopher have asthma which is worse in the colder months. The central heating at the flat is not very effective and there is dampness in the building. Additionally, since money is tight, they are not able to run the heating for very long. Bob tells you that Christopher has started to ask about his mother more since becoming a teenager. He is not sure how much to tell the children about the death because when she died the children did not attend the funeral, nor were they told how she died. Bob would like to know if you can assist him. He's not sure where to start, but feels that the family are struggling.

HOW TO USE RESEARCH TO ASSIST THE OSCAR FAMILY

There are many issues which are present in the case study which could eventuate in different approaches, courses of action and outcomes. Your response would depend on the agreement between Bob and yourself and the children about what areas might be important to begin with and which areas require future work together. Here is a summary of some of the potential areas of work and how research can be used in varying ways in social work practice:

Bob's financial situation

Your organisation may already have information about how much parents are entitled to for a range of things such as housing assistance, support for electricity and/or gas costs, school related expenses and childcare benefit. Discussing with Bob the support he is entitled to could address and help to alleviate some of the problems with asthma that Ruby and Christopher have experienced because of the dampness and cold in the home. Discussing medical support with Bob is also relevant here since asthma is a potentially life-threatening condition if untreated or not managed appropriately.

A cursory glance at the research literature about this kind of financial hardship which impacts upon decisions about whether to use the heating (or cooling) shows that it has been named as a kind of poverty called 'fuel poverty'. In the UK, the Department of Energy and Climate Change define fuel poverty in the following way:

> A household is said to be in fuel poverty if it needs to spend more than 10% of its income on fuel to maintain a satisfactory heating regime (usually 21 degrees for the main living area, and 18 degrees for other occupied rooms). (www.decc.gov.uk/en/content/cms/statistics/fuelpov_stats/fuelpov_stats.aspx)

A search in the *British Journal of Social Work* highlights an article about health inequality in which fuel poverty is mentioned. This seems relevant to Bob's situation because the lack of income has affected whether he heats his home, which, in turn, has had consequences for his children's health. The article:

> ... presents arguments for recognizing and tackling health inequalities as a major new challenge for social work. Four underpinning points provide the building blocks for this case, that health inequalities are a matter of social justice and human rights, that the causes of health inequalities are primarily social, that poverty and poor health are common characteristics of social work service users and, that, therefore, health inequalities are a vital issue for social workers in all settings. A number of implications for social work practice and policy are outlined. The paper concludes that addressing health inequalities implies that social work has to become more actively engaged with critical global social, economic, environmental and political issues. (Bywaters 2009, p. 353)

This paper reports on a range of existing research which has taken place around health inequality and poverty. It makes the argument that social work ought to be more active in being aware of inequalities, such as those brought about by fuel poverty, in day-to-day practice. Yet what is the connection between this piece of research and Bob and his children? How might you use it as his social worker?

Being able to name Bob's situation and link it with the growing number of people who are under financial hardship because of rising costs of fuel can be a powerful thing for clients. That there is something called 'fuel poverty' can help to name individuals' experiences and highlight that this is a new phenomenon and something that needs to change. As a social worker, using this research to help to frame your search to find financial assistance for Bob, you will be more informed.

Similarly, you may recognise other clients in the organisation for whom this is an issue. Arranging a space for people to meet in order to frame a collective response is one way to help to address this problem. Facilitating social action, helping with advocacy activities—these too help to enable people to address the problems brought about by fuel poverty. In some countries certain groups of vulnerable people (such as very young and very old people with health conditions) have been highlighted as being particularly at risk of heat or cold related health problems as a result of the rising costs of fuel. Some countries have introduced financial relief for these groups in the form of credits and tariff reductions. Searching for information on behalf of Bob or providing him with the information about tariffs is an example of how research can be used in social work practice.

Anxiety

During your search into anxiety, you find that *The Medical Journal of Australia* evaluated studies which looked at the efficacy of programmes in schools to address anxiety. The finding was as follows:

> A number of schools programs produce positive outcomes. However, even well established programs require further evaluation to establish readiness for broad dissemination as outlined in the standards of the Society for Prevention Research. (Neil & Christensen 2007, p. 305)

You do not think this article is helpful to your direct practice with Ruby. However, reading this gives you an idea: you plan to talk to Bob about meeting with Ruby to talk about school and whether there are any supports in place at her school to help her deal with her anxiety. This plan of action could lead to you working alongside Ruby and the school to help reduce the impacts of the anxiety for Ruby.

What if Ruby asked you: 'what is the best way to treat anxiety?' A search of the literature in peer reviewed journals in which approaches are evaluated highlights some of the key ways anxiety is addressed in a clinical setting. Through reading this literature you begin to wonder about the role of health and whether Ruby has been assessed as having anxiety. Given her asthma and other recent events, you go back to Ruby and discuss whether there has been an involvement from health professionals. Your concern relates to the possibility that there could be an underlying health issue which has been self-diagnosed as anxiety. Ruby tells you she has looked it up on the internet and self-diagnosed anxiety. Her heart pounds and she feels sick. Following up with health might offer opportunities for working with other professions alongside Ruby. This means that any findings that are made can be responded to alongside other services, with Ruby at the centre of these relations.

Grief and loss in children and young people

After a further meeting with Bob and Christopher, Christopher tells you he would like to talk to you about his mother. You, Christopher and Bob all agree this is a good way forward. Before you meet with Christopher for the first time, you want to 'read up' about grief and loss in young people as it will help you frame your responses to him. Although you remember studying grief and loss at university, you do not feel that you are up to date with your knowledge in this area. You suspect that children ought to be included in rituals around death but wonder if this has changed since you studied.

After conducting a search of the literature you find that there is some debate surrounding grief that does not reach some sort of resolution in a timeframe which you might expect (Worden 1983). This, you find, is called 'complicated grief' or 'complicated mourning'. There is some research which suggests that complicated grief is not a social disorder but one characterised by negative thoughts about one's self. In this study:

> The data revealed a profile of processing in CG [complicated grief] characterized by significant relationships between CG symptoms or diagnosis and both self-devaluation and negative self-related cognitions about the future. (Golden & Dalgleish 2012)

You find an article written by American scholars published in a respected psychology journal. The paper summarises practice approaches to working with children who have lost a parent and the ideas fit with your theoretical and ethical social work perspective. Reading the following text from the article makes you curious about how Christopher must be feeling given that his father never speaks of his late mother and that he did not participate in the funeral or mourning rituals:

> Parental death is one of the most traumatic events that can occur in childhood ... several reviews of the literature have found that the death of a parent places children at risk for a number of negative outcomes. (Haine *et al.* 2008, p. 113)

The authors of the study outline specific ways to work positively with a bereaved child. These include helping to build the capacity of the child to feel positively about themselves, express emotion and communicate with their caregiver, and reducing stressors for the child (Haine *et al.* 2008, pp. 115–119). The same article also highlights some important factors which have been found in research to affect children who are grieving. These include (Haine *et al.* 2008, pp. 120–121):

- The child's developmental stage
- The child's gender
- The cause of death
- How long it's been since the death
- The cultural background of the family and child

This gives you a lot of material which will help to shape your work with Christopher. You plan to meet with him and discuss working together and you will 'check in' with the notes you have made about the research into children and grief. Although the research has been very helpful in terms of summarising studies into grieving children and the outcomes, you do not allow the research to let you leap to any conclusions about what is going on for Christopher. Rather, using a 'client-centred' approach (Rogers 1951), you wish to see how he is experiencing the problem and what he would like to happen. Although the research cannot speak for Christopher, he may be interested in some of the findings: this will be evaluated as the work with him progresses.

HOW WAS RESEARCH USED?

In this case study in which we considered the Oscar family, we looked at how research could be applied to the situation and to our practice. The ways in which research can be applied to social work can be summarised as follows:

- To inform about new terms, movements and phenomena
- To highlight shared problems and possible solutions
- To uncover more questions which help you and the client understand the problem more fully
- To uncover any hidden risks
- To frame practice; this is also referred to as 'evidence-based practice' or 'research-based practice'

How research is applied

The push for social work to be more 'evidence based' is part of a broader shift in which professions are increasingly asked to justify particular responses to their clients. Medical doctors use the evidence from research trials to pick the best medication for their clients. This is an example of the ways in which research *informs intervention*. However, the ways in which clinical trials have been reported on have come under scrutiny (Goldacre 2012). In the social sciences, however, often research does not claim to be generalisable. Research reporting on the positive evaluation of a group for young people who are at risk of homelessness may inform another social worker's work but the process is more than the logical application of 'what works' to a problem. This means that social workers must ask questions of the research they encounter and assess its suitability to the context in which they are interested in it. As we have seen in this chapter, there are many kinds of research approaches and without knowledge about such approaches, critical appraisal of research findings becomes impossible. Here are some suggestions about questions to ask when reading a research report or journal article or book which reports on research:

Research questions to find are relevant

- Where did the research take place? Is it applicable to your context?
- Who undertook the research? What is the professional world-view of the researchers? Are they biologists or social workers? Is it a multidisciplinary team?
- Who published the research? Is the journal well-respected? Does the publisher review book proposals or do they publish them without review?
- Who was involved in the research? How many people?
- Do you understand how the researchers came to the findings? Are you convinced of the arguments being made in the piece?
- Do the authors cite other research? Are any of these references worth looking at? Are there any studies which have counter findings to this one?

There are many, many questions which can be asked when evaluating research. Fortunately, students of social work develop a critical eye for written material during their university studies: essays and the like enable students to develop these skills. It is crucial that these skills continue to be applied post qualification.

HOW TO FIND INFORMATION

In the university setting students are often taught how to use the library's databases. This is the most important skill to master early on in one's social work academic career. Students who are unable to access key pieces of research can struggle to make clearly supported arguments in their written work.

In this chapter there have been some references to 'peer reviewed journals'. Students are sometimes confused about what this means. Generally speaking, journals only agree to publish articles once others have read and critically evaluated them. Researchers, academics or practitioners who write an article—for example about some research into older people and intimate relationships—and would like this published submit it to a journal of their choice. The journal then sends the article to experts in the field. In our example, they will be experts in the field of older people and intimacy. These are the 'peers' who review the article (also known as referees). They read the article, which has been anonymised so they do not know who has written it, and decide if they think it should be published.

There are usually recommendations to do one of the following: reject the article as it is not suitable; accept the article provided the author(s) make major revisions to the paper; accept the article provided minor revisions are made; or accept the article for publication. Generally speaking, it is more likely that there will be changes required or a rejection than a straight-out acceptance. If the paper requires changes, the reviewers will outline what they think are the problems with the paper. When the authors have made the changes (either minor or major depending on what has been suggested), it is likely to go back to the referees for another round of reviews. Journals differ in how many people review but it is usually around three. Because of the 'peer review' process, authors must make sure their arguments are sound and supported by research or theory, and that they have structured the paper appropriately. Peer reviewed papers, having gone through this process, are therefore more respected than other forms of publication such as blogs, self-published material and other non-peer reviewed outputs.

Students who move from the university setting to the organisational setting can find it difficult to find information once their university library membership has expired. Some organisations have their own libraries which may have access to databases and journals and this can be an excellent resource for staff. There are online journals which do not require institutional or individual membership for access: the trick is to ensure that the material is peer reviewed. If it is not peer reviewed, this does not mean the contents are of no use, but that claims about research have not been through the peer review process.

As technology enables quick searching, it can be tempting to use a popular search engine to search for research. Although there are some gateways which contain scholarly articles, social work students and social workers need to be careful that the material they are accessing has been through peer review and that it is up to date. Other sources which contain information which might assist in social work practice can come from non-government organisations and government organisations. If accessing material, it is important to understand who the author is and how they are able to make the claims they make. Similarly, newspaper articles can be based upon opinion and public perception: if reading a newspaper report about new research, try to access the original research to assess for yourself.

CHAPTER SUMMARY

This chapter has introduced some of the key ideas in social research. Developing your own research mindedness is an important skill, particularly since increasingly social workers are undertaking their own research in organisational settings. We have begun to explore some of the key methods used in research such as interviews, focus groups and questionnaires and we have examined objectivism and constructionism as epistemological influences on research design, methodology and analysis (Crotty 2007). Throughout the chapter we have seen how important it is to be clear about methodology and reasons for making decisions about the design of research. The application of social work values and ethics was argued to be relevant to research decisions. We have also considered how to use research in social work. The critical application of research must occur in the context of our work with others: it is not a separate process. We have outlined the specific ways that research can assist in our work with others through the consideration of a case study. We now move on to Chapter 8 where the key ideas of the book are highlighted and the future social work self is explored.

FURTHER READING

ALSTON, M. & BOWLES, W. (1998) *Research for Social Workers: An Introduction to Methods*. Abingdon: Routledge.

BLANKSBY, P. E. & BARBER, J. G. (2005) *SPSS for Social Workers: An Introductory Workbook*. Boston: Pearson.

CROTTY, M. (2007) *The Foundations of Social Research: Meaning and Perspective in the Research Process*. London: Sage Publications.

D'CRUZ, H. & JONES, M. (2004) *Social Work Research: Ethical and Political Contexts*. London: Sage Publications.

DODD, S-J. & EPSTEIN, I. (2012) *Practice-based Research in Social Work: A Guide for Reluctant Researchers*. Abingdon: Routledge.

DYSON, S. & BROWN, B. (2006) *Social Theory and Applied Health Research*. Berkshire: Open University Press.

HENN, M., WEINSTEIN, M. & FOARD, N. (2009) *A Critical Introduction to Social Research*, 2nd edn. London: Sage Publications.

LETHERBY, G. (2003) *Feminist Research in Theory and Practice*. Buckingham: Open University Press.

LIAMPUTTONG, P. & EZZY, D. (2006) *Qualitative Research Methods*. South Melbourne: Oxford University Press.

MCLAUGHLIN, H. (2012) *Understanding Social Work Research*, 2nd edn. London: Sage Publications.

SARANTAKOS, S. (2005) *Social Research*, 4th edn. Basingstoke: Palgrave Macmillan.

SILVERMAN, D. (ed.) (2011) *Qualitative Research*, 3rd edn. London: Sage Publications.

WHITTAKER, A. (2012) *Research Skills for Social Work*, 2nd edn. Exeter: Learning Matters.

8

'Doing' Social Work: Constituting the Professional Self

This chapter:

- Summarises the key theoretical ideas in this book

- Articulates the purpose of the reflexive exercises

- Considers how learning continues post qualification

- Offers a summary of the chapters

- Outlines suggestions for the future about how to be a social worker

Reflexive thinker → social work self

Socialisation of childhood ⟶ social skills
⟶ social rules
(learning B)
aquisition)

learning through interaction

Empathising & social relationships

Break routine through supervision &
reflexive self

learning how to be a social work
requires engagement → only then
do you develop

interdisciplinary working

This book has examined the key knowledge required in social work education. We have explored this knowledge through various forms of learning. From reflexive thinking to active engagement with scenarios, case studies and other targeted activities, material relevant to social work has been presented to help you engage with your social work self. This book has also, hopefully, encouraged the reader to think about their emerging social work identity in a new way and to make the connection between new forms of relating and existing skills, knowledge and experiences.

In Chapter 1 the process of socialisation was examined by looking at the importance of childhood in the acquisition of social skills and learning about social rules. Similarly, social work students enter a period of rapid knowledge acquisition when they enter university and begin to engage with the vast array of materials which help them to *become* social workers.

Research shows that learning in contemporary life can occur through varying, seemingly unrelated contexts (West *et al.* 2011). Becoming a social worker occurs through the reflexive intersection of biography (one's own personal life history and experiences), scholarly ideas, traditional learning materials and imagination: none of which are possible to engage in without human interaction (Mead 1934). In the same way that childhood learning or socialisation occurs through interaction with others in games and play, so too can adult learning (West *et al.* 2011) about social work.

Therefore the activities contained within this book have been designed to:

- Help you engage creatively with the purpose of deeper learning
- Prompt reflexive engagement with your professional self
- Help you identify the social work theories, ethics and values which 'fit' for you
- Re-iterate, mirror and begin to challenge some of the key ideas encountered through traditional learning materials

The subjects brought together in this book will make sense to each social work student in differing ways at differing times. For example, the theories used in interaction with a client in a particular situation will differ to those which underpin practice in another setting or with another client or client group. Figure 8.1 shows one way for you to think about how the material contained within this book is brought together.

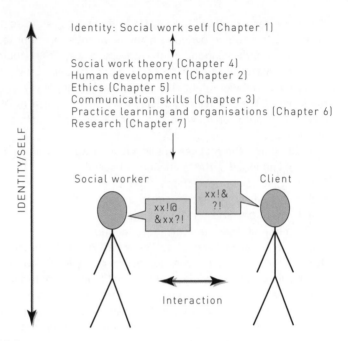

IDENTITY/SELF

Identity: Social work self (Chapter 1)

Social work theory (Chapter 4)
Human development (Chapter 2)
Ethics (Chapter 5)
Communication skills (Chapter 3)
Practice learning and organisations (Chapter 6)
Research (Chapter 7)

Social worker   Client

xx!&
?!

xx!@
&xx?!

Interaction

FIGURE 8.1 Using knowledge in social work practice

Think about how the information and knowledge contained in this text can be conceptualised and draw a map of this. You could use stick figures in the same way as in Figure 8.1 or you could come up with a different sort of diagram.

WHAT HAPPENS ONCE I'M A SOCIAL WORKER?

As we have seen in Chapter 1, socialisation is central to learning about empathising with others and understanding relationships in social life (Mead 1934). For the student of social work, the same kind of socialisation occurs. This socialisation process involves understanding the ways in which social workers interact with others, what theories they use and which values and ethical ideas are associated with the profession. Once students finish their course, this process of learning should not end, even though it can *feel* that it has.

Post qualification, social workers can often feel that they are, in fact, not ready to be social workers. Since social work students are engaging in a socialisation process during their studies, once the conditions for learning are removed, this feeling of 'not being ready' is understandable. Some social workers who have been working for some time insist that they do not 'use theory'. What happens once social workers qualify?

To understand, we must return to our traffic metaphor from the beginning of the book. In the same way that people can forget the specifics of a journey—'Did I cross that road? Was the light back there green or red? Which way did I travel to get here?'—so too does behaviour become routinized (Mead 1934). Similarly, social workers can wonder 'What did I say that really helped that client?', 'Did I let that client have enough "air time" in the group setting?', 'Did that session go well?' In social work, the way to periodically break routinization is through supervision and reflexive practice. Students learn the skills to reflexively engage with their learning and these are further developed through the placement experience and professional practice. Writing reflections, case studies, critical incidents, process recordings and more enable students to fully engage with their emerging professional selves.

While social work students interact in their practice learning they are trying out their professional identities—relating to clients, building professional relationships with colleagues and external organisations.— All of these social interactions help to reinforce student identities as student social workers. Once qualified, social workers will likely abandon the written requirements associated with university work. However, they may write reflections, present at conferences, engage in research for their organisation and review their practice with the help of clients. All of these involve a level of reflexivity and an external prompt for doing so. Supervision provides a space where some reflexive engagement with the work can take place and it is crucial for social workers to engage in this thinking. Organisational limitations can affect the frequency of supervision so developing one's own tools for reflection can be a useful strategy for maintaining the social work self. We will now return to a reflective activity which considers your broader view about social work.

At the very beginning of this book you were asked to reflect upon your beliefs about social work. How have these changed throughout your reading and practice experiences? Take some time now to complete Exercise 8.1.

EXERCISE 8.1

Put the following statements in order from most important (1) to least important (10).

Social workers ... need to change the world
Social workers ... need to work hard
Social workers ... are always on duty
Social workers ... should make people do things
Social workers ... are like the police
Social workers ... help people to change
Social workers ... work with communities
Social workers ... should be able to work anywhere in the world
Social workers ... need career goals
Social workers ... should be caring

You may find that the statements in Exercise 8.1 are no longer enough for you to articulate what social work means to you. Hopefully this is because you now see social work as a central part of your self or who you are. Your professional self will continue to change and respond to the shifts in your external environment and profession. Monitoring this can occur through increased opportunities for reflexive engagement with practice, as we discussed in Chapter 6.

This book has aimed to teach the reader how to understand their professional social work identity. This has meant not only learning about social work itself. How to *be* a social worker means understanding that the self is made through its relationships with others. Learning how to be a social worker requires engagement with:

• Formal knowledge through texts, readings, research and other reports
• Engagement in activities which assist in better understanding this knowledge
• Experimentation with social work skills such as communication
• Experimentation with practice as a social work student on placement working with clients (individuals, groups, communities, globally)
• One's self. This includes reflexive engagement with one's biography and the socio-cultural setting within which the self is constituted
• A political lens which enables power and inequality to be identified at interpersonal, local, national and global levels
• Other students, academic staff and practice teachers, colleagues

Crucially, it is only through the awareness of the interactionist nature of self production that we can consciously fashion a social work self. This is a process that must continue throughout our careers. The ways in which we engage in this process shape the local, national and even international social work identities. In the same way that our social work selves are constantly developing and changing, so too is our profession. Therefore the professional self *you* constitute becomes part of the future generation of social workers who are also constitutive of social work itself.

WORKING WITH OTHERS

Throughout this book we have examined some of the possibilities, limitations and positives to working with other professions. Interdisciplinary working can help to highlight what social work brings to the work. There is a long-held belief that social workers are not very good at articulating who they are. This may be because social work, since its inception, has searched for an ontology: the elusive, clearly articulated set of values, beliefs, theory base and skills has been present since social work began (Gibelman 1999, p. 299).

This book has focused on the social work self and in reading it and considering your own social work self, you take this knowledge with you into your work with others. Working with other groups can help to promote our individual and shared identity as social workers because, as we have seen throughout this book, interaction and relationships with others is central to self-making. George Herbert Mead says:

> A self is a composite or interaction of ... two parts of our natures—the fundamental impulses which make us cooperating neighbors [sic] and friends, lovers and parents and children, and rivals, competitors, and enemies; on the other side the evocation of this self which we achieve when we address ourselves in the language which is the common speech of those about us. We talk to ourselves, ask ourselves what we will do under certain conditions, criticize and approve of our own suggestions and ideas, and in taking the organized attitudes of those engaged in common undertakings we direct our own impulses. (Mead 1925 [2011], p. 316)

The power of language and communication help to promote—or even denigrate—the ways in which social workers view their profession. Our sense of self as a profession is projected upon those with whom we work and other professional groups. The ways in which we make the connection between who we are and what we do need to go beyond reflexivity (Reupert 2009, p. 775). It is a useful (and emancipatory!) exercise to try to move beyond our historical difficulties and 'have a go' at articulating in just one sentence what you think is social work.

SOCIAL WORK IS............

In thinking about the question: 'what is social work?' you may have reflected upon all that you have learned in your studies so far as well as the opportunities available through employment. A definition of social work can be found in Chapter 1 as well as in the Glossary at the end of this book. Each definition, including your own, is equally relevant. We bring our own meanings to the work and interpret our theory and ethical foundation in slightly differing ways: this promotes social work as a dynamic and ever changing profession. We now move on to think more about the key issues which have an impact on our social work selves and the ways in which we conceptualise the social work profession.

PERIODISATION AND SOCIAL WORK

Hopefully this book has highlighted the importance of viewing social work and the social work self through a sociological lens. Such a perspective highlights the ways in which various forces coincide to create a particular reality. What social work means today is not what social work meant 30 years ago. National and international contexts and events which occur serve to continuously shape and help to define what social work means. In the same way as our relationships with others shape who we are as a social worker, so too do these broader contexts have an impact on the profession as a whole.

In Chapter 1 we explored the historical context within which this text has been written. Some of the themes that occupy social work scholarship, practice and research are to do with risk; the role of the state; the shifting social and geographical landscape; global issues; ethical debates about the role of social work, and increased complexity to name but a few. Yet why are these things of concern to us?

As we have noted, late modernity—or contemporary life—has brought with it new challenges. The continuing improvement of technology and the speed with which it brings new products and services has had a massive impact on our lives. As little as a few generations ago, communicative technologies were very different to those used today. Email, the internet and mobile telephones have all had an impact on the ways we communicate. Such new technologies have changed the social landscape because they have led to an increase in the speed at which exchanges occur between cultural settings (for example, see Bauman 1998, 2000; Beck *et al.* 1994; Giddens 1991; Lash 1994b; Urry 2000). No longer constrained by different time zones, people are able to communicate with others around the clock: this has been argued to have an emotional and social cost (Elliott & Lemert 2006).

Additionally, increasingly people in wealthier nations have been able to travel internationally. This increase in mobility has been marked in recent years. The greater availability of affordable travel has led to a significant rise in global movements, and has earned this new social world the description 'borderless' (Urry 2000). Yet travellers do not disembed from their lived experiences once they are away from their homeplace, 'unmarked by the traces of class, gender, ethnicity, sexuality and geography' (Cresswell 1997, p. 377). The ability to travel can, on the one hand, be seen as liberating. Yet it is important to consider that increased mobility is more available to some people than to others. Additionally, people's lived experiences of the broader categories of class, gender, culture, sexual identity and geography do not disappear with travel.

As we discussed in Chapter 1, the late modern life is said to be detraditionalised. Our move away from traditional roles can be seen in the new ways we relate to one another and live out our intimate—and subsequently, family— relationships (Bauman 2003). No longer is social life regulated through tradition. This, coupled with the increased travel and global dimension which is evident in day-to-day life, has been argued to have reduced traditional boundaries. Therefore it is the very fabric of our lives which has been transformed. In this way, life is unstable. It is 'fluid' or 'liquid' (Bauman 1998, 2000) and unable to take a shape or form for very long. The 'scapes and flows' that characterise new 'mobile' lives (Urry 2000, p. 13) are in constant ebb and flow. In this scheme, ' "everyday life" become[s] less clear cut' (du Gay 1993, p. 583).

Late modernity is important to consider in social work (Ferguson & Powell 2002). Yet what does this mean for social work and everyday social work practice? What impacts do increased communication, changing relationships and familial patterns and our new 'mobile' lives (Urry 2000, p. 13) have on social work? What relevance do these theories have to our work? The answers to these questions lie in how social work makes sense of the current historical period: it must both engage in debates about complexity, risk, global and environmental concerns, technology and economic shifts while at the same time being grounded by what social work is good at—fighting against inequality.

In social work we must continue to value the importance of everyday social life and understand the patterns in which our social and cultural environments shape the day-to-day level of experience. As Heaphy (2007, p. 4) notes:

> The reconstructivist theory of reflexive modernity proposed by Giddens and Beck, for example, has argued the emergence of new universalities and commonalities in global and individualized experience where there are no 'others'. This argument may be (relatively) convincing when it is focused on the abstract theoretical working out of the 'reflexivity' of modernity, but it fails to be convincing when the theory is brought down to earth and compared to other arguments about how otherness and difference are centrally important—locally and on a global scale—to shaping personal and day-to-day experience, and to strategies of power.

This means that in social work we need to engage in new movements and theories about the world around us (Dominelli 2010) and our relationships with others; we must seek to recognise that this concern fits within a particular historical point in time and therefore a critical lens helps us understand the reasons for these concerns, and finally, we must continue to address the causes of inequality and injustice in our work.

The increased use of technologies has enabled greater communication between social workers. The desire to come together as a profession and address the issue of inequality through a 'global' means has been expressed through a manifesto called 'The Global Agenda for Social Work'.

> As social workers, educators and social development practitioners, we witness the daily realities of personal, social and community challenges. We believe that now is our time to work together, at all levels, for change, for social justice, and for the universal implementation of human rights, building on the wealth of social initiatives and social movements. We, the International Federation of Social Workers (IFSW), the International Association of Schools of Social Work (IASSW), and the International Council on Social Welfare (ICSW), recognise that the past and present political, economic, cultural and social orders, shaped in specific contexts, have unequal consequences for global, national and local communities and have negative impacts on people. (www.globalsocialagenda.org)

This movement is an example of the ways in which social work is responding to the new 'liquid' environment. Following are the key areas to which this group is committing. It is useful to read through these to see how social work is responding to issues such as economic change, environmental concern, conflict and war, extreme weather events and changing social relationships and landscapes.

- The full range of human rights are available to only a minority of the world's population: unjust and poorly regulated economic systems, driven by unaccountable market forces, together with non-compliance with international standards for labour conditions and a lack of corporate social responsibility, have damaged the health and well-being of peoples and communities, causing poverty and growing inequality.
- Cultural diversity and the right to self-expression facilitate a more satisfactory intellectual, emotional, moral and spiritual existence, but these rights are in danger due to aspects of globalisation which standardise and marginalise peoples, with especially damaging consequences for indigenous and first nation peoples.
- People live in communities and thrive in the context of supportive relationships, which are being eroded by dominant economic, political and social forces; people's health and well-being suffer as a result of inequalities and unsustainable environments related to climate change, pollutants, war, natural disasters and violence to which there are inadequate international responses. Consequently, we feel compelled to advocate for a new world order which makes a reality of respect for human rights and dignity and a different structure of human relationships.

Therefore:

We commit ourselves to supporting, influencing and enabling structures and systems that positively address the root causes of oppression and inequality. We commit ourselves wholeheartedly and urgently to work together, with people who use services and with others who share our objectives and aspirations, to create a more socially-just and fair world that we will be proud to leave to future generations. We will prioritise our endeavours to these ends. (www.global socialagenda.org)

These kinds of movements demonstrate the creative ways in which the profession is moving forward and facing the challenges which present themselves, whilst remaining committed to a clearly articulated value and theory base. The commitment to social justice, eradicating systems and structures which continue to oppress others and working with and on behalf of vulnerable people is clearly articulated. However, importantly, community, social connectedness, health and well-being and self-expression are also stated as being important aspects of social life which enable individuals, families, groups and communities to thrive. Social work has a role to play not only in addressing inequality but also equally in highlighting and working to promote well-being.

Throughout this book we have seen that the answer to 'how to be a social worker' is to establish and develop one's social work self. The ways we engage in this process shape the local, national and even international social work identity. There is a school of thought within the literature about couples which argues that the ability to thrive in an intimate relationship requires people to 'hold on' to their own identities while committed to the 'couple' identity (Schnarch 1997). In this literature, 'differentiation involves balancing two basic life forces: the drive for individuality and the drive for togetherness' (Schnarch 1997, p. 55). Similarly, the ability to work with other professional groups requires social workers to 'hold on' to their own identity. The individual social work self—your individual social work self—realises the 'drive for individuality' and the collective identity of social work in its interprofessional context realises the 'drive for togetherness'. As we have seen throughout this book, this is no easy task, but one which is fraught with dilemmas, differences and points of division, as well as similarities and points of unity. The ways in which we work with other professions will continue to change. This means the trust we put in our own profession and our own practice must be present in our everyday interactions. Ultimately, it is the people we work with to whom we are committed and therefore any trust we put in our own practice and profession must be earned.

Additionally, being able to articulate the values and theories which help to propel the social work self into its role with clients helps in firming up the social work identity. In this book, the ways in which the social work self is constituted have been explored. Specifically, the following are examples of activities which help in the process of professional self-making:

- Use knowledge about one's self. This includes reflexive engagement with one's biography and the socio-cultural setting within which the self is constituted
- Acquire formal knowledge through texts, readings, research and other reports
- Engage in activities which assist in better understanding this knowledge
- Experiment in the classroom with social work skills such as communication
- Experiment (under supervision) with practice as a social work student on placement working with clients (individuals, groups, communities, globally)
- Develop one's political lens which enables power and inequality to be identified at interpersonal, local, national and global levels
- Engage with other students, academic staff and practice teachers, colleagues

How to be a Social Worker contains the idea that social workers must regain confidence in selfhood. This applies both to understanding the importance of self—how it is constituted, socially situated and contextual—as well as being able to answer the question: 'what is social work?' In answering this question, our ethical, value and theoretical foundations are revealed. Social work students beginning their studies and entry into the profession, equipped with this self-knowledge, are perfectly positioned to continue to positively shape the profession of social work and the important role it has in society.

The centrality of interaction to self-production in social work has been of key concern in this book. In other words, becoming a social worker has been argued to occur through the intersection of biography, scholarly ideas, imagination and reflexivity: none of these are possible to engage in without human interaction (Mead 1934). It is therefore imperative that social workers retain their social focus. Professional development, interaction with other professions and reflexive engagement with the self and social work itself: all of these are required in order to continue good practice and development in our field.

In this book we have seen that awareness of the interactionist nature of self is required so that we understand both who we are as a social worker and also who we are as a profession. Individuals do not come to social work with a 'clear slate'. Rather, social work students bring their own identities to their learning and to their profession. As a reminder, here is a final quote from C. Wright Mills who sums up this need to incorporate one's self into one's work:

> What this means is that you must learn to use your life experience in your intellectual work: continually to examine and interpret it. In this sense craftsmanship is the centre of yourself and you are personally involved in every intellectual product upon which you may work. (Mills 1959, p. 196)

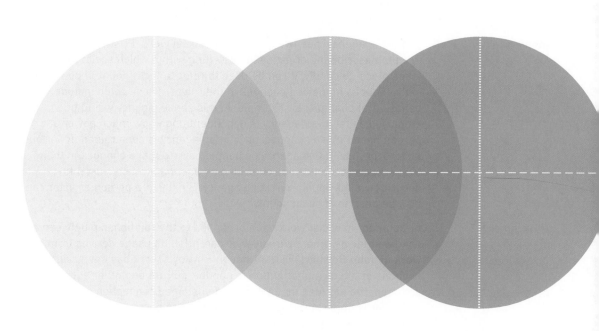

Glossary of Key Terms

Actor	In sociology, the term 'actor' refers to individuals in society. The term is also used in social work to denote an individual.
Agency	The term 'agency' has two meanings in social work. Firstly, it can be used to describe the organisational setting within which social work takes place. Secondly, it can be used to refer to the amount of power an individual has in making changes in their lives. These could include behavioural changes, for example. In this sense, agency would be employed as follows: 'agency is dependent upon how much power a person has to make changes' or 'human agency is constrained by various factors' or 'how much agency do people have to make changes in their lives?' Social action can be classified as *agential*, which is used to describe an individual exercising agency. Similarly, a person or actor can also be described as an agent.
Attachment	Attachment in social work usually applies to the relationship between a child and their primary caregiver or parent(s). Its usage derives from the work of John Bowlby (1951). Although Bowlby's work has been criticised because of the lack of attention to gender, culture and other aspects of selfhood, the key idea that a deep and sustained connection with a caregiver is important to early life continues to persist. Giddens' (1991) concept of ontological security, for example, argues that intimate relationships formed in adulthood are affected by the level of personal security which is derived from early social interactions in the child–caregiver dyad. Theories such as this make the leap between early experiences in childhood and adult patterns of behaviour and interaction. Social workers need to be careful when applying theories about attachment. Having a nuanced understanding of the historical context within which Bowlby's empirical work and subsequent theorising was carried out helps to better understand how to apply notions of attachment to the needs of children.
Client	The term 'client' is used to depict the person or persons receiving a service from a social worker. There are various terms which mean the same as client, and these come in and out of fashion in social work. They include consumer, service user and customer. In some settings, particular language is used to describe a person receiving a service from a social worker. For example, a client of a hospital service might be referred to as a patient since this is the term used in health and allied professions.
Culture	Culture is notoriously difficult to define, and there are many social work and social science texts which discuss culture in great depth. It is important to recognise that everyone in society has a culture. Culture refers to historically significant, shared beliefs, patterns of behaviour, knowledge, customs, rituals and values. Culture is an important part of the self and is embedded in actions and social interactions. Because culture is so embedded in social interaction it can be difficult to discern and name, particularly for the dominant group in society. Recent

scholarship about culture therefore focuses on 'whiteness studies', which seek to uncover the hidden aspects of culture that are interlinked in existing systems and create inequality based on culture and race.

Detraditionalisation

Detraditionalisation (Giddens 1991) refers to the gradual removal of tradition which results in people's roles, which were traditionally prescribed, being upturned. An example of detraditionalisation is the shift in gender roles in the family. Whereas a few generations ago it was common for women in western cultures to be at home raising children and participating in domestic chores, women's roles in relationships have now changed. For example, the increase in more women being in paid work has meant that the traditional role of 'housewife' has decreased. Detraditionalisation is a theory and opponents to this theory argue that society has always evolved and shifted and tradition has always been complex so this is not a new issue (Alexander 1989).

Epistemology

Broadly speaking, epistemology can be described as a world-view. Epistemology is a way of describing the attitude to knowledge which relates to the world around us. For example, imagine I took the view that there are universal truths and therefore believe that some things are true regardless of the context or situation or the people involved. This attitude might be summed up by saying that I had an *objectivist* epistemology. On the other hand, imagine I took the view that there are no universal truths and that people construct their own meanings in individual ways. Although these meanings may share characteristics, we all see the world in slightly—or markedly—differing ways. This way of viewing the world might be described as a *constructionist* epistemology.

Ethics

A consideration of ethics means thinking about how we *should* act towards other people (Rhodes 1986, p. 21). Ethics entails thinking about what we think should occur in our behaviours towards other people. In social work, professional ethics are enshrined in our theoretical frameworks and outlined in professional codes of conduct and codes of ethics. There are many traditions which contribute to scholarship on ethics: these can come from philosophy or applied disciplines such as medical sciences and allied health.

Identity

Generally speaking, 'identity' is a term used to describe who we are. The term came to prominence in the 1990s, and is used in varying disciplines (Jenkins 2000, p. 8). In contrast to the word 'self', the term identity is usually associated with a psychoanalytic or psychological tradition. Identity, for example, can be used to describe one's 'personality'.

Intimate relationship, Sexuality, Sexual identity

Intimate relationships are varied but include marriages, couples living together or living apart and de facto relationships. Intimate relationships can be single sex relationships or opposite sex relationships. Couples can be committed to one another (monogamous) or not committed (non-monogamous). Sexuality refers to a range of emotions and behaviours and desires whereas sexual identity refers to particular categories which define attractions and behaviours and desires. Some sexual identities are bisexual, lesbian, gay, transgender, intersex, fluid and heterosexual.

Late modernity

Various disciplines interested in the study of social life employ periodisation which divides particular epochs into named, historically recognisable points in time. The names given to each of these periods signify particular forms of expression and resonate with a large audience. For example, the term 'postmodern' can be used to describe various things, from architecture to the design of a cereal box. The term 'late modernity' is used in this book to denote the current historical period. The term has been chosen because of its recognition within sociological literature about identity, but can just as easily be substituted with 'contemporary life' or something similar.

Norm

A norm is an unspoken social 'rule'. Norms govern the ways in which we behave towards others.

Reflexivity and reflexiveness

Reflexivity is a well-established concept in social work. Reflexivity relates to the idea that we reflect upon our social work practice to get better and better (see Schon 1983, for example). In social work, reflection is the act of thinking about an event whereas reflexivity relates to the change in action as a direct result of prior reflection. For example, a social worker may begin to facilitate a group for adult survivors of child sexual abuse. In the group the social worker is using art therapies for the first time. The session does not go well. In supervision, the social worker talks about her disappointment with using art. In thinking back and *reflecting* upon what went well and what did not go well, the social worker identifies a new approach to using the art which she plans to try in the next group. The social worker has therefore *reflected* upon her work. In a subsequent group, the social worker tries a new approach as a direct result of her supervision session in which she analysed her previous work. She changes the way she does things in the group and the way she uses art with the group members because of these insights. The social worker has therefore become *reflexive* since her present behaviour has been shaped by her *reflection*. Reflexivity involves three interrelated processes (Bogo & Vayda 1987; Schon 1983). Firstly, we think about, or reflect upon, something specific. Secondly, we critically evaluate that activity. Thirdly, we change future relations of actions based on a conscious decision to change the particular activity (Bogo & Vayda 1987). Although there is a clear difference between reflection and reflexivity in social work, there are complexities involved in the distinction between the terms in the work of George Herbert Mead and social theorists such as Anthony Giddens. Mead argues that 'reflexiveness' means being an 'other' to oneself, only through continual interaction with social processes. Mead says that 'reflexiveness', or what can be called 'reflexivity', is not merely a tool for self-fashioning but is required for social functioning (Jackson 2007, p. 8). What people think of as their 'minds' are, in fact, firmly locatable outside their selves (in contrast to psychoanalytic notions of subjectivity which see identity as related to an 'inner' world of individual thoughts and reflections): minds 'arise' only through social interactions. Mead (1934, p. 134) argues that 'reflexiveness' then, is the essential condition, within the social process, for the development of mind'. Giddens argues that in contemporary society people treat themselves as 'a project' which requires constant evaluation and improvement: this is said to occur through reflexivity (Giddens 1991). Whilst Giddens' 'extended reflexivity' (Adams 2003) means that reflexivity is linked as a product of late modernity, Mead argues that what he calls 'reflexiveness' is merely a feature of social relations. Both Giddens and Mead highlight the importance of the social setting from the onset of human life (Adams 2003, p. 232). Mead's conception of the self is neither the decentred postmodern depiction nor the psychoanalytic subject (Jackson 2007, p. 7): reflexiveness is a part of an overall process in which social interaction produces the self (Mead 1925 [2011]). Whilst it is important not to confuse or conflate these two concepts of reflexiveness and reflexivity, it can be noted for the purpose of providing a simple definition of what is meant by these in relation to sociology that they both suggest varying degrees of awareness of one's self and its relationship to the surrounding world. In social work the terms are more easily separated and distinct from one another.

Scripting

Just as a film or play is scripted, individuals may engage in acts of spontaneity akin to dramatic improvisation, but they are limited by the choices available to them. Thus, although actors can choose their scripts to some extent, their choices do not fall outside a predetermined set of actions and interactions. Scripting theory can help to make sense of the degree to which actors have agency. See also *Agency* and *Structure*

Self

Self is a way to describe who a person is. This can encompass one's attitudes, behaviours and biography and the term suggests that each person has uniqueness. Whereas 'identity can imply a fixity about who one is' (Jackson & Scott 2010a, p. 122), the term 'self' is less fixed. Thus, the use of the term self is associated with particular sociological theories such as those advanced in symbolic interactionism. The term self is primarily employed throughout this book because of its association with Meadian traditions (Mead 1934; Da Silva 2011) in which the changeable and dynamic process of sociality is central to self-making. Mead's notion of the self implies a changeable form of identity (Jackson & Scott 2010a, p. 123).

Self-making

The 'construction of the self' refers to the processes that make up or constitute the self. Throughout this book I use the term 'self-making' (Skeggs 2004) to mean this ongoing process of the constitution or 'making' of the self. These ongoing social processes are made up of various types of social interactions—from discussions with colleagues and communications with others through both verbal and non-verbal means to the intimate communications and actions between lovers.

Service user	See *Client*
Social constructionism	Social constructionism is the idea that individuals each construct the world around themselves. In this way, there is no universal 'truth' which is true for everyone.
Social work	There is much debate about what social work is and is not and this has endured throughout its history (Gibelman 1999). Social work is a broad term used to describe the professional grouping of a range of interventions at the following levels: individual, couple, family, group, community, nationally and globally/internationally. Social work is supported by clear theoretical and ethical foundations. Social work is generally conceived as being a profession which seeks to promote positive change. The particular type of work undertaken in social work is varied and depends on the context. Social workers may have skills in counselling or therapy, casework, group work, advocacy, community development, policy analysis and development and/or research.
Sociality	The notion of sociality is what is important in interactionist appreciations of the self. Sociality consists of the processes involved in social interactions. Sociality is theorised by George Herbert Mead (1934) as the process through which the self is constituted.
Socialisation	Socialisation is the process of learning about the rules which govern behaviour in a given society. Socialisation occurs primarily in childhood, but in some areas of life people become socialised in new ways. For example, social work students become socialised in social work during their studies: they learn the norms, ethics and theories which underpin the profession.
Structure	Structure, or social structure, is a concept which refers to identifiable patterns of relating in social life. In speaking about the relationship between social structure and society, Giddens (2005, p. 699) describes social structure as 'like the girders which underpin a building and hold it together'. See also *Agency*

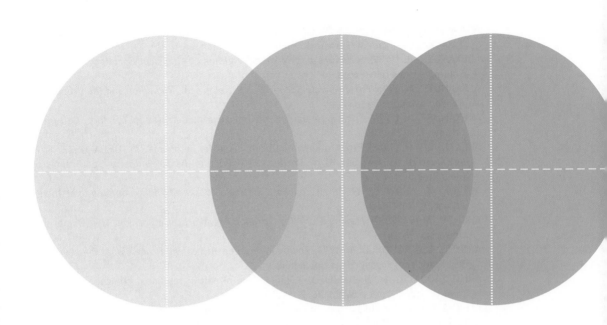

References
and Further
Reading

ADAMS, M. (2003) The reflexive self and culture: A critique. *British Journal of Sociology*, 54, 221–238.

ADAMS, R., DOMINELLI, L. & PAYNE, M. (2005) *Social Work Futures: Crossing Boundaries, Transforming Practice*. New York: Palgrave Macmillan.

ALEXANDER, J. (1989) *Structure and Meaning: Rethinking Classical Sociology*. New York: Columbia University Press.

ALEXANDER, J. (1995) *Fin-de-siecle Social Theory: Relativism, Reduction and the Problem of Reason*. London: Verso.

ALEXANDER, J. (1996) Critical reflections on 'reflexive modernisation'. *Theory, Culture & Society*, 13, 133–138.

ALEXANDER, P. (1988) Prostitution: A difficult issue for feminists. *In:* DELACOSTE, F. & ALEXANDER, P. (eds) *Sex Work: Writings by Women in the Sex Industry*. San Francisco: Cleis Press.

ALSTON, M. & BOWLES, W. (1998) *Research for Social Workers: An Introduction to Methods*. Abingdon: Routledge.

ARCHER, M. S. (2007) *Making Our Way Through the World*. Cambridge, UK: Cambridge University Press.

ARGYRIS, C. & SCHON, D. A. (1974) *Theory in Practice: Increasing Professional Effectiveness*. San Francisco: Jossey-Bass Publishers.

ARND-CADDIGAN, M. & POZZUTO, R. (2008) Use of self in relational clinical social work. *Clinical Social Work Journal*, 36, 235–243.

ATHENS, L. (2005) Mead's lost conception of society. *Symbolic Interaction*, 28, 305–325.

AULL DAVIES, C. (2008) *Reflexive Ethnography: A Guide to Researching Selves and Others*. London: Routledge.

BAILEY, D. & LIYANAGE, L. (2012) The role of the mental health social worker: Political pawns in the reconfiguration of adult health and social care. *British Journal of Social Work*, 42, 1113–1131.

BALGOPAL, P. R. & VASSIL, T. V. (1983) *Groups in Social Work: An Ecological Perspective*. New York and London: Macmillan/Collier Macmillan.

BANDURA, A. (1986) *Social Foundations of Thought and Action: A Social Cognitive Theory*. Englewood Cliffs: Prentice-Hall.

BANKS, S. (2012) *Ethics and Values in Social Work*, 4th edn. Basingstoke: Palgrave Macmillan.

BARKER, R., MILLER, S., PLACE, M. & REYNOLDS, J. (2003) Children with difficulties, parenting training and action research. *International Journal of Child and Family Welfare*, 6, 103–112.

BARNARD, A. M. (2011) The self in social work. *Work Based Learning e-Journal*, 2.

BAUMAN, Z. (1990) *Thinking Sociologically*. Oxford: Blackwell.

BAUMAN, Z. (1993) *Postmodern Ethics*. Oxford: Blackwell.

BAUMAN, Z. (1998) *Globalization: The Human Consequences*. Cambridge, UK: Polity Press.

BAUMAN, Z. (2000) *Liquid Modernity*. Cambridge, UK: Polity Press.

BAUMAN, Z. (2003) *Liquid Love: On the Frailty of Human Bonds*. Cambridge, UK: Polity Press.

BEAUCHAMP, T. L. & CHILDRESS, J. F. (1979) *Principles of Biomedical Ethics*. New York: Oxford University Press.

BEAUCHAMP, T. L. & CHILDRESS, J. F. (1989) *Principles of Biomedical Ethics*, 3rd edn. New York: Oxford University Press.

BECK, U. (1992) *Risk Society*. London: Sage Publications.

BECK, U. (1994) *Reflexive Modernization: Politics, Tradition and Aesthetics in the Modern Social Order*. Cambridge, UK: Polity Press in association with Blackwell Publishers.

BECK, U. & BECK-GERNSHEIM, E. (2001) *Individualization*. London: Sage Publications.

BECK, U. & BECK-GERNSHEIM, E. (2002) *Individualization [electronic resource]: Institutionalized Individualism and its Social and Political Consequences.* London and Thousand Oaks: Sage Publications.

BECK, U., GIDDENS, A. & LASH, S. (1999) *World Risk Society.* Malden, Mass.: Polity Press.

BECKETT, C. (2006) *Essential Theory for Social Work Practice.* London: Sage Publications.

BELLINGER, A. (2010) Talking about (re)generation: Practice learning as a site of renewal for social work. *British Journal of Social Work*, 40, 2450–2466.

BENKO, G. & STROHMAYER, U. (1997) *Space and Social Theory: Interpreting Modernity and Postmodernity.* Oxford, UK and Malden, Mass.: Blackwell Publishers.

BERGER, P. L. (1971) *The Social Construction of Reality: A Treatise in the Sociology of Knowledge.* Harmondsworth: Penguin.

BERGER, P. L. & LUCKMANN, T. (1973) *The Social Construction of Reality: A Treatise in the Sociology of Knowledge.* Middlesex: Penguin Books.

BERK, L. (2010) *Exploring Lifespan Development*, 2nd edn. Boston: Allyn & Bacon.

BHIMJI, F. (2009) Identities and agency in religious spheres: A study of British Muslim women's experience. *Gender, Place & Culture*, 16, 365–380.

BIERNACKI, P. & WALDORF, D. (1981) Snowball sampling. *Sociological Methods and Research*, 10, 141–163.

BLANKSBY, P. E. & BARBER, J. G. (2005) *SPSS for Social Workers: An Introductory Workbook.* Boston: Pearson.

BLIWISE, N. G. (1999) Securing attachment theory's potential. *Feminism and Psychology*, 9, 43–52.

BLOOM, L. (1998) *Under the Sign of Hope: Feminist Methodology and Narrative.* Albany: State University of New York Press.

BOGO, M. & VAYDA, E. (1987) *The Practice of Field Instruction in Social Work.* Toronto: University of Toronto Press.

BONDI, L. & BURMAN, E. (2001) Women and mental health: A feminist review. *Feminist Review*, 68, 6–33.

BOYD, D. A. & BEE, H. L. (2011) *Lifespan Development.* Boston: Pearson.

BOWLBY, J. (1951) *Maternal Care and Mental Health.* New York: Schoken.

BOWLES, W., COLLINGRIDGE, M., CURRY, S. & VALENTINE, B. (2006) *Ethical Practice in Social Work: An Applied Approach.* Crows Nest: Allen & Unwin.

BRONSTEIN, L. R. (2003) A model for interdisciplinary collaboration. *Social Work*, 48, 297–306.

BROWNMILLER, S. (1976) *Against Our Will: Men, Women and Rape.* Harmondsworth: Penguin.

BRUNER, C. (1991) *Ten Questions and Answers to Help Policy Makers Improve Children's Services.* Washington, DC: Education and Human Services Consortium.

BRYMAN, A. (1984) The debate about quantitative and qualitative research: A question or epistemology? *British Journal of Sociology*, 35(1) (March).

BUCHANAN, F. (2008) *Mother and Infant Attachment Theory and Domestic Violence: Crossing the Divide.* Sydney: Australian Domestic and Family Violence Clearinghouse.

BUDGEON, S. & ROSENEIL, S. (2004) Editors' introduction: Beyond the conventional family. *Current Sociology*, 52, 127–134.

BURR, J. (2009) Exploring reflective subjectivity through the construction of the 'ethical other' in interview transcripts. *Sociology*, 43, 323–339.

BUTLER, J. P. (1993) *Bodies that Matter: On the Discursive Limits of "Sex".* New York: Routledge.

BYWATERS, P. (1986) Social work and the medical profession: Arguments against unconditional collaboration. *British Journal of Social Work*, 16, 661–677.

BYWATERS, P. (2009) Tackling inequalities in health: A global challenge for social work. *British Journal of Social Work*, 39, 353–367.

CARMICHAEL, L. (1970a) *Carmichael's Manual of Child Psychology*, 3rd edn. New York: Wiley.

CARMICHAEL, L. (1970b) Piaget's theory. *In:* MUSSEN, P. H. (ed.) *Carmichael's Manual of Child Psychology*, 3rd edn. New York: Wiley.

CARPENTER, J., SCHNEIDER, H., BRANDON, T. & WOOFF, D. (2003) Working in multidisciplinary community mental health teams: The impact on social workers and health professionals of integrated mental health care. *British Journal of Social Work*, 33, 1081–1103.

CARROLL, J. (2007) *The Existential Jesus*. Carlton North, Vic.: Scribe Publications.

CHENOWETH, L. & MCAULIFFE, D. (2005) *The Road to Social Work and Human Service Provision: An Introductory Text*. Southbank: Thomson.

CHISHOLM, D. (2008) Climbing like a girl: An exemplary adventure in feminist phenomenology. *Hypatia*, 23, 9–40.

CLEAK, H. & WILSON, J. (2004) *Making the Most of Field Placement*. Australia, Brazil, Japan, Korea, Mexico, Singapore, Spain, United Kingdom, United States. Sydney: Cengage Learning Australia Pty Ltd.

CLEAK, H., HAWKINS, L. & HESS, L. (2000) Innovative field options. *In:* COOPER, L. & BRIGGS, L. (eds) *Fieldwork in the Human Services*. St Leonards: Allen & Unwin.

CLEAVER, H., NICHOLSON, D., TARR, S. & CLEAVER, D. (2007) *Child Protection, Domestic Violence and Parental Substance Misuse: Family Experiences and Effective Practice*. London and Philadelphia: Kingsley Publishers.

COHEN, E. (1992) Pilgrimage centers: Concentric and excentric. *Annals of Tourism Research*, 19, 33–50.

COHEN, E. D. & COHEN, G. S. (1999) *The Virtuous Therapist: Ethical Practice of Counselling and Psychotherapy*. Belmont: Wadsworth Publishing Company.

COLOMBO, M. (2003) Reflexivity and narratives in action research: A discursive approach. *Forum: Qualitative Social Research*, 4.

COMPTON, B. R. & GALAWAY, B. (1989) *Social Work Processes*, 5th edn. Pacific Grove: Brooks/Cole Publishing Company.

COMPTON, B. R. & GALAWAY, B. (1999) *Social Work Processes*, 6th edn. Belmont: Brooks/Cole Publishing.

COOPER, L. & BRIGGS, L. E. (eds) (2000) *Fieldwork in the Human Services: Theory and Practice for Field Educators, Practice Teachers and Supervisors*. St Leonards: Allen & Unwin.

COULSHED, V. & ORME, J. (2012) *Social Work Practice*, 5th edn. Basingstoke: Palgrave Macmillan.

COURNOYER, B. (2010) *The Social Work Skills Workbook*, 6th edn. Florence: Cengage Learning Inc.

CRESSWELL, T. (1997) Imagining the nomad: Mobility and the post modern perspective. *In:* BENKO, G. & STROHMAYER, U. (eds) *Space and Social Theory: Interpreting Modernity and Postmodernity*. Oxford: Blackwell.

CRISP, B. R. (2010) *Spirituality in Social Work*. Surrey: Ashgate.

CROOK, S. (1998) Minotaurs and other monsters: 'Everyday life' in recent social theory. *Sociology*, 32, 523–540.

CROSSLEY, N. (2001) *The Social Body: Habit, Identity and Desire*. London: Sage Publications.

CROTTY, M. (2007) *The Foundations of Social Research: Meaning and Perspective in the Research Process*. London: Sage Publications.

CUNNINGHAM, J. & CUNNINGHAM, S. (2008) *Sociology and Social Work*. Exeter: Learning Matters Ltd.

CURTIS, L., MORIARTY, J. & NETTEN, A. (2010) The expected working life of a social worker. *British Journal of Social Work*, 40, 1628–1643.

DA SILVA, F. C. (ed.) (2011) *G. H. Mead: A Reader*. London: Routledge.

DAVIES, M. (ed.) (2012) *Social Work with Children and Families*. Basingstoke: Palgrave Macmillan.

D'CRUZ, H. & JONES, M. (2004) *Social Work Research: Ethical and Political Contexts*. London: Sage Publications.

DENSCOMBE, M. (1998) *The Good Research Guide: For Small-scale Social Research Projects*. Buckingham: Open University Press.

DENZIN, N. K. (1978) *Sociological Methods: A Sourcebook*. New York: McGraw Hill.

DEWANE, C. (2006) Use of self: A primer revisited. *Clinical Social Work Journal*, 34, 543–558.

DICKENSON, D., JOHNSON, M. & KATZ, J. S. (eds) (2000) *Death, Dying and Bereavement*, 2nd edn. London, Thousand Oaks, New Delhi: Sage Publications in association with the Open University.

DIXON, J. (2012) Effective strategies for communication? Student views of a communication skills course eleven years on. *British Journal of Social Work*.

DODD, S. J. & JONES, M. (2004) *Practice-based Research in Social Work: A Guide for Reluctant Researchers*. Abingdon: Routledge.

DOEL, M. (2010) *Social Work Placements: A Traveller's Guide*. Abingdon: Routledge.

DOKA, K. J. (ed.) (1989) *Disenfranchised Grief: Recognizing Hidden Sorrow*. Lexington: Lexington Books.

DOKA, K. J. (ed.) (2002) *Disenfranchised Grief: New Directions, Challenges, and Strategies for Practice*. Champaign: Research Press.

DOMINELLI, L. (1989) Betrayal of trust: A feminist analysis of power relationships in incest abuse and its relevance for social work practice. *British Journal of Social Work*, 19, 291–307.

DOMINELLI, L. (2002) *Feminist Social Work: Theory and Practice*. Basingstoke: Palgrave Macmillan.

DOMINELLI, L. (2003) *Anti-oppressive Social Work Theory and Practice*. Basingstoke: Palgrave Macmillan.

DOMINELLI, L. (2004) *Social Work: Theory and Practice for a Changing Profession*. Oxford: Polity Press.

DOMINELLI, L. (2010) *Social Work in a Globalizing World*. Cambridge, UK: Polity Press.

DU GAY, P. (1993) 'Numbers and souls': Retailing and the de-differentiation of economy and culture. *British Journal of Sociology*, 44, 563–587.

DUNK, P. (2007) Everyday sexuality and social work: Locating sexuality in professional practice and education. *Social Work and Society*, 5, 135–142.

DUNK-WEST, P. (2011) Everyday sexuality and identity: De-differentiating the sexual self in social work. *In*: DUNK-WEST, P. & HAFFORD-LETCHFIELD, T. (eds) *Sexual Identities and Sexuality in Social Work: Research and Reflections from Women in the Field*. Surrey: Ashgate.

DUNK-WEST, P. & HAFFORD-LETCHFIELD, T. (eds) (2011) *Sexual Identities and Sexuality in Social Work: Research and Reflections from Women in the Field*. Surrey: Ashgate.

DUNK-WEST, P. & VERITY, F. forthcoming. *Sociological Social Work*. Surrey: Ashgate.

DUTTON, J. E., ROBERTS, L. & MORGANBEDNAR, J. (2010) Pathways for positive identity construction at work: Four types of positive identity and the building of social resources. *Academy of Management Review*, 35, 265–293.

DYSON, S. (2006) *Social Theory and Applied Health Research*. Maidenhead: Open University Press.

EGAN, G. (2006) *Essentials of Skilled Helping, Managing Problems, Developing Opportunities*. Canada: Thomson Wadsworth.

ELLIOTT, A. (1996) *Subject to Ourselves: Social Theory, Psychoanalysis and Postmodernity.* Cambridge, UK: Polity Press.

ELLIOTT, A. (2001) Sexualities: Social theory and the crisis of identity. *In:* RITZER, G. & SMART, B. (eds) *Handbook of Social Theory.* London: Sage Publications.

ELLIOTT, A. (2005) The constitution of the subject. *European Journal of Social Theory*, 8, 25–42.

ELLIOTT, A. & LEMERT, C. (2006) *The New Individualism: The Emotional Costs of Globalization.* Abingdon: Routledge.

ERIKSON, E. H. (1968) *Identity, Youth and Crisis.* New York: W. W. Norton.

EVA, K. W. & REGEHR, G. (2008) "I'll never play professional football" and other fallacies of self-assessment. *Journal of Continuing Education in the Health Professions*, 28, 14–19.

EVANS, S., HILLS, S. & ORME, J. (2012) Doing more for less? Developing sustainable systems of social care in the context of climate change and public spending cuts. *British Journal of Social Work*, 42, 744–764.

EVERITT, A., HARDIKER, P., LITTLEWOOD, J. & MULLENDER, A. (1992) *Applied Research for Better Practice.* Basingstoke: Macmillan.

FERGUSON, H. (2001) Social work, individualization and life politics. *British Journal of Social Work*, 31, 41–55.

FERGUSON, H. (2009) Driven to care: The car, automobility and social work. *Mobilities*, 4, 275–293.

FERGUSON, H. (2011) *Child Protection Practice.* Basingstoke: Palgrave Macmillan.

FERGUSON, H. & POWELL, F. W. (2002) Social work in late-modern Ireland. *In:* PAYNE, M. & SHARDLOW, S. (eds) *Social Work in the British Isles.* London: Jessica Kingsley.

FIELDING, N. (1996) Qualitative Interviewing. *In:* GILBERT, N. (ed.) *Researching Social Life.* London: Sage Publications.

FOOK, J. (1991) Is casework dead? A study of the current curriculum in Australia. *Australian Social Work*, 44, 19–28.

FOOK, J. (1993) *Radical Casework: A Theory of Practice.* St Leonards: Allen & Unwin.

FOOK, J. (1999) Critical reflexivity in education and practice. *In:* PEASE, B. & FOOK, J. (eds) *Transforming Social Work Practice: Postmodern Critical Perspectives.* St Leonards: Allen & Unwin.

FOOK, J. (2012) *Social Work: Critical Theory and Practice*, 2nd edn. London: Sage Publications.

FORTE, J. A. (2004a) Symbolic interactionism and social work: A forgotten legacy, Part 1. *Families in Society*, 85, 391–400.

FORTE, J. A. (2004b) Symbolic interactionism and social work: A forgotten legacy, Part 2. *Families in Society*, 85, 521–530.

FRANZBLAU, S. H. (1999) Historicizing attachment theory: Binding the ties that bind. *Feminism and Psychology*, 9, 22–31.

FREUD, S. (1914) *Psychopathology of Everyday Life.* [S.l.], [s.n.].

FREUD, S. (1949) *An Outline of Psychoanalysis.* New York: W. W. Norton.

FREUD, S. (1965) *Three Essays on the Theory of Sexuality.* [New York], Avon.

FRIEDAN, B. (1965) *The Feminine Mystique.* Harmondsworth: Penguin Books.

FUREDI, F. (2004) *Therapy Culture: Cultivating Vulnerability in an Uncertain Age.* London: Routledge.

GAGNON, J. H. (1999) Sexual conduct: As today's memory serves. *Sexualities*, 2, 115–126.

GAGNON, J. & SIMON, W. (1973) *Sexual Conduct: The Social Sources of Human Sexuality.* Chicago: Aldine.

GAGNON, J. & SIMON, W. (2011) *Sexual Conduct: The Social Sources of Human Sexuality*, 2nd edn, 3rd printing. New Brunswick, USA and London, UK: Aldine Transaction, A Division of Transaction Publishers.

GANZER, C. (2007) The use of self from a relational perspective. *Clinical Social Work Journal*, 35, 117–123.

GARDINER, M. (2004) Everyday utopianism. *Cultural Studies*, 18, 228–254.

GARFINKEL, H. (1984) *Studies in Ethnomethodology*. Cambridge, UK: Polity Press.

GARRETT, P. M. (2012) Re-enchanting social work? The emerging 'spirit' of social work in an age of economic crisis. *British Journal of Social Work*.

GAUNTLETT, D. (2007) *Creative Explorations: New Approaches to Identities and Audiences*. London: Routledge.

GAUNTLETT, D. (2011) *Making is Connecting: The Social Meaning of Creativity, From DIY to Knitting to YouTube and Web 2.0*. Cambridge, UK: Polity Press.

GAVRON, H. (1966) *The Captive Wife: Conflicts of Housebound Mothers*. London: Routledge & Kegan Paul.

GEERTZ, C. (1973) *The Interpretation of Cultures*. New York: Basic Books.

GERMAIN, C. B. & GITTERMAN, A. (1980) *The Life Model of Social Work Practice*. New York: Columbia University Press.

GIBELMAN, M. (1999) The search for identity: Defining social work—past, present, future. *Social Work*, 44, 298–310.

GIDDENS, A. (1976) *New Rules of Sociological Method: A Positive Critique of Interpretative Sociologies*. London: Hutchinson.

GIDDENS, A. (1979) *Central Problems in Social Theory: Action, Structure, and Contradiction in Social Analysis*. London: Macmillan.

GIDDENS, A. (1984) *The Constitution of Society: Outline of the Theory of Structuration*. Berkeley: University of California Press.

GIDDENS, A. (1990) *The Consequences of Modernity*. Stanford: Stanford University Press.

GIDDENS, A. (1991) *Modernity and Self-identity: Self and Society in the Late Modern Age*. Cambridge, UK: Polity Press.

GIDDENS, A. (1992) *The Transformation of Intimacy: Sexuality, Love and Eroticism in Modern Societies*. Cambridge, UK: Polity Press.

GIDDENS, A. (2005) *Sociology*, 4th edn. Cambridge, UK: Polity Press.

GILBERT, N. (2001) *Researching Social Life*, 2nd edn. London: Sage Publications.

GILLIGAN, C. (1982) *In a Different Voice: Psychological Theory and Women's Development*. Cambridge, Mass.: Harvard University Press.

GOLDACRE, B. (2012) *Bad Pharma: How Drug Companies Mislead Doctors and Harm Patients*. London: Fourth Estate.

GOLDEN, A.-M. J. & DALGLEISH, T. (2012) Facets of pejorative self-processing in complicated grief. *Journal of Consulting and Clinical Psychology*, 80, 512–524.

GOTT, M. (2006) Sexual health and the new ageing. *Age and Ageing*, 35, 106–107.

GRAHAM, J. R. & SHIER, M. L. (2010) The social work profession and subjective well-being: The impact of a profession on overall subjective well-being. *British Journal of Social Work*, 40, 1553–1572.

GRAY, M., WEBB, S. A. & MIDGLEY, J. O. (eds) (2012) *The Sage Handbook of Social Work*. London: Sage Publications.

GREEN, A. I. (2007) Queer theory and sociology: Locating the subject and the self in sexuality studies. *Sociological Theory*, 25, 26–45.

GREEN, L. (2010) *Understanding the Life Course: Sociological and Psychological Perspectives*. Cambridge, UK: Polity Press.

GREER, G. (1970) *The Female Eunuch*. London: MacGibbon & Kee.

GROSZ, E. A. (1994) *Volatile Bodies: Toward a Corporeal Feminism*. St Leonards: Allen & Unwin.

HAINE, R. A., SAYERS, T., SANDLER, I. N. & WOLCHIK, S. A. (2008) Evidence-based practices for parentally bereaved children and their families. *Professional Psychology: Research and Practice*, 39, 113–121.

HAMILTON, G. (1954) Self-awareness in professional education. *Social Casework*, 35, 371–379.

HANDEL, W. (2003) Pragmatic conventions: A frame for a theory of action and interaction. *Sociological Quarterly*, 44, 133–157.

HARDWICK, L. & WORSLEY, A. (2011) *Doing Social Work Research*. London: Sage Publications.

HAWKES, G. (2004) *Sex and Pleasure in Western Culture*. Cambridge, UK: Polity Press.

HEALY, K. (2012) *Social Work Methods and Skills: The Essential Foundations of Practice*. Basingstoke: Palgrave Macmillan.

HEALY, K. & MULHOLLAND, J. (2012) *Writing Skills for Social Workers*, 2nd edn. London: Sage Publications.

HEAP, C. (2003) The city as a sexual laboratory: The queer heritage of the Chicago School. *Qualitative Sociology*, 26, 457–487.

HEAPHY, B. (2007) *Late Modernity and Social Change: Reconstructing Social and Personal Life*. Abingdon: Routledge.

HENN, M. W., WEINSTEIN, M. & FOARD, N. (2009) *A Critical Introduction to Social Research*, 2nd edn. London: Sage Publications.

HEYDT, M. J. & SHERMAN, E. (2005) Conscious use of self: Tuning the instrument of social work practice with cultural competence. *The Journal of Baccalaureate Social Work*, 10.

HOLMES, M. (2006) Love lives at a distance: Distance relationships over the lifecourse. *Sociological Research online*.

HOLMES, M. (2007) *What is Gender? Sociological Approaches*. London, Thousand Oaks, New Delhi, Singapore: Sage Publications.

HOLMES, M., BEASLEY, C. & BROOK, H. (2011) Guest editorial. *Australian Feminist Studies*, 26, 3–7.

HOLSTEIN, J. A. & GUBRIUM, J. F. (2002) *Handbook of Interview Research: Context and Method*. Thousand Oaks: Sage Publications.

HOLSTEIN, J. A. & GUBRIUM, J. F. (2011) Animating interview narratives. *In:* SILVERMAN, D. (ed.) *Qualitative Research*. London: Sage Publications.

HOOKS, B. (1986) Sisterhood: Political solidarity between women. *Feminist Review*, 23, Socialist Feminism—Out of the Blue (Summer), 125–138.

HOUSTON, S. (2010) Beyond homo economicus: Recognition, self-realization and social work. *British Journal of Social Work*, 40, 841–857.

HUGMAN, R. (2005) *New Approaches in Ethics for the Caring Professions*. Basingstoke: Palgrave Macmillan.

HUGMAN, R. (2009) But is it social work? Some reflections on mistaken identities. *British Journal of Social Work*, 39, 1138–1153.

HUGMAN, R. & SMITH, D. (eds) (2005) *Ethical Issues in Social Work*. Abingdon: Routledge.

HUMPHREY, G. M. & ZIMPFER, D. G. (2008) *Counselling for Grief and Bereavement*, 2nd edn. London, Thousand Oaks, New Delhi, Singapore: Sage Publications.

HUNTINGTON, J. (1981) *Social Work and General Medical Practice*. London: George Allen & Unwin.

IFE, J. (2001) *Human Rights in Social Work: Towards a Rights-based Practice*. Cambridge, UK: Cambridge University Press.

IFE, J. (2008) *Human Rights and Social Work: Towards a Rights-based Practice*. Cambridge, UK: Cambridge University Press.

IFSW (2012) *Definition of Social Work* [Online]. International Federation of Social Workers. Available at: http://ifsw.org/policies/definition-of-social-work/.

INHELDER, B. (1964) *The Early Growth of Logic in the Child: Classification and Seriation.* London: Routledge & Kegan Paul.

IRIGARAY, L. (1985) *This Sex Which is Not One.* Ithaca: Cornell University Press.

JACKSON, S. (1999) Feminist sociology and sociological feminism: Recovering the social in feminist thought. *Sociological Research Online*, 4.

JACKSON, S. (2007) The sexual self in late modernity. *In:* KIMMEL, M. (ed.) *The Sexual Self: The Construction of Sexual Scripts.* Nashville: Vanderbilt University Press.

JACKSON, S. (2008) Ordinary sex. *Sexualities*, 11, 33–37.

JACKSON, S. (2011) Material feminism, pragmatism and the sexual self in global late modernity. *In:* JONASDITTOR, A. G., BRYSON, V. & JONES, K. B. (eds) *Sexuality, Gender and Power: Intersectional and Transnational Perspectives.* New York: Routledge.

JACKSON, S. & SCOTT, S. (1996) *Feminism and Sexuality: A Reader.* Edinburgh: Edinburgh University Press.

JACKSON, S. & SCOTT, S. (2007) Faking like a woman? Towards an interpretive theorization of sexual pleasure. *Body & Society*, 13, 95–116.

JACKSON, S. & SCOTT, S. (2010a) *Theorizing Sexuality.* Maidenhead: Open University Press.

JACKSON, S. & SCOTT, S. (2010b) Rehabilitating interactionism for a feminist sociology of sexuality. *Sociology*, 44, 811–826.

JAMIESON, L. (1998) *Intimacy: Personal Relationships in Modern Societies.* Cambridge, UK: Polity Press.

JENKINS, R. (2000) Categorization: Identity, social process and epistemology. *Current Sociology*, 48, 7–25.

JOAS, H. (1997) *G. H. Mead: A Contemporary Re-examination of His Thought.* Cambridge, Mass.: MIT Press.

JONASDITTOR, A. G., BRYSON, V. & JONES, K. B. (eds) (2011) *Sexuality, Gender and Power: Intersectional and Transnational Perspectives.* New York: Routledge.

JONES, L. & GREEN, J. (2006) Shifting discourses of professionalism: A case study of general practitioners in the United Kingdom. *Sociology of Health & Illness*, 28, 927–950.

JORDAN, B. (2012) Making sense of the 'Big Society': Social work and the moral order. *Journal of Social Work*, 12, 630–646.

KADUSHIN, A. (1976) *Supervision in Social Work.* New York: Columbia University Press.

KATZ, J. (1976) *Gay American History: Lesbians and Gay Men in the U.S.A.: A Documentary.* New York: Crowell.

KESSLER, S. J. & MCKENNA, W. (1985) *Gender: An Ethnomethodological Approach.* Chicago: University of Chicago Press.

KIMMEL, M. (ed.) (2006) *The Sexual Self: The Construction of Sexual Scripts.* Nashville: Vanderbilt University Press.

KING, A. (2009) Overcoming structure and agency. *Journal of Classical Sociology*, 9, 260–288.

KINSLEY, A. C. (1953) *Sexual Behavior in the Human Female.* Philadelphia: Saunders.

KOLB, D. A. (1984) *Experiential Learning: Experience as the Source of Learning and Development.* Englewood Cliffs: Prentice-Hall Inc.

KONDRAT, M. E. (2002) Actor-centered social work: Re-visioning 'person-in-environment' through a critical theory lens. *Social Work*, 47, 435–448.

KRISTEVA, J. (1991) *Strangers to Ourselves.* New York: Harvester Wheatsheaf.

LAM, C. M., WONG, H. & LEUNG, T. T. F. (2007) An unfinished reflexive journey: Social work students' reflection on their placement experiences. *British Journal of Social Work*, 37, 91–105.

LAMBERT, M. J. & BARLEY, D. E. (2001) Research summary on the therapeutic relationship and psychotherapy outcome. *Psychotherapy: Theory, Research, Practice, Training*, 38, 357–361.

LASCH, C. (1979) *The Culture of Narcissism: American Life in an Age of Diminishing Expectations*. New York: W. W. Norton.

LASH, S. (1988) Discourse or figure? Postmodernism as a 'regime of signification'. *Theory, Culture & Society*, 5, 311–336.

LASH, S. (1994a) *Economies of Signs and Space*. London: Sage Publications.

LASH, S. (1994b) Reflexivity and its doubles: Structure, aesthetics, community. *In:* BECK, U., GIDDENS, A. & LASH, S. (eds) *Reflexive Modernization*. Cambridge, UK: Polity Press.

LASH, S. (2001) Technological forms of life. *Theory, Culture & Society*, 18, 105–120.

LASH, S. (2003) Reflexivity as non-linearity. *Theory, Culture & Society*, 20, 49–57.

LAURENTIS, T. (1991) Queer theory, lesbian and gay studies. *Differences: A Journal of Feminist Cultural Studies*, 3, iii–xviii.

LEE, J. (1994) *The Empowerment Approach to Social Work Practice*. New York: Columbia University Press.

LEFEVRE, H. (1992) *Critique of Everyday Life*. London: Verso.

LEFEVRE, M. (2010) *Communicating with Children and Young People: Making a Difference*. Bristol: The Policy Press.

LEMING, M. R. & DICKINSON, G. E. (2002) *Understanding Dying, Death and Bereavement*, 5th edn. Fort Worth: Harcourt College Publishers.

LETHERBY, G. (2003) *Feminist Research in Theory and Practice*. Philadelphia: Open University Press.

LEVER, J. (1978) Sex differences in the complexity of children's play and games. *American Sociological Review*, 43, 471–483.

LEVER-TRACY, C. (ed.) (2010) *Routledge Handbook of Climate Change and Society*. New York: Routledge.

LEYS, R. (1993) Mead's voices: Imitation as foundation, or, the struggle against mimesis. *Critical Inquiry*, 19, 277–307.

LIAMPUTTONG, P. & EZZY, D. (2006) *Qualitative Research Methods*. South Melbourne: Oxford University Press.

LILJEGREN, A. (2011) Pragmatic professionalism: Micro-level discourse in social work. *European Journal of Social Work*, 15, 295–312.

LISHMAN, J. (2009) *Communication in Social Work*, 2nd edn. Basingstoke: Palgrave Macmillan.

LOEWENBERG, F. M., DOLGOFF, R. & HARRINGTON, D. (2000) *Ethical Decisions for Social Work Practice*. Itasca: Peacock Publishers, Inc.

LOMAX, C., JONES, K., LEIGH, S. & GAY, C. (2010) *Surviving your Social Work Placement*. Basingstoke: Palgrave Macmillan.

LUHMANN, N. (1977) Differentiation of society. *Canadian Journal of Sociology/Cahiers canadiens de sociologie*, 2, 29–53.

LUHMANN, N. (1984) The self description of society: Crisis fashion and sociological theory. *International Journal of Comparative Sociology*, XXV, 59–72.

LUHMANN, N. (1986) *Love as Passion: The Codification of Intimacy*. Cambridge, UK: Polity Press.

LYMBERY, M. (2006) United we stand? Partnership working in health and social care and the role of social work in services for older people. *British Journal of Social Work*, 36, 1119–1134.

LYMBERY, M. (2012) Social work and personalisation: Fracturing the bureau-professional compact? *British Journal of Social Work*.

LYNN, R. (2010) Mindfulness in social work education. *Social Work Education*, 29, 289–304.

MACINTYRE, G. & PAUL, S. (2012) Teaching research in social work: Capacity and challenge. *British Journal of Social Work*.

MACKEY, R. A. (2008) Toward an integration of ideas about the self for the practice of clinical social work. *Clinical Social Work Journal*, 36, 225–234.

MACKINNON, C. (1982) Feminism, Marxism, method and the State: An agenda for theory. *Signs*, 7, 515–544.

MACKINNON, C. A. (1989) *Toward a Feminist Theory of the State*. Cambridge, Mass.: Harvard University Press.

MACLAREN, C. (2008) Use of self in cognitive behavioral therapy. *Clinical Social Work Journal*, 36, 245–253.

MAINES, D. R. & MARKOWITZ, M. A. (1979) Elements of the perpetuation of dependency in a psychiatric halfway house. *Journal of Sociology and Social Welfare*, 6, 52–69.

MALINOWSKI, B. (1927) *Sex and Repression in Savage Society*. London: Kegan Paul.

MALINOWSKI, B. (1929) *The Sexual Life of Savages in North-western Melanesia: An ethnographic account of courtship, marriage and family life among the natives of the Trobriand Islands, British New Guinea*. New York: Eugenics Publishing.

MANDELL, D. (2008) Power, care and vulnerability: Considering use of self in child welfare work. *Journal of Social Work Practice*, 22, 235–248.

MANGAN, J. A. & NAURIGHT, J. (eds) (2000) *Sport in Australasian Society: Past and Present*. London: F. Cass.

MANTLE, G., WILLIAMS, I., LESLIE, J., PARSONS, S. & SHAFFER, R. (2008) Beyond assessment: Social work intervention in family court enquiries. *British Journal of Social Work*, 38, 431–443.

MARTIN, J. (2006) Reinterpreting internalization and agency through G.H. Mead's perspectival realism. *Human Development*, 49, 65–86.

MAYWALD, S. (2000) Two pedagogical approaches to group supervision in the human services. *In:* COOPER, L. & BRIGGS, L. (eds) *Fieldwork in the Human Services*. Sydney: Allen & Unwin.

MCLAUGHLIN, H. (2012) *Understanding Social Work Research*, 2nd edn. London: Sage Publications.

MCNAY, L. (1992) *Foucault and Feminism: Power, Gender and the Self*. Cambridge, UK: Polity Press.

MCNAY, L. (1994) *Foucault: A Critical Introduction*. Cambridge, UK: Polity Press in association with Blackwell Publishers.

MCNAY, L. (2000) *Gender and Agency: Reconfiguring the Subject in Feminist and Social Theory*. Malden, Mass.: Polity Press.

MCTIGHE, J. P. (2011) Teaching the use of self through the process of clinical supervision. *Clinical Social Work Journal*, 39, 301–307.

MEAD, G. H. (1913) [2011]. The social self. *In:* DA SILVA, F. C. (ed.) *G. H. Mead: A Reader*. Abingdon: Routledge.

MEAD, G. H. (1922) [2011]. A behavioristic account of the significant symbol. *In:* DA SILVA, F. C. (ed.) *G. H. Mead: A Reader*. Abingdon: Routledge.

MEAD, G. H. (1925) [2011]. The genesis of the self and social control. *In:* DA SILVA, F. C. (ed.) *G. H. Mead: A Reader*. Abingdon: Routledge.

MEAD, G. H. (1934) *Mind, Self and Society from the Standpoint of a Social Behaviourist*. Chicago: Chicago University Press.

MELTON, J. G. (2007) Perspective: New new religions: revisiting a concept. *Nova Religio: The Journal of Alternative and Emergent Religions*, 10, 103–112.

MIEHLS, D. & MOFFATT, K. (2000) Constructing social work identity based on the reflexive self. *British Journal of Social Work*, 30, 339–348.

MILLER, W. R. (2003) Commentary. *Addiction*, 98, 5.

MILLETT, K. (1970) *Sexual Politics*. PhD 0265025, Columbia University.

MILLETT, K. (1972) *Sexual Politics*. London: Abacus.

MILLS, C. (1958) *The Causes of World War Three*. New York: Simon & Schuster.

MILLS, C. & SCHNEIDER, H. (1948) *The New Men of Power: America's Labor Leaders*. New York: Harcourt Brace and Co.

MILLS, C. W. (1951) *White Collar: The American Middle Classes*. New York: Oxford University Press.

MILLS, C. W. (1956) *The Power Elite*. New York: Oxford University Press.

MILLS, C. W. (1958) The structure of power in American society. *British Journal of Sociology*, 9, 29–41.

MILLS, C. W. (1959) *The Sociological Imagination*. New York: Oxford University Press.

MILLS, C. W. (1962) *The Marxists*. New York: Dell Publishing. Also Harmondsworth: Penguin (1962/63).

MILLS, C. W. (1963) *Power, Politics, and People*. New York: Ballantine Books.

MILLS, C. W. (1964) *Sociology and Pragmatism: The Higher Learning in America*. New York: Paine-Whitman Publishers.

MILLS, C. W. (2000) *The Sociological Imagination*. New York: Oxford University Press.

MILNER, J. & O'BYRNE, P. (2002) *Assessment in Social Work*. Basingstoke: Palgrave Macmillan.

MINTY, B. & PATTINSON, G. (1994) The nature of child neglect. *British Journal of Social Work*, 24, 733–747.

MITCHELL, J. (1974) *Psychoanalysis and Feminism*. London: Allen Lane.

MOON, D. (2008) Culture and the sociology of sexuality: It's only natural? *Annals of the American Academy of Political and Social Science*, 619, 183–205.

MORGAN, A. (2000) *What is Narrative Therapy? An Easy-to-read Introduction*. Adelaide, South Australia: Dulwich Centre Publications.

MORRIS, A. (2008) Too attached to attachment theory? *In:* PORTER, M. & KELSO, J. (eds) *Theorising and Representing Maternal Realities*. Newcastle: Cambridge Scholars Publications.

MORRIS, L. (2012) Citizenship and human rights: Ideals and actualities. *British Journal of Sociology*, 63, 39–46.

MORRISSEY, G. & HIGGS, J. (2006) Phenomenological research and adolescent female sexuality: Discoveries and applications. *The Qualitative Report*, 11, 161–181.

MULHOLLAND, M. (2011) When porno meets hetero. *Australian Feminist Studies*, 26, 119–135.

MULLALY, R. P. (1997) *Structural Social Work: Ideology, Theory and Practice*, 2nd edn. Toronto, New York: Oxford University Press.

MUNRO, E. (2011) *The Munro Review of Child Protection: Final Report – A Child-centred System*. London: Department for Education.

NAYAK, A. & KEHILY, M. J. (2006) Gender undone: Subversion, regulation and embodiment in the work of Judith Butler. *British Journal of Sociology of Education*, 27, 459–472.

NEIL, A. L. & CHRISTENSEN, H. (2007) Australian school-based prevention and early intervention programs for anxiety and depression: A systematic review. *Medical Journal of Australia*, 186, 305–308.

NELSON, A. (2011) *Social Work with Substance Users*. London: Sage Publications.

NELSON-JONES, R. (2012) *Basic Counselling Skills, A Helper's Manual*, 3rd edn. London: Sage Publications.

NEUMANN, I. B. (2006) Pop goes religion. *European Journal of Cultural Studies*, 9, 81–100.

NEWBURN, T. & STANKO, E. (1994) *Just Boys doing Business?: Men, Masculinities and Crime*. London: Routledge.

NICHOLSON, L. & SEIDMAN, S. (eds) (1995) *Social Postmodernism: Beyond Identity Politics.* Cambridge, UK: Cambridge University Press.

OAKLEY, A. (1981) Interviewing women: A contradiction in terms. *In:* ROBERTS, H. (ed.) *Doing Feminist Research.* London: Routledge & Kegan Paul.

O'DONNELL, M. H. (2003) Radically reconstituting the subject: Social theory and human nature. *Sociology*, 37, 753–770.

PARSONS, T. (1956) *Family: Socialization and Interaction Process.* London: Routledge & Kegan Paul.

PARTON, N. (2008) Changes in the form of knowledge in social work: From the 'social' to the 'informational'? *British Journal of Social Work*, 38, 253–269.

PATTON, M. Q. (2002) *Qualitative Research and Evaluation Methods*, 3rd edn. Thousand Oaks: Sage Publications.

PAYNE, M. (2005) *Modern Social Work Theory*, 3rd edn. Basingstoke: Palgrave Macmillan.

PAYNE, M., ADAMS, R. & DOMINELLI, L. (2005) *Social Work Futures: Crossing Boundaries, Transforming Practice.* New York: Palgrave Macmillan.

PEASE, B. & FOOK, J. (1999) *Transforming Social Work Practice: Postmodern Critical Perspectives.* St Leonards: Allen & Unwin.

PERLMAN, H. H. (1957) *Social Casework: A Problem-solving Process.* Chicago: University of Chicago Press.

PETERSON, C. (2004) *Looking Forward through the Lifespan: Developmental Psychology*, 4th edn. Frenchs Forest, NSW: Prentice-Hall.

PIAGET, J. (1964) *The Early Growth of Logic in the Child.* London: Routledge & Kegan Paul.

PIAGET, J. (1973) *The Child's Conception of the World.* London: Paladin.

PINCUS, A. & MINAHAN, A. (1973) *Social Work Practice: Model and Method.* Itasca: Peacock Publishers, Inc.

PINEO, P. C. (1961) Disenchantment in the later years of marriage. *Marriage and Family Living*, 23, 3–11.

PLANTE, R. F. (2007) In search of sexual subjectivities: Exploring the sociological construction of sexual selves. *In:* KIMMEL, M. (ed.) *The Sexual Self: The Construction of Sexual Scripts.* Nashville: Vanderbilt University Press.

PLUMMER, K. (1975) *Sexual Stigma: An Interactionist Account.* London: Routledge & Kegan Paul.

PLUMMER, K. (ed.) (1981) *The Making of the Modern Homosexual.* London: Hutchinson.

PLUMMER, K. (2008a) Queers, bodies, and postmodern sexualities: A note on revisiting the 'sexual' in symbolic interactionism. *In:* KIMMEL, M. (ed.) *The Sexual Self: The Construction of Sexual Scripts.* Nashville: Vanderbilt University Press.

PLUMMER, K. (2008b) Studying sexualities for a better world? Ten years of sexualities. *Sexualities*, 11, 7–22.

PLUMMER, K. (2010) Generational sexualities, subterranean traditions, and the hauntings of the sexual world: Some preliminary remarks. *Symbolic Interaction*, 33, 163–190.

QUINNEY, A. & HAFFORD-LETCHFIELD, T. (2012) *Interprofessional Social Work: Effective Collaborative Approaches.* Exeter: Learning Matters.

REAMER, F. (1990) *Ethical Dilemmas in Social Service: A Guide for Social Workers.* New York: Columbia University Press.

REAMER, F. (1992) *The Impaired Social Worker.* Faculty Publications, Paper 171. Available online at: http//digitalcommons.ric.edu/facultypublications/171.

REAMER, F. (2001) *The Social Work Ethics Audit: A Risk Management Tool.* Washington: NASW Press.

REED, K., BLUNSDON, B., BLYTON, P. & DASTMALCHIAN, A. (2005) Introduction, perspectives on work–life balance [online]. *Labour and Industry*, 16, 5–14.

REIFF, P. (1966) *The Triumph of the Therapeutic: Uses of Faith after Freud*. New York: Harper and Row.

REINHARZ, S. & CHASE, S. (2002) Interviewing women. *In:* HOLSTEIN, J. A. & GUBRIUM, J. F. (eds) *Handbook of Interview Research: Context and Method*. Thousand Oaks: Sage Publications.

REUPERT, A. (2006) The counsellor's self in therapy: An inevitable presence. *International Journal for the Advancement of Counselling*, 28, 95–105.

REUPERT, A. (2007) Social worker's use of self. *Clinical Social Work Journal*, 35, 107–116.

REUPERT, A. (2009) Students' use of self: Teaching implications. *Social Work Education*, 28, 765–777.

REYNOLDS, J. (2007) Discourses of inter-professionalism. *British Journal of Social Work*, 37, 441–457.

RHODES, M. L. (1986) *Ethical Dilemmas in Social Work Practice*. Boston: Routledge & Kegan Paul.

RIBNER, D. S. & KNEI-PAZ, C. (2002) Client's view of a successful helping relationship. *Social Work*, 47, 379–387.

RICH, A. (1980) Compulsory heterosexuality and lesbian existence. *Signs*, 5, 631–660.

RITZER, G. & SMART, B. (eds) (2001) *Handbook of Social Theory*. London: Sage Publications.

ROBERTS, H. (1981) *Doing Feminist Research*. London: Routledge & Kegan Paul.

ROGERS, C. (1951) *Client Centred Therapy*. London: Constable and Company Limited.

ROGERS, C. R. (1957) The necessary and sufficient conditions of therapeutic personality change. *Journal of Consulting Psychology*, 21, 95–103.

ROGERS, C. R. (1961) *On Becoming a Person: A Therapist's View of Psychotherapy*. Boston: Houghton Mifflin.

RONEN, T. (1997) *Cognitive Developmental Therapy with Children*. Chichester: Wiley.

ROSE, A. (ed.) (1962) *Human Behavior and Social Processes: An Interactionist Approach*. Boston: Houghton Mifflin.

ROSENAU, P. V. (1997) [untitled]. *Contemporary Sociology*, 26, 246–247.

RUBIN, G. (1992) Thinking sex: Notes for a radical theory of politics and sexuality. *In:* VANCE, C. S. (ed.) *Pleasure and Danger: Exploring Female Sexuality*. [New ed.] London: Pandora Press.

RUCH, G. (2009) Identifying 'the critical' in a relationship-based model of reflection. *European Journal of Social Work*, 12, 349–362.

RYAN, A. (2005) From dangerous sexualities to risky sex: Regulating sexuality in the name of public health. *In:* SCOTT, J. & GAIL, H. (eds) *Perspectives in Human Sexuality*. South Melbourne: Oxford University Press.

SALEEBEY, D. (1992) *The Strengths Perspective in Social Work Practice*. New York: Longman.

SALEEBEY, D. (1996) The strengths perspective in social work practice: Extensions and cautions. *Social Work*, 41, 296–305.

SALEEBEY, D. (2006) *The Strengths Perspective in Social Work Practice*, 4th edn. Boston: Allyn & Bacon.

SANDERS, T. (2006) Sexing up the subject: Methodological nuances in researching the female sex industry. *Sexualities*, 9, 449–468.

SARANTAKOS, S. (2013) *Social Research*, 4th edn. New York: Palgrave Macmillan.

SCHNARCH, D. (1997) *Passionate Marriage: Keeping Love and Intimacy Alive in Committed Relationships*. Carlton North: Scribe Publications Pty Ltd.

SCHON, D. A. (1983) *The Reflective Practitioner: How Professionals Think in Action*. New York: Basic Books.

SCHUTZ, A. (1954) Concept and theory formation in the social sciences. *In:* THOMPSON, K. & TUNSTALL, J. (eds) *Sociological Perspectives*. Middlesex: Penguin Education.

SCHUTZ, A. (1967) *The Phenomenology of the Social World*. Evanston: Northwestern University Press.

SCHWARTZ, P. (2007) The social construction of heterosexuality. *In:* KIMMEL, M. (ed.) *The Sexual Self: The Construction of Sexual Scripts*. Nashville: Vanderbilt University Press.

SCHWARTZ, W. (1974) Private troubles and public issues: One social work job or two? *In:* KLENK, R. W. & RYAN, R. W. (eds) *The Practice of Social Work*, 2nd edn. Belmont: Wadsworth.

SCOTT, J. & GAIL, H. (eds) (2005) *Perspectives in Human Sexuality*. South Melbourne: Oxford University Press.

SCOTT, S. (2010) *Theorising Sexuality*. Maidenhead: Open University Press [Imprint].

SEDGWICK, E. K. (1990) *Epistemology of the Closet*. Berkeley: University of California Press.

SEIDMAN, S. (1993) Identity and politics in a 'postmodern' gay culture: Some historical and conceptual notes. *In:* WARNER, M. (ed.) *Fear of a Queer Planet: Queer Politics and Social Theory*. Minneapolis: University of Minnesota Press.

SEIDMAN, S. (1995) Deconstructing queer theory or the under-theorisation of the social and the ethical. *In:* NICHOLSON, L. J. & SEIDMAN, S. (eds) *Social Postmodernism: Beyond Identity Politics*. Cambridge, UK: Cambridge University Press.

SEIDMAN, S. (1997) *Difference Troubles: Queering Social Theory and Sexual Politics*. New York: Cambridge University Press.

SEIDMAN, S. (2004) *The Social Construction of Sexuality*. New York: W. W. Norton.

SHARDLOW, S. (1995) Confidentiality, accountability and the boundaries of client–worker relationships. *In:* HUGMAN, R. & SMITH, D. (eds) *Ethical Issues in Social Work*. Abingdon: Routledge.

SHAW, I. (2011) Social work research—an urban desert? *European Journal of Social Work*, 14, 11–26.

SHIER, M. L. & GRAHAM, J. R. (2011) Mindfulness, subjective well-being, and social work: Insight into their interconnection from social work practitioners. *Social Work Education*, 30, 29–44.

SHILLING, C. (1999) Towards an embodied understanding of the structure/agency relationship. *British Journal of Sociology*, 50, 543–562.

SILVERMAN, D. (1985) *Qualitative Methodology and Sociology: Describing the Social World*. Aldershot: Gower Publishing Co.

SILVERMAN, D. (2007) *A Very Short, Fairly Interesting and Reasonably Cheap Book about Qualitative Research*. London: Sage Publications.

SILVERMAN, D. (ed.) (2011) *Qualitative Research*. London: Sage Publications.

SINGER, P. (1993) *How are We to Live?: Ethics in an Age of Self-interest*. Melbourne: Text Publishing.

SINGER, P. (2004) *One World: The Ethics of Globalisation*. Melbourne: Text Publishing.

SINGER, P. (2009) *The Life You Can Save: Acting Now to End World Poverty*. New York: Random House.

SIPORIN, M. (1972) Situational assessment and intervention. *Social Casework*, 53, 91–109.

SKEGGS, B. (1997) *Formations of Class and Gender: Becoming Respectable*. London: Sage Publications.

SKEGGS, B. (2004) *Class, Self, Culture*. London: Routledge.

SMITH, D. E. (1987) *The Everyday World as Problematic: A Feminist Sociology*. Boston: Northeastern University Press.

SMITH, E. E., ATKINSON, R. L. & HILGARD, E. R. (2003) *Atkinson and Hilgard's Introduction to Psychology*. Belmont: Wadworth/Thomson Learning.

SMITH-ROSENBERG, C. (1975) The female world of love and ritual: Relations between women in nineteenth-century America. *Signs*, 1, 1–29.

STANLEY, L. (ed.) (1990) *Feminist Praxis: Research, Theory, and Epistemology in Feminist Sociology*. London: Routledge.

STANLEY, L. (1993) On auto/biography in sociology. *Sociology*, 27, 41–52.

STANLEY, L. & WISE, S. (1990) Method, methodology and epistemology in feminist research processes. *In:* STANLEY, L. (ed.) *Feminist Praxis: Research, Theory, and Epistemology in Feminist Sociology*. London: Routledge.

STAR, C. (2008) Locating justice in a warming world: Developing notions of climate justice in the UK and the USA. *Australasian Political Science Association Conference 2008*.

STEIN, Z. & SUSSER, M. (2000) The risks of having children in later life. *BMJ*, 320, 1681–1682.

STRAUSS, A. & CORBIN, J. (1990) *Basics of Qualitative Research*. London: Sage Publications.

TAYLOR, B. J. (2011) Developing an integrated assessment tool for the health and social care of older people. *British Journal of Social Work*.

THOMPSON, N. (2012) *Anti-discriminatory Practice*, 5th edn. Basingstoke: Palgrave Macmillan.

THOMPSON, N. (2011) *Effective Communication: A Guide for the People Professions*, 2nd edn. Basingstoke: Palgrave Macmillan.

TREVITHICK, P. (2012) *Social Work Skills and Knowledge: A Practice Handbook*, 3rd edn. Maidenhead: Open University Press.

UNGAR, M. (2008) Resilience across cultures. *British Journal of Social Work*, 38, 218–235.

URDANG, E. (2010) Awareness of self—a critical tool. *Social Work Education*, 29, 523–538.

URRY, J. (2000) *Sociology beyond Societies: Mobilities for the Twenty-first Century*. London: Routledge.

URRY, J. (2005) The complexities of the global. *Theory, Culture & Society*, 22, 235–254.

VASILAKI, E. I., HOSIER, S. G. & COX, W. M. (2006) The efficacy of motivational interviewing as a brief intervention for excessive drinking: A meta-analytic review. *Alcohol and Alcoholism*, 41, 328–335.

VYGOTSKY, L. S. (1962) *Thought and Language*, Cambridge, Mass.: MIT Press.

VYGOTSKY, L. S. (1978) *Mind in Society: The Development of Higher Psychological Processes*. Cambridge, Mass.: Harvard University Press.

WAGNER, G. (1998) Differentiation as absolute concept?: Toward the revision of a sociological category. *International Journal of Politics, Culture, and Society*, 11, 451–474.

WARNER, D. N. (2004) Towards a queer research methodology. *Qualitative Research in Psychology*, 1, 321–337.

WARNER, M. (ed.) (1993) *Fear of a Queer Planet: Queer Politics and Social Theory*. Minneapolis: University of Minnesota Press.

WEBB, S. A. (2010) (Re)assembling the Left: The politics of redistribution and recognition in social work. *British Journal of Social Work*, 40, 2364–2379.

WEBER, M. (1949) *The Methodology of the Social Sciences*. New York: Free Press.

WEEKS, J., HEAPHY, B. & DONOVAN, C. (2001) *Same Sex Intimacies: Families of Choice and Other Life Experiments*. London: Routledge.

WEINSTEIN, J. (2008) *Working with Loss, Death and Bereavement: A Guide for Social Workers*. London, Thousand Oaks, New Delhi, Singapore: Sage Publications.

WEST, B., PUDSEY, J. & DUNK-WEST, P. (2011) Pedagogy beyond the culture wars. *Journal of Sociology*, 47, 198–214.

WHITE, M. & EPSTON, D. (1990) *Narrative Means to Therapeutic Ends*. New York: W. W. Norton.

WHITTAKER, A. (2012) *Research Skills for Social Work*. Exeter: Learning Matters.

WILSON, J. (2000) Approaches to supervision in fieldwork. *In:* COOPER, L. (ed.) *Fieldwork in the Human Services: Theory and Practice for Field Educators, Practice Teachers and Supervisors*. St Leonards: Allen & Unwin.

WITKIEWITZ, K. & MARLATT, G. A. (2004) Relapse prevention for alcohol and drug problems: That was Zen, this is Tao. *American Psychologist*, 59, 224–235.

WOLCOTT, H. F. (1994) *Transforming Qualitative Data: Description, Analysis and Interpretation.* London: Sage Publications.

WORDEN, J. W. (1983) *Grief Counselling and Grief Therapy.* London and New York: Tavistock Publications.

WRIGHT, C. M. (1960) *Listen Yankee: The Revolution in Cuba.* New York: McGraw Hill.

YIP, K. (2006) Self-reflection in reflective practice: A note of caution. *British Journal of Social Work*, 36, 777–788.

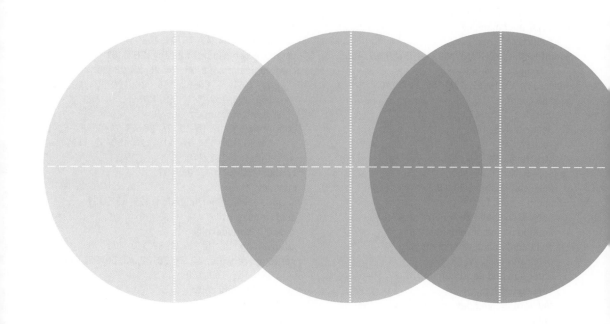

Index

* How do global conglomerates cause!
social inequalities and injustice
· GREED DRIVES INEQUALITY
· MORE FOR one BUT LESS FOR MANY.

* social work - A profession promoting
well-being & Human Rights. changing
individual situations as well as
acting upon larger scales to prevent
inequalities & injustice.

* Global economic inequalities: Are
they are the Rise or Decline
- 1% → Richest wont allow this to happen
- Gap between everyone else is shrinking
2014 GUARDIAN
- unpaid interns -

* Economic inequality → as bad as
all other inequality → as damaging
in effect